Claregalway

Parish History
750 Years

Stair pharóiste Bhaile Chláir na Gaillimhe

Copyright © 1999 Published by Claregalway Historical and Cultural Society

Printed by JayCee Printers Ltd., Galway, Ireland.

ISBN   0-9536210-0-6
First printed in 1999
Reprinted in 2002

Table of Contents

FOREWORD I

INTRODUCTION III

ACKNOWLEDGEMENTS IV

CHAPTER 1: THE CLARE RIVER 1

CHAPTER 2: AGRICULTRE 14

CHAPTER 3: 1916 RISING AND TROUBLES 33

CHAPTER 4: LANDLORDS 44

CHAPTER 5: THE FRANCISCAN FRIARY .55

CHAPTER 6: CASTLES IN THE AREA 72

CHAPTER 7: TRADES AND OCCUPATIONS 79

CHAPTER 8: POEMS, PRAYERS AND RECITATIONS 92

CHAPTER 9: SCHOOLS AND EDUCATION 106

CHAPTER 10: IRISH 123

CHAPTER 11: LOCAL FOLKLORE AND SUPERSTITIONS 134

CHAPTER 12: WELL KNOWN PEOPLE 144

CHAPTER 13: SPORTS, RECREATION AND PASTIMES 149

CHAPTER 14: THE FAMINE 181

CHAPTER 15: TOWNLANDS AND PLACENAMES 186

CHAPTER 16: THE CHURCH AND PARISH PRIESTS 209

CHAPTER 17: SNIPPETS 231

CHAPTER 18: PARISH ORGANISATIONS AND CLUBS 237

APPENDIX A: SCHOOL ATTENDANCE ROLLS 255

APPENDIX B: DEATHS AND MARRIAGES .276

Foreword

There has always been a healthy interest in local history in Ireland. Whether, and if so to what extent, this may be ultimately attributable to the importance of genealogy and of topographical learning among the learned class in the old Gaelic system, it is impossible, perhaps futile, to speculate. But in more recent centuries works of distinction on the history of parishes, dioceses and counties constitute a significant contribution to the professional writing of history in Ireland.

However deep-rooted this interest may be, the explosion of interest – and involvement – in local history projects in recent decades in Ireland has been quite phenomenal and without precedent. The causes of this extraordinary growth of interest, and of output, in local studies are both general and highly particular. The improvement in the availability and accessibility of an ever-widening range of source materials; the growth in the number of adults pursuing courses of formal study in history, archaeology and other branches of local studies; the growth in general interest in history and 'the human environment' prompted by engrossing documentaries on television; these may be counted among the general factors which have contributed to the current high levels of interest in local studies.

Two particular factors, however, deserve special notice. The support provided by FÁS – largely through its community employment schemes – towards projects in local studies and community improvement, has been an important stimulus and resource to researchers and community groups engaged in local studies. From graveyard inventories to placenames research and modest works of restoration to buildings, an immense amount of useful work and a significant output of publications have resulted from various FÁS schemes, to say nothing of the interest ignited and the skills developed among local community groups. A second vital factor in stimulating interest in the history of many local communities has been the rapid rate of social and indeed physical, change being experienced by many communities, particularly by communities on the outskirts or within the growth radius of expanding cities and towns.

There is widespread concern in these communities that the traditional bonding based on 'old stock', close-knit social rituals, shared memories and secure community institutions, is weakening and giving way before increasing mobility, in-migration ('suburbanisation') and the bewildering changes in work and leisure patterns. It should also be said, however, that many new settlers coming in to older communities and parishes share these concerns and are themselves anxious to create, or to contribute to, a new sense of community based on rootedness and social solidarity. Knowing the history, the folklore and the 'seanchas' of a local community, is a powerful asset in deepening a sense of place and belonging, for native or newcomer.

These impulses and ambitions are clearly identifiable in the laudable project which has produced this parish history of Claregalway. All associated with this project are deserving of praise and gratitude. Its compilation was an act of collective celebration and an affirmation of community identity and solidarity. The book is a rich compendium of information, stories and perspectives on the lives and times of Claregalway and its people down through the centuries. From placenames to politics, superstitions to sport, religion to recreations, landscape to local lore, the reader, whatever his or her interests, will find much that is informative and entertaining in this volume.

Tá dúchas na Gaelige, idir theanga agus eile, láidir sa pharóiste seo leis na cianta. Is deas mar atá cuid den oidhreacht sin le fáil sa leabhar seo: is iodhreacht í nár chóir ligint i ndearmad ná i léig.

Finally, the people of Claregalway can take satisfaction in this account of their 'story'. No doubt, there will be debate and argument on various details, and new information will be unearthed in the ensuing discussion. This is only as it should be. The past – and any account of the past, however scrupulously presented – will always be interrogated and interpreted afresh by each generation. But the account presented in this volume will certainly enable the living community of Claregalway to know their parish better and to feel better about themselves. It will also enable all others who read it to take the pulse of a Galway parish with a rich past, a vibrant present and, one hopes, a confident future as a cohesive parish community.

An t-ollamh Gearóid ó Tuathaigh
Dept. of History
NUI, Galway

Introduction

Claregalway is a rural parish rich in history and tradition. This book covers about 750 years of history and culture, beginning around the year 1250 with the foundation of the Franciscan Friary. There are a lot of interesting historical references about Claregalway from the 13th Century onwards, because of its strategic importance to the defence of Galway and also its situation on the lowest crossing point of the Clare River. There are many ancient ruins in the parish, such as the Friary, the De Burgo castle and the Nine Arch Bridge that are mentioned in old documents. The history includes details of the church and its many parish priests, and of schools and education throughout the ages. The culture and folklore in the book captures old sayings and traditions, old ways of doing things and attempts to paint a picture of the way people lived. You can see from the table of contents that there is a wide variety of topics addressed.

The Claregalway Cultural and Historical Society produced this book. Information on all the items mentioned in the previous paragraph were scattered around in different places such as letters, books, articles, newspaper cuttings and so on. The Society felt it was important to gather these together into a single source and to help preserve them as a kind of legacy for future generations. With the growing urbanisation of Claregalway it is very easy for this unique information to be forgotten or lost.

This book should satisfy the serious reader with all the detail contained in it. Alternatively, for the casual reader, it can be skimmed, put to one side and then dipped into or used as a reference when needed. Hopefully you will find it attractive to read and the photographs interesting.

Acknowledgements

The compiling and writing of this book was a true community effort - no one individual did it all. A large number of people helped in various ways.

There was the initial research and gathering of information by the FÁS workers. This was done from a variety of sources. Newspapers were examined, books were read and articles were scrutinised. Interviews were held with senior members of the parish who shared with us their memories and thoughts of days gone by. With these we were able to enhance the facts written down in books. People searched through old photo albums and cupboards to unearth photographs of historical interest. First drafts of chapters were written by individuals and then were re-drafted and polished by others. Many people showed a great commitment and interest in this project by giving of their time and by attending many meetings.

We wish to acknowledge and thank all those who helped along the way. Our gratitude also extends to those whose photographs, interviews or articles were eventually not included in the book.

Committee
The Claregalway Historical and Cultural Society

Committee – the Claregalway Historical and Cultural Society
Back Row (L to R): *Sean Concannon, Michael Hession, Brendan Noonan and Mícheál Ó'Heidhin*
Seated (L to R): *Gearóid Hartigan, Tom Lenihan (chairman) and Seamus O'Connell (treasurer)*

Acknowledgements

Mattie Boyle
Marie (née Moore) Buckley
Canon Gerard Callanan
Johnny Casserley
Johnny Clarke
Mrs. Cloherty (Mary Ellen Lally)
Larry Coady
Mary Coady
Pat Coen
Luke Concannon
Padraic Concannon
Paul Concannon
Sally Concannon
Seamus Concannon
John Conroy
Ursula Cribbin
Philip Cribbin
Kathleen Crowe
Dominick Duggan
Evelyn Duggan
Marie Duggan
Mary Duggan
Kathleen Dunleavy
Mary Earley
Brian Fahy
Josette Farrell
Peter Feeney
Rita Feeney
Denise Flaherty
Enda Flaherty
Tom Flaherty
Madeleine Flanagan
FÁS
Ann Marie Forde
Martin Forde
Tara Forde
Evelyn Fox
Mrs. Fox
Rachael Freaney
Brona Gallagher

John Geraghty
Patrick Giles
Aodáin Gloinn
Angela Glynn
Dawn Glynn
Kate Glynn
Michael Glynn
Nora Glynn
John Grealish
Noel Grealish
Paddy Greaney
Eddie Hanley
Mairtin Hanley
Mary Hanley
Ciaran Hartigan
Mary Helebert
Paddy Heneghan
Annie Hession
James Hession
Patrick Hession
Rita Hession
Martina Hughes
Michael Hughes
Brigie Hurney
Patrick Hurney
Tom Keaney
Frank Kearney
Mary Kearney
Sharon Kearney
Sean Kelly
Mary Kenny
Andrea Kingston
Joanna Kyne
Vincent Lyons
Maura (née Gillespie) Manning
Pat Maye
Meitheal Forbartha na Gaeltachta
Jarlath McDonagh
Ann McKiernan
Patrick Monaghan

Pat Moore
Bernadette Moran
Jimmy Moran
Josephine Moran
Mary Moran
Mary Moran (Senior)
Maudie Moran
Mrs. Paddy Moran (Annie McGrath)
Sarah Moran
Tom Moran
Tommy Moran
Billy Morris
Seoirse Morris
Canon Noel Mullin
Maura Murphy
Tommy Murphy
Carmel Naughton
Mary Newell
Marian Noonan
Sadie Noone
Nora O'Brien
Padraig O'Conaire
Joe O'Connell
Margaret O'Connell
Mary O'Connell
Nonie O'Connell
James O'Dea
Caroline O'Hara
Thomas Reilly
Nora Ruane
Paddy Ruane
Maura Ryan
Maurice Semple
Michael Smith
Jarlath Walsh
Michael Walsh
Nellie Walsh
Sean Walsh
Claregalway Community Centre

Chapter 1: The Clare River

Introduction

The Clare River takes its name from the old Clár an Diabhail or Devil's Flat, a name derived from the fact that the river at this place was formerly crossed on planks supported on pillars. This name also had an anglicised version, in that Claregalway was once known as Clár-yn-dowl.

An aerial view of the Clare River, also showing the Franciscan Friary and the De Burgo Castle

Outline of the Clare River

The River Clare rises in Ballyhaunis, Co. Mayo, and is roughly 85km in length. It passes through towns such as Dunmore and Milltown, through the neighbouring parish of Lackagh before entering Claregalway.

The Clare River is used as a boundary mark for many of the townlands in the Claregalway parish. Kiniska is the first townland to the north of the river. To the south of the river is Gortatleva and next to this is one field in Lydacan. The townland of Lakeview runs along with the river, out on to the N17 (Galway to Tuam) road. On crossing the road it divides Cahergowan from the Claregalway townland. After this it forms the dividing line between Montiagh North and South. Curraghmore is located to the north. Finally the river pours into the Corrib.

Bridges

The first mention of a bridge over the Clare River was in 1349 and was probably a wooden structure.

The nine arched bridge, known locally as the Nine Arches, was erected in stone probably in the early 1700's. This bridge is a very impressive sight and an attractive reminder of Claregalway's past. At that time, probably a large number of men would have been working on the project. These would have included skilled stone masons and cutters. They would have cut and dressed rock from a local quarry to the required shape, giving the facing stones the finest finish and all this done by hand. They would have mixed mortar of local sand, water and lump lime (made by burning limestone in a local kiln). Their work has lasted over 300 years. The Claregalway Amenity Group is presently arranging to have this bridge restored.

The old bridge prior to 1957 with the Friary and Castle.

In 1765, shortly after the construction of the Nine Arches, John Borkin, a local landlord from nearby Lackagh, changed the course of the river. He diverted it away from under the Nine Arches to a deeper channel about 30 metres further north. He did this in order to improve the drainage in the area. Also he wanted to deepen it so as to make it navigable up to Tuam, however his plan was thwarted by rock in Lackagh that could not be broken. This work was done with grants from the then Irish Parliament and the Commissioners for Inland Navigation, which were developing canals all over the country. Presumably another bridge would have been built at that time, although there is no record available about this.

The Clare River

There are two old stone plaques set in the wall on either side of the north end of the bridge that commemorate the work by Borkin. These stones were taken from the original bridge that stood there. The one at the castle side reads:

> *This canall was made by*
> *John Borkin of Lacka Esq.*
> *to induce the draining Ye*
> *Lands and make it navigate from*
> *Galway to Tuam*
> *and other parts*
> *1765*

The one at the friary end is not so clear, some letters and words are indecipherable, however it's still possible to get the general meaning. It reads as follows:

> *nall was made y gre__*
> *John Borkin of Lacka Esq^R __*
> *our members of parliment coi_*
> *Rs of the inland navigation _u__*
> *_ors the flooded grounds this*
> *the county drain the lands _*
> *way ___ from Galway &*
> *___ parts of the county 1765*

The present bridge was constructed in 1957 and replaced the previous narrow humpback bridge. The main road was also widened at that time. Up to then, the Galway to Tuam road passed over the Nine Arches. The commemorative plaque placed on the new bridge reads as follows:

> *1957*
> *This bridge was constructed by the Galway County Council*
> *John Higgins Eyre St. Galway Contractor*
> *Martin Quinn   Chairman*
> *C.L. O'Flynn   County manager*
> *L.O. Luanaigh   County Engineers*
> *G. Lee J.B. Collins   County Engineers*
> *F.S.Rishworth)*
> *Ed. Ralph Ryan)   Constructing Engineers*

The Clare River

The 1765 stone plaque (the castle side one) commemorating the changing of the Clare River

Flooding and Drainage

Flooding has been a constant problem in the Claregalway area over the centuries, mainly because of the relatively flat and low-lying terrain and of course the West of Ireland rain. Numerous attempts were made at drainage, either through changing the course of the Clare River or deepening it. The following newspaper articles give details of the suffering and hardships caused by this flooding and the efforts made to remedy it.

The Tuam Herald, dated 13th January 1838:
"TAKE NOTICE
That pursuant to an Act passed in the 1st and 2nd years of the reign of his late Majesty King William the IV, entitled 'an Act to empower landed proprietors in Ireland to sink, embank and remove obstructions in rivers' an application will, 40 days after due publication hereof, be made to the Lord Lieutenant or other Chief Governor or Governors of Ireland, to issue a commission authorising and constituting a company of undertakers under the said act, within the district of Lough Corrib, its rivers and the lands contiguous thereto, for the purpose of draining, reclaiming and improving the said lands, by keeping the waters of Lough Corrib at or near summer level, and that it is proposed to execute the authority of said commission in the townlands of Claregalway, Curraghmore, Gortcloonmore, Gortadoo, Kiniska, Loughgeorge, Montiagh North and Waterdale in the parish of Claregalway in the Barony of Clare; and in the

The Clare River

townlands of Cloon, Gortatleva, Lakeview, Lydacan, Montiagh south, Pollaghrevagh, Summerfield and Rocklawn in the parish of Claregalway in the Barony of Dunkellin, ..."

Note the mention that the Claregalway parish is split between the Baronies of Clare and Dunkellin.

Flooding in Montiagh

The Tuam Herald, dated 18th May 1844:
"IMPROVEMENT OF LOUGH CORRIB
I am happy to say that the survey and specification are made and ready for the drainage of the lands bordering on the river of Claregalway from Ballygaddy bridge below Tuam to Claregalway. After considerable delay and trouble I have succeeded so far and I now trust there will be no difficulty in getting the necessary assents. The distance is 22 miles, the money to be expended £22,000, all in labour, all that labour to be performed by the tenants of the different lands on the banks of the river, 5,500 acres to be saved and relieved, profit of 10 percent on the outlay and money to be repaid by ten or twelve instalments. Besides the other advantages to be derived, a better climate, the crops of the upland saved and sheep saved from rottenness. Two or three crops will repay the whole outlay."

The Tuam Herald, dated 24th October 1891:
"MONTIAGH – DESTRUCTIVE FLOODS
Montiagh, situate in the parish of Claregalway is at present completely flooded by the overflowing of the river from the recent wet weather. The entire district

along the river at Claregalway to the Corrib presents the appearance of a large lake and the poor Montiagh people of whom there are about 40 families suffer periodically from these destructive floods. At the present time they have their cattle tied up in the houses so the grasslands are under water of considerable depth. The potato crop is ruined, as what has been dug from the ground is in pits and these too are covered by the flowing of the river. The hay crop also is lost and the grass will be of very little use after the floods subside. The condition therefore of the poor people of Montiagh is most pitiable. And were it not that their worthy pastor, the Rev. Father Commins. PP comes to their assistance on these sad occasions which, as we have said, are periodic, there would be dire destitution in the district."

The Connacht Tribune, dated 3rd September 1910:

"PEASANT'S PERIL

CROPS DESTROYED BY FLOODS ALL OVER THE COUNTY

Half a dozen houses in the Waterdale district, about seven miles from Galway, stand in danger of being submerged owing to the overflowing of the river Liscananaun a tributary of the Corrib. Already the house of Thomas Glennane has been flooded, a few acres of hay and other crops, together with a large quantity of turf, have been destroyed. About five acres are under water, but there is no foundation for the report of an impending bogslide.

The people of Waterdale live on the edge of a bog and in what is perhaps the most low-lying district around Galway. Fronting the house is a wretched specimen of a by-road about a mile in length and connected with the main road to Loughgeorge. The Liscananaun River runs collaterally with this road and is a sort of canal, 20 feet deep in parts.

Since the rains of Thursday week the water in the drains has been driven backward and yesterday it overflowed the roadside to such an extent that the alarm of the poor people was pitiable to witness. A few stalwart peasants, seeing the danger in which their houses would be placed if the flood crossed the bye-road, built up a retaining dam of turf along it for about 200 yards. This primitive dam is about 3 feet in height and so far has succeeded in keeping back the water, which has risen over two feet above the level of the bye-road. In one instance the water burst up through the floor of a house on the other side of the road and extinguished the fire, and it is feared if the dam bursts the bye-road will be carried away and the half dozen houses on the verge of the bog submerged.

Some strange sights may be witnessed at the scene of the flood. In one field a number of men and women were seen engaged in taking away potatoes, submerged to their waists. Haycocks have been carried away, but with the improvement in the weather more serious damage will be averted.

The Clare River

The Nine Arches taken from inside the field

The tenants of the district place the cause of the flood at the door of the Lough Corrib Drainage Trustees. Professor Townsend, the engineer to the Trustees, has the floodgates at Galway raised to allow the surplus water away.

A drive along the road from Galway to Headford will speedily convince one that there is no exaggeration in the statements that have been made in reference to the floods. Curraghmore bog, lying on the main road from Galway and about 6 miles from the city, is entirely under water owing to the Claregalway River having overflowed its banks. Well nigh 40 acres of meadow have been submerged and the small 'tramp-cocks' which were in the fields might be seen floating down the stream. The people have turned out with boats and endeavoured to save at least some portion of the ruined harvest. The turf in the bog has also been carried away. A house about 220 yards from the bridge that spans the river on the public road is surrounded by water to a depth of about 18 inches. The people had to leave the building and take refuge in an outhouse."

The Connacht Tribune, dated 10th September 1910:

"MEMORIAL TO THE CONGESTED DISTRICTS FROM THE PEOPLE OF THE PARISH OF CLAREGALWAY.

Gentlemen – We, the undersigned, on behalf of the people of the parish of Claregalway, respectfully beg to bring under the notice of the Congested Districts Board the condition of the people. There are in the parish 320 families of whom 246 are of the valuation of £7 and under. The total valuation of the parish is about £4,000. Portion of the parish has been purchased under the

Lands Acts of 1903, but a large portion has not yet been sold. There are in the parish grasslands in the possession of Mr. R. St. Ffrench, Mr. H. Holmes and Mr. Burke, which we understand can be obtained by the Board for the purpose of relieving congestion. The tenants in congested estates are quite prepared to migrate to other holdings either in this parish or elsewhere.

The parish contains two rivers, viz. The Clare and Cregg, both of which are liable to floods. Some years ago the Clare River overflowed and flooded all the tenants along the banks for some miles, so that the entire crops were damaged and the people driven from their homes. On that occasion the distress occasioned by the flood was so great that a public subscription had to be started to relieve the poor people.

During the past three weeks the Clare River again overflowed its banks and caused widespread destruction of the crops and compelled the people to leave their houses and remove the family and stock to their neighbour's. The villages affected are Montiagh, Waterdale, Cloonbiggen, Cahergowan, Cloon, Clogher, Gortadooey and Gortcloonmore. In these villages there were destroyed about 25 acres of hay, 6 acres of crops (potatoes, oats and turnips) and over £57 worth of turf. A large number of the inhabitants are tenant purchasers, but their holdings are so small and low-lying that they have to plant their crops along by the river bank, with the result that every rise of the river places their holdings in great danger.

The condition of the Clare river is largely responsible for the flooding as the Board of Drainage Trustees have utterly failed to clean the river, with the result that it has silted up and the outlet to the lake is blocked. The closing of the weir in Galway also keeps water back. There is no board to whom we can appeal save the Congested Districts Board as the latter alone possesses the power and funds necessary to relieve the condition of affairs which exist.

At a public meeting of the people of the parish, held on Sunday, 4th September, we were appointed a committee to approach the Board with a view to asking the Board to take immediate steps to purchase the estates in this parish which are still unsold and to resettle the people in the lands.

Signed: Redmond MacHugh PP, W. Duffy MP, Joseph A. Glynn solicitor, Chairman Galway County Council P. Ryan RDC, J. Connell RDC, Michael Murphy RDC, Malachy Hession, Thomas Casserley, J. Concannon."

The Connacht Tribune, dated 15th February 1913:

"CORRIB FLOODS

Colonel Kilkelly DL, JP, presided at the meeting of the Drainage Trustees on Saturday and the others present were Messrs. Lawrence Walsh, Owen Kyne RO, Thomas Crowe, Michael Hannon, R.H. Ffrench JP, P. Lyons and J.G. Alcorn.

Mr. O'Dea solicitor: I appear here for 30 tenants from the parish of Claregalway and Liscananaun and they have land around Cregg and Waterdale and they have instructed me that for the last two years their lands have been flooded more than ever before. They had hoped for great things from the new committee but they have been disappointed and things have been worse than before. Last year may have been a bad year but they say there is another river there not under your control and it was perfectly dry, while theirs is not at all as it ought to be.

They instruct me to say that if this kind of thing goes on they will refuse to pay any more assessments – that is if they don't get an undertaking that things will be put right and if necessary they will only pay at the point of the bayonet. I come here before you because I know that you are with us in sympathy and sympathy is all very good in its way but it won't make a man's land dry or save his hay from being ruined. What we want is that you will make your overseer do his duty. I am informed that there is £31 spent on this work this year for which previously £10 was granted and the land is actually worse that previously. We don't wish to press unduly and we will be satisfied if for a start you see that the weeds are cut."

The Tuam Herald, dated 22nd March 1913:

"THE CORRIB DRAINAGE

The following points in the report of the Board of Works show that the Corrib Drainage is in a bad way, and that the tributary rivers flowing into it are not kept in proper order and efficiently cleared. The consequence is continual overflowing when any excessive rains come on. The Board should insist on the local drainage being properly done and not botched as it is:

There are 31 miles of main rivers flowing into the Corrib.

The Claregalway River 81/2 miles long, is full of shoals and obstructions, specially from Claregalway downstream and its bad condition increases the damage by floods as it can only carry them off when they are of small dimensions.

The Cregg and Waterdale rivers, 91/2 miles long is blocked and shoaled in numerous places and are therefore capable of discharging little more than summer water properly. The only attempt to maintain these rivers appears to have been by the clipping of grass edges and the partial cutting of weeds, which is not effective river cleaning and tends to increase the growth of weeds and ultimately to create impassable barriers to flood waters."

In 1954 the largest arterial drainage scheme of its kind ever undertaken in this country commenced. This was known as the Corrib Drainage Scheme. It benefited farmers in Galway, Mayo and Roscommon and the Clare River and its tributaries came within the scheme. 400 miles of river and stream were widened and deepened to carry water off an area of 400 square miles of land.

The Clare River

Sean Concannon remembers the first drainage excavators arriving outside Lenihan's public house in Claregalway in the summer of 1954. There was a lot of local people employed on the project; driving machines, blasting rocks, building bridges, building walls, and bring oil and diesel for the machines. During the summer, the working day started at 8.00am and finished at 7.30pm. The dinner break was at 1.00pm, while the next break was at 5.30pm. The water for tea was boiled on the riverbank by lighting a fire and keeping it going with diesel. Needless to relate, the kettles got very black. Sean's first job was filling sandbags for dams. Working with Sean were Michael Dolly from Waterdale, Peter Newell from Gortadooey and Patrick Spellman from Carnmore. In 1955 machines moved down from Claregalway bridge to Montiagh while others moved upstream to Crusheen. The scheme stopped men from having to emigrate to look for work. Sean has memories of many happy days on the banks of the Clare River!

Draining the Clare River at Mointeach South.

The Tuam Herald, dated 19th March 1955:

"Particulars of the progress being made on the Scheme are given in a statement by Mr. Michael Donnellan, TD, Parliament Secretary to the Minister for Finance......... It will cost some £2,120,000 in all......... The Corrib-Clare Scheme, which will take some ten years to complete, will involve the excavation of about 2 1/4 million cubic yards of material, including nearly half a million of rock...... Continuous excavation will be carried out for the whole length of the Clare River. The principal points on this at which deepening and widening

operations will be undertaken are the Lackagh Rock cut about 12 miles upstream of the outfall (where a solid wall of rock, 30 feet deep and 20 feet wide is being removed), the Corofin Rock cut and the shallow stretch of river about a half mile long at Conagher above Milltown

At Lackagh the widening of the rock cut will probably have been completed and this will largely eliminate the flooding between Lackagh and Tuam. The rock cuts above Claregalway and Cregmore will also be dealt with this year, and a start will be made on the Corofin rock cut as well as the rock cut at Conagher near Milltown. By the time the scheme reaches its peak about 500 men will be in employment on the scheme and about 50 excavators will be in use.

When the scheme is completed, Mr. Donnellan said, more than 50,000 acres of land now subject to flooding and waterlogging will benefit and up to 23,000 acres of bog will be available for drainage. The level of Lough Corrib will have been lowered by two feet and lands on the shores of the lake, as well as lands in the lower reaches of the Clare and Cregg rivers will be freed from the severe, prolonged and widespread flooding and waterlogging to which they are now subjected.

It is estimated, said Mr. Donnellan, that the annual improvement in the value of the land drained by the Scheme will be about £43,000."

Finally it must be recorded that some people interviewed stated that there was no problem until Borkin changed the course of the river in 1765. Two theories which they had were, firstly, that the new river was narrower, which helped flooding, and that also the building of the Salmon Weir caused the level of Lough Corrib to rise, which in turn meant that the river level also rose.

Transport

River transport was mostly on the lower stretches of the Clare, from Claregalway to Lough Corrib. The transport of turf accounted for the major part of it, but the Claregalway boatmen also took part in the general trade on the lake. Many of them were from Montiagh with about 40 boats in all from that village. They used flat-bottomed boats called 'flats'. These were about 17 feet long and were designed to carry a load on shallow water. The boat would be pushed along with an ash pole about 8 foot long called a 'cliath'. They were very stable and safe although there was a story mentioned about one such boat that sprung a leak and the occupants had to save the turf by throwing it onto the bank, before saving themselves, which they did.

Boats returning home to Claregalway had difficulty in finding the mouth of the Clare, as the shore of Lough Corrib around that area was overgrown. A long pole was set up at the river mouth to help in guiding the boats in.

The Clare River

Fishing and Poaching

Fishing has long been an important practice associated with the River Clare. However many people have not always been strictly within the law, regarding this. The fact that some people reverted to poaching may have been as a direct result of the fishing restrictions that existed. For the people of Montiagh, fishing and the sale of turf was their livelihood. The river was noted for salmon poaching, for the locals, knowing the pools where the fish rested at night, easily caught them with nets. The salmon were nearly always sold, much of it in Galway city.

The fishing rights from the Claregalway bridge to the lake belong to the castle owners, as do those on the castle side above the river. The rights on the opposite side of the river belong to the farmers. Some farmers bought fishing rights and later sold them or rented them to angling clubs.

According to local accounts, poachers would seek out deep areas, with few rocks, with one man going on each side of the river. They used nets like those used at sea. They would organise a lookout so that if the Gárdai or bailiffs arrived the nets would "disappear" to safety. In the 1940's and 1950's the walkie-talkies and speedboats changed the odds against the poachers, as did the introduction of heavy fines. Any fish that were caught were usually sold to hotels in Galway.

Cregmore Bridge

This apparently easy way of making some extra money did not always have a happy outcome. One man, Michael Murphy, was sent to jail even though he was innocent, and more tragically John Duggan, a young poacher, died at Curraghmore trying to evade the Gárdai.

Hayworth described the river as "slow flowing and fishful" and newspapers in 1910 highly praised the river for its salmon and trout.

The Tuam Herald, dated 15th May 1915:

"Galway Notes

I believe that the fishing on the Claregalway River has been fairly good of late. Captain R.E. Palmer on his waters in Kilcolgan succeeded in landing a fine spring fish 13$^{1/2}$ lbs. But unfortunately lost another about 18 lbs. having him played out to the gaff when the hook came out. Mr. R. Joyce got one 11$^{3/4}$ lbs. in Claregalway at Curraghmore bridge."

Pollution

The Connacht Tribune, dated 18th November 1939:

THOUSANDS OF FISH POISONED IN CLAREGALWAY RIVER

Salmon weighing from twenty to thirty pounds have been taken from the Clare River, County Galway, known locally as the Claregalway River, during the last two weeks, and have been boiled and fed to pigs and dogs. This amazing story was told to our correspondent when he visited the area in question on Monday evening. During the last fortnight residents along the river bank were dumbfounded when they found thousands of salmon, trout, pike and eels floating on top of the water dead.

This amazing phenomenon has not yet been satisfactorily explained, but the unanimous opinion of fishermen west of the Shannon is that the fishing in this, the best salmon and trout-fishing river west of the Shannon has been ruined. Salmon and trout and eels worth approximately ten thousands pounds have been totally destroyed and this estimate does not include the enormous destruction valued at hundreds of thousands which has been done to the spawn.

At this time of the year it is customary for the salmon and trout to go up the Claregalway River from Lough Corrib to spawn. In the middle of the spawning season the fish were suddenly poisoned and riparian fishermen who have their homes along the river bank were treated to the spectacle of thousands of valuable fish floating along the top of the river.

Chapter 2: Agriculture

Introduction

Claregalway has been and continues to be largely a farming community with its rich limestone soil ideal for tillage farming and grazing for stock and other animals. The typical size of the farms in the parish varies from twenty to seventy acres. Farmers kept pigs and cows. Some also kept some sheep, horses, turkeys, geese and chickens. The fowl were kept to produce eggs, which would be consumed for home use or sold at the fair. It was mostly dry stock in Claregalway but some farmers did produce milk. In the olden days, all milk was consumed at home; either drank fresh or let go sour and churned into butter. In the last 30 years or so most milk has gone to the creamery either in Renmore or Athenry.

Washing the sheep prior to shearing - underneath the old Claregalway bridge

Pigs

Every farmhouse had a pig or two usually a sow and some bonhams. They were easy to keep as they lived on scraps and people generally let them roam around the farm during the day. Up until the 1960's pigs were either sold in the markets or else killed at home, but after that they were sent to the slaughterhouse in Galway.

Pig markets were held at Lenihans, now "the Nine Arches" pub. Lenihans pub was at the site of the fair in Claregalway, and it seems that it was the fair that brought about the pub and not vice versa. Some of the buyers at Lenihans were

Agriculture

McGiverns (who had stores in Galway and Monivea) and the Glynn brothers. James Healy bought pigs in Hessions pub during the summer.

There was also a pig market at Loughgeorge where the weighing, buying and selling occurred. Corbett, another very popular buyer from Headford would visit Loughgeorge on a Monday. There was also another buyer named Kelly who visited Loughgeorge. Most of the pigs fetched 15 shillings or so and went on to the Castlebar or Claremorris factories. Occasionally the farmers sold their bonhams in Galway. As was stated earlier pigs were killed at home for food and although a Mr. Donovan from Mullacuttra was a well-known pig killer, every village had somebody who could be called upon when needed.

A certain basic method was practised for the killing of the pigs. The pigs met their end tied upside down in a horse-cart, which was of course after the simple task of catching them. The pig's legs were tied to the cart and then his throat was cut and his heart stabbed. The unfortunate animal was then shaved with a sharp knife, after boiling water had been poured over him. One person described a wooden implement, similar to a comb without teeth, which also did a satisfactory job. Then the dead pig was transferred to a shed and hung by the legs from the rafters. Some people slit his back legs at this point and then inserted a wooden peg in order to hang the pig from its back legs. Naturally, the shed was secured to prevent any curious, or perhaps hungry, animals entering.

Next day, the pig was taken down and cut up. He was then opened, gutted and washed and the blood was gathered and boiled with oatmeal to make black pudding. The portions of the pig were then put into a salted barrel of water. When an egg could float on top of the water then this was a sign of enough salt. Some farmers removed most of the bones at this stage and when these parts were taken from the brine they were hung up upon spikes near the chimney. In this way the bacon was smoked and thus would last for a long time. Some of those interviewed recalled that as children they felt that the taste was very strong but they eventually got used to it.

Beet

Beet was first grown as a serious cash crop in 1933 and despite the hardships that were initially related to achieving a good yield, it continued to be grown until the Tuam Sugar Factory closed in 1984. That is not to say that the odd farmer doesn't still plant beet, but no longer is his shoulder strained as regularly as of old with carrying loads of sugar beet.

Back in the 1930's a horse machine was used to sow the beet but this was a luxury compared to sowing by hand. Billy Morris, Cregboy recalled how he was *"on his knees all the time"* one summer singling and weeding the beet. Another hardship he recalled was when he had to fill the lorry by hand, as there was no

Agriculture

beet fork. The beet was weighed in Oranmore Station and fetched over 30 shillings a ton. An advantage in growing beet was that the pulp was returned to the farmers who made good use of it, feeding it to calves and sheep. During the war, beet farmers were fortunate during the rationing as the Sugar Factory gave them permits to buy sugar. The final advantage to the beet growers was that they were always guaranteed a fixed price.

Turf

The bogs in Claregalway are located in the townlands of Cloon, Curraghmore, Gortcloonmore, Waterdale and as its name suggests, Montiagh. One man who had a bog in Gortcloonmore described the old procedure, which was used in the days before the turf machine. Parties of three were necessary for a successful day. The first, a cutter would go down with his "slean" and cut the sods and throw them up to the two spreaders who would fill a barrow with 10-12 sods, wheel it out and spread the turf out flat where it was left for a fortnight. After this it was put standing in "groigins" and eventually brought home in carts and creels. Generally the turf was cut once a year but this was changed to twice a year during the 'Emergency'. When the people from Montiagh had no other work, they used to travel to Oranmore nearly every second day to sell their turf.

Barrow for spreading turf. Used up to the early 1960s.

Eggs and Fowl.

Many people kept fowl as they could throw scraps to them or just let them pick. Hens, geese, chickens, turkeys and ducks were to be found to varying degrees around. The belief was 'more poultry, better woman', so anyone who had their gaggle of geese was doing well. At the time of the pig markets near the castle, women from Gortatleva, Ballymurphy and other areas brought large baskets of eggs to these markets to sell. One women remembered a lorry coming from Athenry once a week to buy these eggs. There were people who sold sugar and tea at the markets so if all the eggs were sold you could buy a pound of one or the other.

Horses

Not all farmers in the parish had horses but nonetheless, there were a few in each townland and consequently the machinery of the time was all horse-drawn. It is known that all the big houses had horses. The farmers who had to do without were lent horses and also whatever implements they needed. In the 1920's and 1930's some of these included horse ploughs, harrows, reapers and binders. For hay, there was also a horse-mowing machine, but the horses weren't too keen on it, as it was noisy and uncomfortable. This mower could also be adapted for cutting corn. Various attachments were added and the driver used to sit up on a seat with a rake, which he used to lay the sheaves.

A number of people in the parish remember the races at Loughgeorge which mainly consisted of common working horses and lasted for about two days.

In 1906, the Galway Committee of Agriculture offered nominations to farmers mares to be served by thoroughbred stallions. The value of each nomination was £2. Preference was given to the best young mares under six years of age. Each mare had to be the property of a farmer whose holding did not exceed a valuation of £300, but three-fourths of the nomination was reserved for farmers under the £30 valuation. Claregalway got 17 nominations.

Old horse carts.

Agriculture

The horses of Claregalway achieved certain notoriety in 1929 when the Connacht Tribune stated that they *"could not make any hand of tarred roads"*. Mr N Kyne spoke on behalf of the Claregalway farmers, many of whom were present in the public gallery, saying that horses could not draw loads over the tarred half of the road, so that they all had to travel on the sanded half. Horses shoes could be "sharpened" for 3s. to travel on tar and unsharpened afterwards for another 3s. but this was both expensive and time consuming. Tarred roads suited lorries, cars and buses and the county surveyor said it was hard to reconcile the two forms of traffic. It was also felt as strange that it was only Claregalway horses, which seemed to have a problem. The situation was so bad that at areas near Holmes Hill and Rockwood the council had placed empty tar barrels to stop horses using one side of the road only!

Stands for building up stacks of corn

Crops

Oats were grown in all parts of the parish and were thrashed, originally by flail. The flails in Claregalway were as others made from hazel and holly joined together by a leather thong. In some places it was called a "suist". After thrashing came the winnowing and this involved letting the oats fall in a windy shed. The wind blew the chaff away and the heavier seed fell straight down, where it was gathered later. Some people had a winnowing machine, which involved putting oats in and then turning the handle, but nobody seemed too keen to praise this particular machine. Originally thrashing was a community effort but many of the labourers that used to get work in Claregalway were let go after mechanisation.

Agriculture

Trashing corn with the old trashing mill. About the 1940s.

Wheat was also grown and was taken to the mill to make wholemeal from which bread was made. Mangles, turnips, and potatoes were the other crops, which many farmers grew. Children were given special holidays from school for 4 or 5 days during the potato-picking season. Hay was originally harvested with the use of a scythe. The horse mower then arrived but the scythe still had to be used to cut an initial strip. The arrival of the tractor in the 1960's brought new machinery like the plough, rotary mower and combine harvester. These and other machines helped do away with old sights such as cocks of hay (usually small to prevent heating), and horses working in the field.

Barley was another crop grown in Claregalway, originally for malting but now used as feed for animals. The malting barley went to Guinness but farmers eventually opted to grow feeding barley that could be sold either to Flynns of Lackagh or else to the local farmers.

Hand operated winnowing machine, which separated seed from chaff. Used up to the 1940s.

Agriculture

The Claregalway Co-operative Agricultural Society.

It seems that the Claregalway Co-Operative Society was founded in 1899 according to a report in the Tuam Herald on the 4th February 1899. A meeting was held at Claregalway of the Irish Agriculture Organisation on the 22nd of January 1899 for the purpose of establishing a Co-operative Agricultural Society. Mr R.H French who had been most earnest to bring about a spirit among his neighbours took the chair. After Mr French had addressed the meeting, Mr Thomas Casserly delivered a short address in Irish. It was probably in conjunction with this that a public lecture was organised in 1903, which took place in the Claregalway National School on topics like "Manures and Manuring" also "Food and Feeding" amongst others. Rev M. Commins took the chair.

The Society was officially registered on 28th January 1915 under the Industrial and Provident Societies Act of 1893. Its registry reference was 1206 and from that date it had to submit annual returns, audited by a public auditor, to the Registrar in Dublin. These returns provided for detailed accounts and indicated how it traded.

The society had serious cash flow problems. It sold goods to farmers on credit who were either slow to pay or could not pay. Meanwhile it ran up an overdraft with the bank. Records show that it ceased to function since the 31st December 1923 owing to bad debts and the difficulty in collecting balances. It made efforts to collect these debts and correspondence by Mr. George Carter, a local schoolteacher who was the Society's secretary, shows that the debtors were all small farmers and they found it hard to meet their obligations. A resolution was passed to put the Society into voluntary liquidation on 3rd October 1926.

After much correspondence between the secretary and the Registrar, with threats of legal proceedings by the Registrar for the non-completion of annual returns, the registry of the Society was cancelled on the 29th November 1933.

The following is an extract from the official annual returns for the Society. Consider that the pound was worth more in the 1920's that it is now.

Agriculture

FORM A.R. 27.

FOR OFFICIAL USE.
Reg. No. 1206 R galway

FOR OFFICIAL USE.

REGISTRY OF FRIENDLY SOCIETIES
IRELAND **IMPORTANT.**
This Return does not apply to State Insurance, holding &c. and particulars relating to the operations of Society under the National Insurance Act must not be included.

INDUSTRIAL AND PROVIDENT SOCIETIES ACTS, 1893 TO 1913.

ANNUAL RETURN PRESCRIBED by the CHIEF REGISTRAR for AGRICULTURAL SOCIETIES in IRELAND carrying on Business under the above Acts.

Year ending (1) 31/38 December, 1915

This Return, together with a copy of each Balance Sheet made during the period included therein, is to be sent to the Registrar as soon as possible after the close of the Society's financial year and in any event not later than the 31st March, 1916.

Name of Society Clare Galway Cooperative Ag. Society _____ Limited.

Description of Trading { Agricultural Requirements manures & seeds
{ Agricultural Produce

Does the Society issue a printed Statement of Accounts (2) ? **No** } If so, a copy should be forwarded with the Annual Return.

Has the Public Auditor made a *Special* Report other than the usual certificate as to the correctness of the Accounts ? **No**

State name of any organisation to which Society is affiliated I. A. O. S.

State number of Rule under which Shares are issued to Members 16

Date of Establishment 28th Jany 1915. When first Registered 28th Jany 1915.

Number of Branch Establishments at end of year

Do the Rules of the Society authorise operations under the Small Holdings and Allotments Act, 1908 ?

Do the Rules of the Society provide for security to be given by Officers, &c. ? Yes If so, state the number of the Rule 53

OFFICERS, &c., IN RECEIPT OR CHARGE OF MONEY.				
NAME. (3)	ADDRESS. (4)	Maximum amount of Cash held.	SECURITY. Amount.	Whether by Bond or Guarantee Society
George Carter	Claregalway	510/-	—	—

Does the Society give Credit ? Yes State to what extent as decided by Committee

If Credit is given, state number of Rule authorising it 4. d. ; or, if not authorised by Rule, state circumstances in which it is allowed

State amount deducted during the year from Members' Share Capital in payment of debts : £ — s. — d.

State upon what basis the value assigned to the Stock-in-Trade at end of year has been calculated, and by whom it has been certified

State what provision is made for Bad and Doubtful Debts none

The Audit for the year has been conducted by Mr. Bussain , Public Auditor under the Industrial and Provident Societies Act, appointed to conduct the Audit by the Shareholders.

under the authority of Rule No. 40

Registered Office of Society, (4) Claregalway

in the County of Galway.

RETURN AS TO MEMBERS.	Ordinary Members.	Societies or Companies.
Number of Members at the beginning of the year (5)	—	—
Number of Members admitted during the year	132	—
Together	144	
Number of Members whose membership has ceased during the year ...	1	—
Number of Members at the end of the year	131	—

(1) This date must be within four months before or one month after 31st December, 1915.
(2) If no printed statements are issued, a written "copy of each balance sheet made during the period included in the return" will be accepted (see Sec. 3 (2) of 1913 Act).
(3) If the names are more than can be conveniently inserted here, they may be added (with the particulars required) on a separate sheet.
(4) State full postal address.
(5) This must agree with the number at the end of the previous year, as shown in the Annual Return for that year, or an explanation of the difference must be furnished on this form.

(J 3573—r.) Wt. 15483—18. 2000. 8/15. D & S.

Copy from the first annual return of the Claregalway Co-operative Agricultural Society for 1915

- 21 -

Agriculture

Year	Number of Members	Sales	Bank Overdraft	Debtors
1915	131	£700	£342	£315
1916	180	£1,370	£793	£777
1917	211	£2,182	£740	£912
1918	225	£2,387	£975	£810
1919	241	£2,323	£1,431	£1,316
1920	245	£2,491	£1,801	£882
1921	245	£3,250	£1,824	£1,461
1922	245	£1,074	£1,687	£1,218
1923	251	£995	£1,370	£1,205
1924	251	£77	£858	£694
1925	253	----	£608	£435

Debtors refers to the money owing to the Society for goods sold on credit.

People in the Carnmore townland joined a Co-op in the neighbouring Oranmore but this suffered the same fate as the one in Claregalway. In the 1950's there was a similar failure, this time involving branches of Macra Na Feirme and the Young Farmers Association. They bought manure and other items in a co-operative manner, but it did not work out. As regards the manure, it arrived loose in lorries leaving the farmers with a lot of work. They firstly had to get in weighing equipment and then weigh, bag, and distribute the manure. All in all this proved to be time consuming and messy; so it was not repeated.

The Connacht Tribune, 10th September 1910:

PROTEST AGAINST INACTIONS OF CONGESTED DISTRICT BOARD AND NEGLECT OF DRAINAGE TRUSTEES

"A special meeting of the Claregalway branch of the United Irish League was held on Sunday last to consider the steps to be taken towards acquiring permanent relief for the parties whose lands were inundated during the floods. The floods were abating slowly, but two square miles of country still continued flooded. There was a very large and representative attendance.

Speech by the The Chairman of the County Council:

Mr J.A. Glynn, the chairman of the County Council, ..., said he regretted that the occasion for the meeting had arisen. He thought the previous meeting held in connection with the flooding of Montiagh would have been the last. At that time they approached the Estates Commissioners with a view of having the people of

- 22 -

Agriculture

Montiagh transferred to the good land around them, where they would be free from floods. He was greatly surprised to see by the papers last week that they were again troubled by the floods and that the work of the Estates Commissioners good as it was, was not sufficient.

The Chairman wrote to him asking him to call to the office of the Congested Board as he was in Dublin with a view to having further relief granted. He did so, but Messrs. Doran and Micks were absent on urgent business in some other part of the country and there was no person there who had the authority to deal with a case like his. When he came home, he received a letter from Fr. MacHugh asking him to attend their meeting on that day. As far as the floods were concerned the people had to bear the loss.

Some years ago they got counsel's opinion as to how they could compel the drainage Commissioners to clear the river. The opinion was very clear that they could approach the Board of Works and compel them to do so, but every penny spent would come out of their own pockets just the same. Previously the drainage rate had been paid by the landlords but now it must be paid by the tenants who purchased the land. The Drainage Commission a few years ago recommended that all drainage boards be abolished and their powers vested in the County Councils. When the Galway County Council asked to be given the powers of the Galway Drainage Board they were refused them. Now the Board was willing to transfer to them the powers, as the rates have to be levied on the tenant farmers. The County Council has now refused to accept them, pending proper legislation.

...... There was an All-Ireland Drainage Committee formed some time ago for the purpose of forcing on the Government the necessity of taking over the drainage boards. The matter would be before Parliament when it assembled and he was sure their interests would be well looked after by Mr Duffy, M.P. .... They came there with a definite purpose and that was to form a committee and that committee would forward to the C.D. Board a memorial requesting them to purchase the grazing ranches in the neighbourhood and transfer the people who live in the bogs to them.

... There are two estates in the neighbourhood and the committee should interview the proprietors of those to know if they were willing to sell. If they are not, the C.D. Board has the fixing of the price and they can be compelled to sell. As regards one of the estates in the neighbourhood, he was sure there would be an offer to sell to the Congested Districts Board before Christmas. ..... They were successful before in getting the land for the tenants in the Clanmorris estate and he was sure they would be successful again. ...

Speech by Mr William Duffy M.P.:

..... It was sad to think that after all the Acts of Parliament that had been framed and reframed that people of Montiagh should still be living under such

Agriculture

conditions – living under constant fear of losing their lives and their crops after their hard year's work. It was most lamentable to see human beings living under such conditions. It is all due to the maladministration of the English Government, and it is a terrible commentary on any country that would allow such a state of things to exist.......

He hoped the Central Districts Board would be induced to purchase the lands belonging to Messrs. Ffrench, Burke and Holmes, which were in the neighbourhood and have them divided amongst the tenants. The only hope for the people of the low-lying districts was to transfer them into the uplands. Their object in holding the meeting that day was to impress upon the Central District Board the necessity for having that done and to request them to enforce their compulsory powers. There may be some landlords who are willing to sell, but if they are not they will be compelled to do so.

The Central District Board was charged with the full responsibility for the relief of the people and unfortunately Montiagh came within their category. The people were living in a perilous position, subject to floods and were as entitled to relief as any people could be. The landlords' greed, exactions, extravagances were allowed to continue too long over the people and would not be allowed any longer. The people of the district may not be altogether blameless for allowing such a state of things to exist so long as their own inaction might have caused it. If the people joined the popular movement and kept united he was sure there would not be a single person living in the bogs.

If the people supported the local branch of the United Irish League, the Irish Party would see that their grievances were addressed. ..... It was through the Irish Party, that the Land Act of 1909, which gave compulsory powers to the C.D. Board, was passed.

Emigration / Migration

Times were bad in Ireland during the 1940's and 1950's. Brendan Behan frequently mentioned the eternal triangle of poverty, pregnancy, and emigration. Massive emigration was a constant feature. Every year dozens of young men and women from the parish emigrated to the Bronx in New York, to Norwood in Boston, to London, to New Zealand, Australia or Canada. Among those of course, were many of our star hurlers never again to wear the jersey for the honour of the village. Some emigrants who immediately come to mind are - the Duggans, Grealishs, Lardners, Killileas, Bodkins and Hanleys. Also Paddy Feaney, Sean Fahy, Martin Murphy, Mattie Fox, Johnny Hynes, Mattie Conneely, Mattie Commins, and Mike Ruane to name but a few.

One interviewee told of two of his uncles in particular who emigrated after the famine. They went off on the ship from Galway in search of a new life. One was supposed to have reached the American coast and settled in New York. There he

Agriculture

set up a shop for himself and married a German girl. He was commonly known, we are told, by some as Black Micheal Forde. He never returned home, as was the fate of many of the Irish emigrants at the time. As for the fate of the other uncle he died on the ship and was buried at sea. The land that was left behind by the emigrants was generally divided amongst the remaining family.

Transporting the Mointeach Migrants to County Kildare in 1960.

In 1908 there were 40 families living in Montiagh who were very close to each other. This probably goes back to before Cromwell's time when they were forced off any good land that was in Claregalway. In that year the Land Commission transferred out a number of families to Kiltrogue and Crusheen in Claregalway. Included in the transfer were the Morans, the Noones, the MacGuinnesses, the Murphys and four Duggan families who were moved to the Kiltrogue area. The Land Commission then divided their lands amongst the people that were left behind.

In the 1950's there were about 20 houses in Montiagh. In 1960 four

Milking the cow by hand. About the 1940s.

- 25 -

Agriculture

families from Claregalway, three from Montiagh and one from Cahergowan moved to Kildare near the Curragh. The Land Commission had taken their property and sub-divided it giving them better and bigger farms in Kildare in exchange. In 1961, the Moran family was moved fom Cloonbiggen to Trim in Co. Meath and in 1962 the Dolly family was moved also from Waterdale to a farm near Maynooth.

Ploughing

The Connacht Tribune - 20th February 1937:

PLOUGHING IN LOUGHGEORGE -
WINNER SPOKE IRISH ALONE

"A ploughing competition which aroused much interest was held on the lands of Mr. Malachy Kelly, Loughgeorge, Claregalway recently. The competition, which was held under the auspices of the County Committee of Agriculture, was organised by Mr. D. Harney, Department's overseer, assisted by Messrs. John Monaghan and Thomas Hughes, Knockdoe. Under good hard weather conditions and before a large gathering, seven teams participated in a competition which, considering that it was the first of its kind in the locality, reached a very high standard.

In class I, (chill plough) the standard reached was particularly high and Mr Thomas Newell, Carraghy, Claregalway was awarded a meritorious first in the class. Mr Martin Fox, Killeen, Castlegar and Patrick Lawless, Anbally, Corofin were awarded second and third respectively for very creditable performances in the same class.

Tom Reilly, former All Ireland Senior Horse Plough Champion.

Agriculture

Claregalway ploughing match participants, about the 1950s.

In class II (swing plough) Mr M Duggan, Montiagh, Claregalway, who plays full-back in his parish hurling teams, was awarded first for really good ploughing. Irish was the only language used by this competitor during the whole competition and by a large following who supported him. Second prize in this class was won by Mr Martin Hughes Claregalway and Mr William Joyce of Caraun, Claregalway was awarded third. The competition was judged by Mr Cotter, county instructor in agriculture."

The Connacht Tribune - 1st February 1947:

GALWAY'S PLOUGHING CHAMPION

"Thomas O'Reilly, Cloon, Claregalway, last year's junior champion, won the Galway County Ploughing Championship, Perpetual Challenge Cup at Caherlistrane on Thursday."

The Connacht Tribune - 8th February 1947:

"Mr Thomas O'Reilly, Cloon, Claregalway who won the County Senior Championships and perpetual challenge cup at the county ploughing championships held in the lands of Mr. Patrick Mangan Caherlistrane on Thursday of last week was the holder of the Co. Junior Championships which he won at Glenamaddy last year. He has competed about 7 times in the championship. Conditions were against good ploughing as the heavy frost the night before made the sod very hard. Some competitors were still ploughing when darkness fell.

Mr D Harney Agricultural Overseer in Claregalway said that even though the standard was not up to previous years he thought that it was very good when conditions were taken into consideration."

Agriculture

The Claregalway ploughing committee pictured at their annual social in 1969.

Thomas O'Reilly from Cloon, Claregalway first started ploughing in 1945. Ploughing was very popular at the time as can be seen from the numerous articles in the Connacht Tribune. Mr O'Reilly recalls that up to 50 or 60 teams of horses would compete in the competitions. There were quite a few from Claregalway involved in the ploughing at county level.

He has won 28 county senior matches. He won the Junior All-Ireland in 1963 and 10 Senior All-Irelands in 1978, 1981, 1982, 1983, 1984, 1985, 1988, 1989, 1991 and 1993. He also won a special horse class in 1990 and 1992. He represented Ireland in the 1984 World Ploughing Championship, which were held in Horn Castle, Lincolnshire, England, where he was runner up. In the Championship the competitors ploughed for two days, then after that marks were given. The World Ploughing Championships are held in different places all over the world each year. He was placed third in the European ploughing championships that were held in Limavaddy, Derry in 1991.

Thomas O'Reilly explained how the condition of the field plays an important part in ploughing. Also he told us that in the beginning he used to borrow horses for the competition but as he *"went at it in earnest"* he purchased his own. Now his son Gerard is also involved in ploughing.

Pat Kilgarriff composed the following poem to the ploughman's daughter on her wedding day.

THE WEDDING

It was up in Claregalway at a wedding one day,
Some came for to look and some came for to pray,
It was James Kilgarriff who built in Rahoon,
And Tom Reilly's daughter, the ploughman from Cloon.

Now Jimmy took Mary and Mary took Jim,
And pictures were taken of her and of him,
You could tell by his smile he was over the moon,
With Tom Reilly's daughter, the champion from Cloon.

We left from Claregalway to drive into town,
And bonfires were blazing around Cahergowan,
We drove into Galway our bellies to fill,
At a place called the Warwick away up in Salthill.
They were singing and dancing and screeching for more,
They knocked lights off the ceiling and sparks off the floor,
They were ploughing with horses around Galway Bay,
And Pat Murphy's meadow was mowed in a day.

They sang of the Claddagh at the foot of Fairhill,
With everyone happy and Tom paying the bill,
Then we departed to give Tom his due,
The All Ireland trophies at a pub in Cloonboo.

Fairs and Markets

A fair existed in Claregalway in the nineteenth century. Proof of this is contained in the Connacht Tribune of 1852, which tells us that the fair day was set for the 12th October. Here people bought and sold bonhams, cows, sheep, cattle and every sort of vegetable as well as oats, wheat and barley. Besides this, the people of the parish travelled to fairs in Galway, Athenry, Tuam and Headford. When the people had to go to Galway this meant leaving home at one or two in the morning to walk to the fair with their livestock. As people didn't have good lights at the time the journey was even harder.

When they arrived in Galway they had to find a place to stand with their animals, anywhere from where Moons is now, all the way out to Bohermore. In the late 1950's cattle and sheep were sold here, and occasionally bonhams, as mentioned earlier. Other produce sold in Galway were oats, turnips and potatoes that were usually brought into town on a horse and cart. There were usually sold opposite the American Hotel, as there was a scale there for weighing. A strange practice

Agriculture

at the time was that it was often incumbent upon the seller to deliver the produce, which meant that the day was made even longer as all the different runs had to be made. Also sold was the rye that was grown in the boggy land, straw which was good for thatching and cart loads of hay. When everything was sold and the day was over, everyone headed for home.

McDonaghs and Palmers were two big oat buyers at the markets. When Martin McDonagh was the most extensive merchant in Galway he employed a man from Claregalway to buy oats for him. A certain story went around that this man used to walk around the sellers with his hands behind his back and if someone "tipped" him some money, McDonaghs would buy their oats. Mr McDonagh, or "Martin Mor" as he was more commonly known, also employed Sean Corcoran from Lydacan to look after his horses.

Persse's distillery, in the early years of this century, had their own buyer at the Galway market, a Martin Cullinan from Claregalway, whose task was to buy good quality oats and barley.

One man from Claregalway gave an account of his memories of the fairs in Galway:

"There was a weighing scale in the square in Galway. It is gone out of it now. They had a great name in our village for having a top class potato. I used to hear my father and my brother say that they wouldn't be allowed pass through Bohermore but they'd have the whole lot of the potatoes sold before they got to the market at all."

Another person recalled how a lot of bargaining went on between the buyer and the seller to get the best possible price going. Finally when the deal was struck (by spitting on the palm of the hand and shaking hands) the farmer would give the buyer a little "luck money". Then they both proceeded to the pub for a drink.

Besides Galway other local fairs were held in Tuam, where the October fairs were the biggest, in Headford on church holy-days and later on the fourteenth of each month in Castlehackett (June 2, October 2) and Turloughmore (August 1 and September 18). The latter two places also had a carnival atmosphere, with drinking booths, peddlers and travelling musicians. Fights might also break out and in the 1840's three men were killed following a faction fight at the fair in Turloughmore.

Fairs changed after the 1960's or so as the marts became more popular. The marts were a lot more organised and the penning and tagging of the animals meant that the farmer didn't have to be constantly minding and looking out for his animals.

Agriculture

General

When land was being valued in the last century, the land of Carnmore was valued at a lower level than other land in the parish because of the fact that there was not much water or wells on the land. The land itself though was probably better than the higher valued land in the west of the parish and since the 1973 water scheme, Carnmore now has an adequate water supply.

Sleán for cutting turf; churn for making butter and a spinning wheel for making thread from wool.

Grievances over land were particularly liable to erupt into violence. In 1837 in Claregalway when tenants were evicted from the Lord Clanmorris estate, the man who took over possession was targeted. He himself was beaten "most unmercifully" as was his son, while their workers, who were ploughing at the time had to run to safety leaving their horses to be chased off the land, and the implements to be broken by the mob. When the Loughgeorge police arrived they saw some distance away on a hill a large number of people shouting and hollering.

The Wyndgam Land Act of 1903, which provided extensive financing with favourable terms to enable tenants to purchase their holdings from the landlords, marked the end of the Land War. Among the landlords who sold out in 1904 was Lord Clanmorris, enabling his Claregalway tenants to buy their farms. The previous October he came to Montiagh, where flooding of the Clare River was causing great hardship, and arranged for an increase in the size of holdings there. Also he set up a relief fund to help those who had lost crops etc. In 1907 the last of the Burkes of Ower, Mrs Margaret Teeling, sold her lands at Ower (665 acres)

Agriculture

and Moyne (752 acres) holding on only to the house and demesne (146 acres) at Ower.

In 1908 the Tuam Herald showed the results of the "County of Galway Scheme of Prizes for Cottages and Small Farms". In first place in the Galway Rural Class was John Duggan, Loughgeorge and second was John Monaghan, Knockdoe, Claregalway.

The farmers of Claregalway also hit the news in the 1970's when the sheep and potatoes, upon which there were large dependencies, had just gone from two years of scarcity and high prices to the situation of high acreage and high yield which was set to plummet prices. Then, at the same time the Clare River could not hold the very heavy rainfall and 100's of acres were affected, with the potato crop worst hit. It was hoped that the drainage scheme of the 1950's (see chapter on Clare River) would ensure that these floods would recede faster than they had previously. Cattle and sheep that had to be taken in were now being fed their winter-feeding which meant that there would inevitably be a shortage in the spring.

Drilling plough; horses hames (on the wall); horse drawn spring harrow for tilling and a milk can.

In the early days when there were no vets, either the farmers themselves or the local quack carried out treatments, which were usually herbal. Two men who did such work in Claregalway were Paddy Feeney from Corbally and Patrick Cullinan from Cahergowan.

Farm-work was easier after the advent of electricity even if only for the advantage of lighting to replace the old lamps with wicks. The electricity arrived and local horses were used to draw up the big poles.

Chapter 3: 1916 Rising and Troubles

1916 Rising

County Galway was one of the few places outside Dublin to have taken an active part in the 1916 Easter Week Rising. On Monday evening of that week news of the insurrection reached the Galway countryside and local volunteers from Claregalway and Castlegar began to mobilise. The supporters of these men of 1916 became known as Sinn Feiners.

The leader of the Claregalway men was Tom Ruane who was also the captain of the Claregalway hurling team. Other officers in the Claregalway Company included Nicko Kyne, George Glynn and Patrick Feeney. Many men from the Claregalway hurling team had joined the IRA. Together with the officers, the men listed below made their way to an initial meeting at Carnmore Cross.

Willie Carr	Carnmore
John Collins	Carnmore
Ned Cummins	Carnmore
John Conneely	Carnmore
John Hughes	Carnmore
William Flaherty	Carnmore
James Grealish (Peter	Carnmore
James Grealish (Roger)	Carnmore
Mairtín Paddy Grealish	Carnmore
Mairtín Watt Grealish	Carnmore
Patrick "Patcheen Eamuin" Grealish	Carnmore
Jack, Mike, Peter and Tom Lally	Carnmore
John, Pat and Stephen Walsh	Carnmore
William Corcoran	Lydacan
Tom "Tailliúr" Hession	Cregboy
Martin Samways	Cregboy
Michael, Philip and Tom Murphy	Gortatleva
Pat Kelly	Caherlea
Henry Duggan (Liam)	Montiagh
Willie Duggan	Montiagh
Henry Duggan (Sean)	Montiagh
Dan Duggan	Montiagh
Thady Corkett	Montiagh
John Concannon	Montiagh

At Carnmore, they rendezvoused with the Castlegar men under Brian Molloy and Pat Callanan. Orders came from Liam Mellows via Padraig Feeney to tell the two companies to proceed to Moyode. This was agreed for daybreak the following day and leaders Tom Ruane and Pat Callanan went to rest for a few hours.

As they rested, a group of policemen travelled on reconnaissance through the Castlegar and Carnmore areas. On arriving at Carnmore Cross, they came across the Volunteers. An initial shot was fired by the Volunteers side killing a Constable Whelan, who was the first fatality of 1916 in Galway. Ruane and Callanan now arrived on the scene to find the men in a buoyant mood and they began marching to Moyode. Despite their limited arsenal of weapons, pikes, forks and a few shotguns, the mood within the camp was optimistic as they awaited orders from Mellows.

Comdt. Pat Feeney from Mullacuttra who was prominent during 1916

As the days went by and no action was ordered, times were getting harder for Mellows men, as food was difficult to come by. After some time Fr. Feeney from Castlegar begged them to go home. Cold and hungry, they left Moyode with whatever weapons they had with them. As they got more tired and hungry, they dropped their weapons, with the result that John Concannon from Montiagh was one of the few to return with his gun. They were so weak that even Henry Duggan came home without his boots, being too weak to carry them.

In the aftermath of 1916, came the hunt for the rebels. Descriptions of those on the run were published in the police bulletin *"Hue and Cry"*. Nicko Kyne from Kiltrogue village was charged with *"having on the 25th April 1916 and subsequent dates at Carnmore and Oranmore, committed various acts of rebellion."* Many others were also accused of similar crimes and were pursued as a result of this bulletin.

Two hundred police from Northern Ireland were drafted into Galway to assist the local force. Houses of suspected rebels were torn apart in an effort to find weapons. In one week alone two hundred and seventy rebels were arrested and sent to Dublin by warship, but later prison trains were used to transport the prisoners. Everyone was housed in Richmond Barracks and while there, many were court-martialled. The leader of the Castlegar Company, Brian Molloy was sentenced to death in relation to the death of Constable Whelan at Carnmore Cross, but this was later commuted to ten years penal servitude. The lists of men from Claregalway sent to prisons in Great Britain included:

Sent to:

Wandsworth Detention Barracks:
Patrick O'Brien	Waterdale
J. Collins	Claregalway

Stafford Detention Barracks:
William Coady	Claregalway
Michael Glynn	Lydacan
Patrick Grealish	Carnmore
Philip Murphy	Gortatleva

Lewes Detention Barracks:
Patrick Concannon	Claregalway

By July 1917 most prisoners were home again, and it was such people who formed the core of the IRA. Included among the people who went on the run was Tom Ruane. He headed for Moycullen and he travelled out onto an island in Lough Corrib whenever he was in danger. The police and the army came looking for him on several occasions. He escaped arrest because the Irish Secret Service was able to inform him in advance of the British plans. A reward of one thousand pounds was offered for his capture. Eventually by a stroke of misfortune, his wife's handbag was snatched by two R.I.C. men in Galway. Contained in the bag was a letter, which bore his address at Bohans, Borra, Moycullen. Tom Ruane was arrested, taken to the police station in Galway and later deported to the internment camp in Frangoch, Wales, where he spent ten months. He was arrested again in 1918, in connection with the so-called German plot, jailed in Wormswood Scrubs and later in Winson Green, Birmingham.

Men who served with Tom Ruane in the Second Battalion of the first Galway Brigade included:

Sgt. W. Coady	Claregalway
Comdt. Patrick Feeney	Mullacuttra
Lieut. T. Fox	Carnmore
Vice Comdt. Martin Grealish	Claregalway

With Sean Collins, T. Cunningham, Seamus Duggan, Martin Fahy, D. Greally, Sean Lynskey and Nicholas Murphy of Kiltrogue and with Sean Lally of Carnmore.

An 1916 Bayonet and old Guards baton belonging to Martin Lally, Carnmore West.

The Black and Tans

In 1920, the Black and Tans arrived in Ireland and brought with them a reign of terror, torture and murder as part of the British response to the Irish Declaration of Independence. The parish of Claregalway suffered along with other parts.

The Tans took their names from their khaki and black uniforms and were said to have been sent to Ireland because of their savagery. They travelled throughout the countryside in "Crossley Tenders" sitting in two rows opposite each other. They shot indiscriminately at everything and everybody would run for cover when they heard the lorries approach. People lived in constant fear for their lives and homes and many slept fully clothed because if they took too long to open a door, the Tans would break the door down. Searches took place in the houses of known Republicans and sympathisers. As well as shooting their intended targets, they often beat or shot other family members.

In a raid on Egans pub in Cashla, the owner of the pub Thomas Egan was shot dead having been accused by the Tans of withholding information. To add insult to injury, the Tans then limited the numbers attending his funeral to the extent where even his closest relatives were afraid to attend. The Tans also killed John Hanlon of Lackagh.

Charles Quinn from Claregalway was injured in a failed ambush on the Black and Tans. People were waiting on both sides of the road but a badly aimed grenade knocked a wall on some of the ambushers exposing them to the Tans gunfire. Quinn was injured and taken to the Infirmary in Prospect hill (what used to be the old county buildings). A nurse in the Infirmary, who was dating an R.I.C. man, told him that Quinn was a patient. However Quinn was taken away before he was to be killed.

Officers of the Second Battalion of the First Galway Brigade of the IRA, taken at Killeen Castle, Claregalway in 1921.
Front Row (reclining): Martin Skerritt and W Cunningham.
Kneeling: J Cunningham, D Greally, Frank Cunnane, Nicholas Murphy, P O'Brien, P Connell and W Cody. *Centre Row:* Martin Grealish, T Cunningham, Padraic Feeney (in uniform), T Fox, Martin Fahy, Seamus Duggan, Craddock, Langan, Michael Feeney, John Healy, Martin Kyne and Tom Ruane. *Back Row:* Tom King, Joe O'Flynn, Sean Lynskey, Sean Lally, P Dooley, Sean Collins, John Melia and Malachy Healy.

Two Tans also threatened Fr. Moran because he was a known Republican sympathiser. It took the intervention of another soldier to prevent his execution. However this did not prevent them plotting to burn his and other big houses in the area. This plot also involved the attempted burning of Cahills Post Office, but for the vigilance of locals who hunted the arsonist/ex soldier from the scene. If the burning had succeeded, it would have given the Black and Tans the ideal excuse for the retaliation that they sought.

Attack on Loughgeorge R.I.C. Barracks

In May 1920, the mid-Galway Brigade I.R.A. launched an attacked on the R.I.C. barracks in Loughgeorge. The barracks was manned by nine R.I.C. men and a sergeant. The Loughgeorge barracks was an important strategic post. The barracks was built of sandstone walls and was surrounded by barbed wire. I.R.A. policy at the time was to make such military posts no longer fit to occupy and to force their complete evacuation.

The roads between Loughgeorge and Galway and between Loughgeorge and Oranmore were to be blocked and mined so as to prevent reinforcements coming. The attack took place at night. A bomb was placed against the wall and it blew up half the gable wall. It also blew the gable of Duggan's workshop next door. Following the explosion the attackers poured rifle and revolver fire through the hole. Nobody was killed in this incident, the only casualty being a constable who was injured by flying glass. Eventually the attackers withdrew, after which the R.I.C. put on a show of force by firing and sending up flares.

The Duggan family who lived next door fled their home until the attack was over, their horse and foal having being killed. Reinforcements from Eglington Street, who had been sent for, were delayed because the attackers, who all escaped, had blocked the road by felling trees and by building a wall.

Thomas Ruane

Tom Ruane was a native of Carnmore and joined the I.R.B. when it was formed in 1908. As we have already seen from the 1916 Rising, he was an active member of the GAA, captaining the hurling side from 1910 to 1916, his favourite position being that of full back. He was also a member of the County Board for a number of years.

Captain Tom Ruane from Carnmore who was prominent from 1916 to 1922

In 1916 he was in Moyode with the Galway Brigade under the command of Liam Mellows and when this was disbanded he went on the run. After his release from Birmingham Prison, he was appointed a justice of the Sinn Fein courts for south and west Galway.

He was subsequently on the run from the Black and Tans when there was a reward of £1,000 for his capture. He took the Republican side in 1920. As a reprisal for the Kilroe ambush, which occurred near Headford, all his farm produce including turf was burned.

Tom Ruane was chairman of the old Galway District Council for seven years.

He was elected to Galway County Council as a Sinn Fein member and was chairman of the Finance Committee.

His horses ran in the local races and he also had an interest in greyhounds. Both his sons were involved in politics. Paddy was in Sinn Fein for 30 years and was elected to Galway County Council six times; he was also a committed GAA member and was local Treasurer for many years. Stephen Ruane was a member of Fianna Fail for many years. Their nephew is presently a British MP.

Thomas Ruane died on 31st August 1937 aged 53 years. He is buried in Claregalway cemetery and the inscription on his headstone reads:

> *Erected by his widow, family and 1916 comrades of the*
> *Old IRA Claregalway, in memory of the Vice-Brigadier*
> *of the Second Western Division. Thomas Ruane*
> *Carnmore August 31st 1937. R.I.P.*

On one side of the base of the headstone are carved crossed rifles and the year 1916.

World War I (1914-1918)

Bernie Fahey from Cregboy killed in action during World War I and buried in France

This would have been a turbulent time in Ireland and as we have already seen in Claregalway and surrounding areas. It would seem that anybody who emigrated to England, the United States, Australia or New Zealand were conscripted into their adopted country's army.

Bernie Fahey, an uncle of Brian Fahey and Evelyn Fox, went to New Zealand before the World War. He was conscripted into the New Zealand expeditionary force. He served in France where he was killed on active duty on 20th April 1917.

John Glynn, from Corofin Parish, had emigrated to America. He was conscripted into the American army when World War I broke out. He served in France, survived and eventually returned home. He married Kate Hughes from Mullacuttra where he lived until his death.

Pat Tynan was a Mayo man who lived with the Lenihans in Lakeview before the War. He returned to Claregalway where he worked as a postman until his retirement. He continued to live in Lakeview where he died on 11th May 1958 aged 81 years. He is buried in Claregalway cemetery.

Thomas Greaney (1888-1974) from Carnmore served with the U.S. Army. He was a step-uncle of Bridgie O'Brien, Carnmore.

World War II (1939-1945)

Known as the Emergency in Ireland, the Second World War epitomised life at it's most cruel, a time of hardship, shortages, and rationing.

Ladies Local Security Force (LSF), taken in Claregalway 1944.
Front Row (L to R): Bridie Morris, Baby Monaghan, Rita Hession, Nurse Keane, Mary Joyce and Julia Greally. *Back Row (L to R):* Bridgie Canavan, Bina Murtagh, Nora Hession, Mary Coady (Flaherty), Nora Moran (Glynn), Kathleen Holland (Fahy), Mary Feeney (Doherty), Winnie Heneghan Feeney and Bid Flaherty.

There were two organisations active in the parish: the Local Defence Force and the Local Security Force. Most people from the age of sixteen upwards were involved in one or the other organisation. Their role was one of security and because of Ireland's neutrality, neither British nor German invaders were welcome.

Because there was very little industry in the country, Ireland was dependent on imports. Everything was scarce. Good quality flour was non-existent and people

Emergency Services Claregalway 1944 comprising men and women of both the Local Defence Force and the Local Security Force.

had to make do with a type of 'black' flour mixed with barley, making it almost impossible to bake. Fruits such as bananas, oranges didn't arrive in the country at all and one could count themselves lucky if they had any currants or raisins at Christmas. Farmers were obliged to become self-sufficient and had to grow wheat by law. The farmers had a reasonable supply of meat as almost every house reared a pig.

There was no mill in Claregalway or Carnmore and some people recall going over to Lishenavella to the mill. T.V.O. (Tractor Vaporising Oil), a kind of paraffin oil, was used to turn the mill.

Rationing: Ration cards were sent out by the Government. The book was supposed to last for twelve months. One had to have so many coupons before getting clothes or shoes. Fabrics, such as threads, were of very poor quality; in fact everything was of a second hand rate. The law forbade the use of a car unless it was for a doctor, priest or soldier.

Bicycle tyres had to be carefully minded because replacements were not available. Candles were also scarce and of a poor quality.

Ted O'Connell of Mullacuttra served in the Second World War.

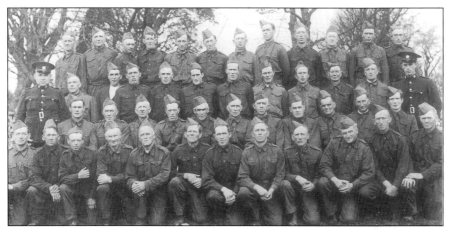

The Claregalway group Local Security Force (LSF) taken in 1944.
Front Row (L to R): John Kearney, Stephen O'Brian, Martin Murphy, Val Duggan (Cull), John O'Keane, Peter Duggan, Willie Corket Duggan, Henry Sean, Sean Johnny Moran, Martin Hughes, Tom Moran and Malachy Moran. *Second Row (L to R):* Mick Lenihan, William Lynskey, Val Duggan (Bailiff), Pat Skerritt, Tim Feeney, George Glynn, John Egan, Dan Hearney, Billy Morris, Martin Fox and Michael Madden. *Third Row (L to R):* Sergeant Gillespie, Dan Duggan, Charlie Quinn, Paddy Carr, Patrick Canavan, James Collins, Johnny Flaherty, James Connell, Sonnie Giles, Seamus Greally (Brack), Martin Hanley and Guard Kavanagh. *Fourth Row (L to R):* Pat Wall, J McGrath, Darby Greally, John Long, Joe Long, James Hession, Paddy Moran, John Concannon, Paddy Moran (Cloon), Michael Skerritt, Dan Noone and Séan Greally.

Claregalway Branch of the FCA in 1957

1916 Rising and Troubles

The Claregalway group Local Defence Force (LDF) taken in 1944.

Chapter 4: Landlords

The Owners of Claregalway Castle

The Earl of Clanricarde was the first to own and live in the present Claregalway Castle, which dates from the 15th century when it was built for Ulick de Burgo.

Tradition has it that the castle was occupied by a **Lord Dunkellin**, whose barony bears his name. Originally it had a thatched roof which had been maintained by a local man by the name of Duggan. The adjoining lodge was once owned by a Mayo cattle-rancher by the name of Mellotte. The lands attached to the castle were divided among local tenants by the Land Commission as a result of the land agitation in the early 1900's, but the fishing and fowling rights were retained by the owners of the castle.

The last landlord to inhabit Claregalway Castle was **Sir James Nelson**, a millionaire horse owner, whose family owned the Nelson Shipping line. He came mainly for the shooting season.

There are contradictory accounts as to the sequence of ownership from this point on. It would appear that the castle and lodge were purchased by a **Captain Palmer**, who was looked after by a local woman, Ellen Glynn. The next occupant seems to have been another English army officer by the name of **O'Connor**, who had seen service in India. He had a son and two daughters, Hyacinth and Geraldine. The castle was then purchased by **Johnson**, yet another officer, who had a taste for oriental decor. He hired many staff to maintain the building and grounds.

The castle and lodge seem to have been unoccupied for a period until after the civil war when the Civic Guards took temporary possession for a few years until the new barracks was built in Loughgeorge. In 1926 the property was taken over by a **Captain Slacey**, who had gas and a water supply installed in the lodge and invested a considerable sum on its refurbishment during his brief tenure. At this stage it seems that the castle had fallen into disrepair. The lodge was occupied for brief periods by **Major John Jordanstaff** and **Mr. Martin**, a County Council engineer, before the property was acquired by **Brigadier General Jobson** and his wife who was a retired nurse. They hired Peter Newell, Mary Greally and Johnny Hughes to maintain the buildings. Their son, Richard, was educated in the Grammar School in Galway. The Jobsons lived in the lodge until the 1960's, when the property was purchased by **Mr. Buckley** from Spiddal.

The present (1999) owner is Mr. E O'Donaghue.

Landlords

Lord Clanmorris

Lord Clanmorris's family name was Bingham. Mary P. Donnellan's article, *Clanmorris Rentals in Co. Galway* in the Journal of the Galway Family History Society, Volume V, 1998, gives fascinating glimpses into the lifestyle of the Bingham family. Her research shows that the first Bingham to be created Baron Clanmorris was in July 1800. The third Baron for whom the 1832/33 rentals were written up - Denis Arthur Bingham, who married Helena Persse, was "both a daring rider and a race horse breeder" and, in an article in *The Daily Telegraph* of December 21st 1895, he was noted as having possessed in his day "the best stud of hunters and steeplechasers that Ireland contained [Bingham Daly, Theresa, *The Mayo Binghams*, p.81]. He died in 1848 and was succeeded by his son, John Charles Robert Bingham, who married another member of the Galway Persse family. This gentleman was Lieutenant Colonel of the North Mayo Militia [*Burke's Peerage and Baronetage*, London 1907]. By 1878, John George Barry Bingham, 5th Baron Clanmorris, was noted as having three addresses - Cregclare and Seamount in Co. Galway and Newbrook, Ballyglass, Co. Mayo. [Hussey de Burgh, O.H., *The Landowners of Ireland*, Dublin, 1878].

The family had added the Cregclare acreage to their holding after the famine when they purchased a section of the Lambert property for £19,000 {Lane, Padraig G., "The Encumbered Estates Court and Galway Land Ownership, 1849-58 in Moran Gerard and Gillespie Raymond [eds.] *Galway History and Society*, Dublin, 1996, p.409}. In 1876/77, John George Barry was paying subscriptions towards membership of eight different clubs including Galway County Club, the Carlton, Marlboro and Kildare Street Clubs as well as yacht clubs in both Ireland and England, all in all a lifestyle that required considerable financial resources.

The last Lord Clanmorris lived in Cregclare near Ardrahan. He suffered two tragedies in a short space of time when two of his sons died. One, the Hon. Bentinck Yelverton, his third son, died at the age of thirty-seven in Brisbane. His other son, the Hon. Henry Derrick Thomas Bingham died in Llandulas after a few days illness at fourteen years of age. Lord Clanmorris owned over 3,000 acres in Claregalway, Kiniska, Montiagh North and South, Curraghmore and Cahergowan-Summerfield. In the townland of Claregalway there was once a police barracks and also a chapel and graveyard. These he leased out to James O' Brien and to the Rev. John Burke and his brother Michael. Lord Clanmorris sold the townlands in 1907.

Valentine O'Connell-Blake

Valentine O' Connell Blake farmed over 1,800 acres in Carnmore West and Carnmore East.

- 45 -

Landlords

The Coach house attached to Waterdale House

The Owners of Waterdale House

There is an interesting account of the occupancy of Waterdale House in the S.M.A Fathers' publication, *Claregalway Abbey*. According to their research the house was built in the 18th century by a member of the Staunton family from Buckinghamshire, who had settled in Galway in the 17th century and married a member of the Lynch family. The entrance to the house was at Mullacuttra, close to the fort on the Loughgeorge/Corrandulla road.

Waterdale House

Landlords

Walter Lambert of Cregclare, Ardrahan, married Catherine Staunton, a granddaughter of the first settler James Staunton. Lambert owned over 1,700 acres in Gortadooey, Gortcloonmore, Mullacuttra, Waterdale and Cloughane. He gave a terminable lease of the house and the demesne[c. 700 acres] to **James Blake**. The house, it was said, "with a judicious outlay could be made a most comfortable residence". Waterdale estate, 1,786 acres, which was heavily in debt in 1855, was saved from being sold off, because funds from the sale of other Staunton properties [including Cregclare House and part of the estate, sold to Lord Clanmorris] were used to "clear off the encumbrance" on Waterdale. In the early 1900's after the departure of Lady Lambert, with the house already vacant and falling into ruin, the lands were "striped", chiefly among the tenants and workers of the estate.

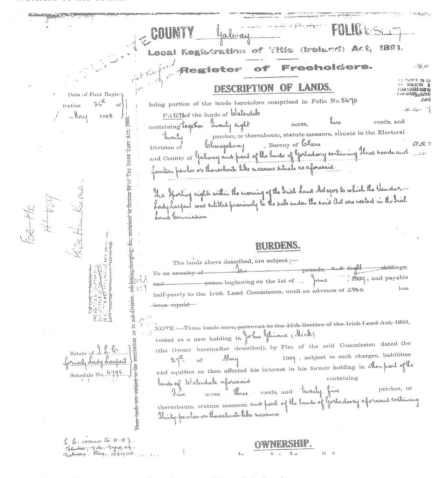

Copy of the land registration title relating to Waterdale lands

The Owners of Lydacan Castle

In the mid 19th century Andrew H. Lynch lived in Lydacan Castle and owned almost 1,700 acres of land in Lydacan, Caherlea, Gortatleva and Lissarulla. Patrick Qualter was caretaker of the estate.

Martin Francis O'Flaherty

The next occupant of the castle was Martin O'Flaherty. He evicted some families in order to enlarge his fields and to let the land to better tenants. This incurred the strong anger of Fr. James Commins, who was parish priest at the time, who preached a sermon against him in which he said that for a Catholic he was turning out as bad as Pollock. This made O'Flaherty disliked and feared. He was disliked for other reasons too. It was said that early in life he was a Young Irelander but that previous to the insurrection of 1848 he had fled to Australia or New Zealand to avoid taking part in it. He returned after some years having made some money.

The circumstances in which he came into possession of the Lydacan property are said to be as follows. The estate had been in the possession of the Lynch family previously and the last of them, a Mrs. Lynch, who was known among the people as *'An tSean Mhaistireas'*, became impoverished and the place was put up for auction by the creditors – whoever they were. No one wished to deprive the lady of her home and those who might be expected to bid agreed tacitly at least not to do so. O'Flaherty, who was described as being a 'hammer man' at the auction, made a bid and the property was knocked down to him.

These two circumstances, the way he acquired the estate and the fact that he was a renegade from the national cause, led to his being feared and also rather despised.

Martin O'Flaherty sold Lydacan Castle to James Greated. O'Flaherty died c.1870.

James Greated

Mr. Greated lived in the castle with his mother, wife and family. He seems not to have been popular with his tenants. The castle was burned in November 1922. The following is an account from the Tuam Herald about this event.

LYDACAN CASTLE GUTTED

'Last Saturday night the residence of Mr. James Greated, known as Lydacan Castle, Claregalway was set on fire by a party of armed and masked men who entered the castle at 9.30pm. The building was completely gutted, causing damage, which was estimated at £12,000.

Mr. Greated, his wife, his mother and his maid were taken to a stable where they

Landlords

Rockwood House, which belonged to the landlord Holmes. Recently renovated.

The gatelodge to the Holmes residence

were guarded by armed men. Later they found the castle ablaze. Republicans who arrived on the scene later helped to save some of the furniture. The household took shelter in the loft until morning.

Agrarianism is assigned to be the cause, Mr. Greated having had some dispute recently with certain parties in the adjoining village in regard to land. A few weeks ago he was driven from his home but returned again only to have it burnt to the ground. When his wife pleaded that the house should be saved, the raiders said that it was better that it should be burned than her husband should lose his life. Mr. Greated said that the question of the land had been referred to the courts and they should await the decision of the courts. Mr. Greated was also told by the raiders that this was the way Catholics were treated in Belfast. The outrage is universally condemned but it is a sorry and scandalous proceeding unworthy of Irishmen.'

James Galbraith

James Galbraith owned over 1,000 acres in Lakeview and Cregboy. Two of his tenants, John Galway and Edmond Morris acted as caretakers of the estate. There was a church in the townland of Lakeview, which was leased by Rev. James Commons. Galbraith sold the land of Lakeview to Mr. Holmes, another landlord, who lived in Rockwood House. The house and 99 acres of land were sold to Mr. Fox in 1922 for £385 [according to local tradition], while the remainder of the estate was taken over by the Land Commission. It is said that Holmes handed in a "scraw" to the Commissioners, symbolising the forfeiture of his ownership of the estate.

Rocklawn House, Cloon, about 1920s, home of the Ffrenches.

Landlords

James Ffrench

James Ffrench, of Rocklawn House, owned over 500 acres in Cloon and Pollaghrevagh. They were a Catholic family. The last of the Ffrenches - Eddie, his wife and sister-in-law - were boycotted in the late 1930's and early 1940's by locals, some of whom destroyed the house. The family was forced to live temporarily in a stable before leaving permanently.

William Burke

He owned close to 500 acres in Knockdoemore and Peake.

Dominick Browne

Almost 300 acres in Rooaunmore and Loughgeorge were owned at various times by Dominick Browne and the Directors of the Alliance Company.

Lord Bishop of Cashel

His estate consisted of 98 acres in the townland of Kiltrogue.

Landlords

Landlords' Estates

Lessor	Townland	Area		
		Acres	**Roods**	**Per**
Lord Clanmorris	Claregalway	479	3	30
	Curraghmore	792	3	11
	Kiniska	505	0	22
	Montiagh North	439	2	17
	Montiagh South	331	2	23
	Cahergowan/			
	Summerfield	585	0	39
	Total:	3085	1	22
Valentine O'Connell-Blake	Carnmore West	1774	1	09
	Carnmore East	88	2	01
	Total:	1862	3	10
Rep. Andrew H Lynch	Lydacan	842	1	26
	Caherlea	147	3	36
	Gortatleva	336	2	37
	Lissarulla	365	3	29
	Total:	1696	1	08
James S. Lambert	Gortadooey	409	1	33
	Gortcloonmore	507	0	39
	Mullaghruttery	180	0	16
	Waterdale	610	1	34
	Cloughaun	11	1	39
	Total:	1719	3	21
James Galbraith	Cregboy	676	1	02
	Lakeview	345	3	03
	Total:	1021	0	05
James Ffrench	Cloon	169	2	35
	Pollaghrevagh	386	0	31
	Total:	555	2	26
William Burke	Knockdoemore	267	1	02
	Peake	220	2	00
	Total:	487	3	02
Directors of the	Rooaunmore	250	1	16
Alliance Company	Loughgeorge	31	3	38
	Total:	282	1	14
Lord Bishop of Cashel	Kiltrogue	98	0	00
Martin Cullinan	Cahergowan/			
	Summerfield	51	1	11

- 52 -

Landlords

Lord Dunsandle	Lecarrowmore	33	2	11
Rep. Robert Faire	Cloonacauneen	29	0	16
Thomas Ruane*	Carnmore West	21	3	15
John Morris*	Carnmore West	0	3	10
		17	1	11
	Total:	18	0	21

Landlords' Estates

Tenant	Townland	Acres	Roots	Per
Michael Grealish (Jas)	Carnmore West	14	1	12
James O'Brien	Lecarrowmore	13	3	09
James Grealish	Carnmore West	10	3	11
John Galway	Lakeview		2	00
James Grealish & Patrick (John)	Carnmore West	6	2	23
John Ryan	Claregalway	5	0	00
Michael Burke	Carnmore West	4	3	20
Thaddeus Carr	Waterdale	4	0	0
James Blake	Carnmore West	3	2	24
Thomas Ruane & Michael Grealish (Jas)	Carnmore West	3	2	24
James Grealish & Michael (James)	Carnmore West	3	2	03
Michael (James)	Carnmore West	3	2	10
Owen Connell	Knockdoemore	2	0	28
Michael Rooney	Carnmore West	2	3	04
John Hanley	Carnmore West	2	1	05
Henry Walsh	Carnmore West	1	2	20
Patrick Reilly	Claregalway [police bks]	0	1	08
James Fahy	Lydacan, house & garden	0	1	00
Patrick Burke	Cregboy	0	0	18

List of lessors with whom there is no area

Lessor	Townland	Tenure
James O'Brien	Loughgeorge	house
Michael Burke	Cahergowan/Summerfield	4 houses
Michael Burke & Edward D. Burke	Curraghmore	house, small & garden
Edmund Lenehan	Lydacan	house
Honoria Casserley	Kiniska	house

Patrick Long (Roe)	Kiniska	2 houses
Gill Herward	Mullacuttra	house
Thomas Browne	Rooaunmore	garden
Edward Grealish	Carnmore West	house
Martin Tully	Cregboy	house
Thomas Casserley & Partners	Claregalway	herd's house
Catherine Kelly	Waterdale	house
Nicholas Kyne	Kiltrogue	house
Edmund Nolan	Cloughaun	house
Francis Carthy	Cahergowan/Summerfield	house
Patrick Concannon	Cloon	house
John Galway & land	Cloon	house, office
Bryan Moran	Pollaghrevagh	house & garden
Walter Collins	Caherlea	house & office
Patrick Kelly	Carnmore West	land

Water and its area

Lessor	Townland	Area		
		A	**R**	**P**
Lord Clanmorris	Claregalway	17	3	33
	Montiagh North	15	0	00
James S. Lambert	Gortcloonmore	10	2	00

Chapter 5: The Franciscan Friary

This chapter on the Franciscan friary is divided into two sections. The first will describe its history, which will be done sub divided by century. The second will describe its architecture.

History

Introduction

The Franciscans or Order of Friars Minor was founded probably in 1208, by St Francis of Assisi and approved by Pope Innocent III in 1209. After devoting himself to a life of preaching, service, and poverty, Francis gathered around him a band of 12 disciples. He led them from Assisi to Rome to ask for the blessing of the pope, who expressed doubt about the practicability of the way of life that the group proposed to adopt. Pope Innocent gave them his blessing, however, on condition that they become clerics and elect a superior. Francis was elected superior and the group returned to Assisi, where they obtained from the Benedictine abbey on Mount Subasio the use of the little chapel of Santa Maria degli Angeli, around which they constructed huts of branches. Then, in imitation of Christ, they began a life of itinerant preaching and voluntary poverty.

In 1223 Pope Honorius III issued a bull (old English for a papal edict) that constituted the Friars Minor a formal order and instituted a one-year noviciate (a period of apprenticeship). St. Francis died in 1226. As time passed, the order grew and the only body of equal power was the Dominicans. The Franciscans, however, became fractionalised, and in 1517 Pope Leo X divided the order into two bodies, the Conventuals, who were allowed corporate property, as were other monastic orders, and the Observants, who sought to follow the precepts of Francis as closely as possible. The Franciscans in Claregalway belonged to the Conventuals.

13th Century

The history of the foundation of the Claregalway friary is obscure, like most other friaries. The founding had been generally ascribed to approximately the year 1290. However in 1956, the chance discovery of a thirteenth century document in the State Paper Office in London had the result of *"bringing the date of the foundation of the Franciscan house at Claregalway to some year between 1250 and 1256, thirty years before the date commonly given hitherto"*.

John de Cogan I, one of the early Normans, built the monastery for the Franciscan friars around 1252 in what was then called 'Clar an Duil'.

The Franciscan Friary

A view of the Friary from the northeast

Claregalway had been granted to John de Cogan as a reward for his part in the conquest of Connaught. The Normans were major patrons of the church and played a large part in the introduction of religious orders. 'Clar an Diabhail' or Claregalway was considered to be in the diocese of Annaghdown. The friary is reputed to be the first known Franciscan house in Connaught.

In 1291, Pope Nicholas IV issued a bull granting an indulgence of one year and one quarantine (old English for forty days) to all penitents who visited the church of the friars minor of Claregalway on certain feast days. Those were the Annunciation of the Blessed Virgin, St. Francis, St. Anthony, St. Clare, or during their octaves, as well as on the anniversary of the dedication of the church.

In 1297, the Franciscan friary was at the centre of an ecclesiastical dispute between the diocese of Tuam and Annaghdown that reached the courts of King Edward I and Pope Boniface VIII in Rome. The diocese of Annaghdown had been created before the coming of the Normans and had the support of the native Gaelic O'Flaherty family, while the Tuam diocese represented the Normans. The Archbishop of Tuam considered that the territory of Annaghdown, or at least part of it, properly belonged to Tuam.

While the Bishopric of Annaghdown was vacant, its ceremonial items such as the mitre, crosier, ring, sandals together with letters and documents detailing the apostolic privileges were left for safekeeping with the friars of Claregalway. William de Bermingham, bishop of Tuam, raided the friary. His Archdeacon, Philip de Blund, had to appear before the court of common pleas in Dublin, charged with seizing forcibly from the Claregalway friars the chest of the bishop of Annaghdown. And that *"he broke it open in the doorway of the mother Church, and with force took away the episcopal mitre, with the pastoral staff and other contents"*.

This dispute seems to have dragged on for a number of years. There is a record of the case being heard before the chief justice in Dublin in 1300. In 1303, Pope Boniface VIII ordered the Bishop of Limerick to effect an agreement between the Archbishop of Tuam and the Dean of Annaghdown and failing this to report to the Pope, however it is not known how this concluded.

14th Century

In 1327, John Magnus de Cogan gave to the guardian and friars of the convent *"all the lands and tenements in Clonmoylan as far as Claredoule."* There is a picturesque condition imposed on the friars in return for this gift of presenting a rose annually to the donor and his heirs on the feast of St. John the Baptist.

In 1328, Robert, Bishop of Annaghdown sued Malachy, Archbishop of Tuam at the justices of the bench in Dublin for having by force carried off his goods and chattels found at "Strothyr Clare" (Claregalway) to the value of £40.

In 1333, another benefactor Philip Hamlin gave ten acres of land to the friars to provide the bread and wine for their Masses.

In 1368, Thomas de Bermingham, Lord of Athenry, gave them all the lands from Clonmoylan to Clare to pay for wine and candles for the altar.

In 1386, John Roch granted the friars as a perpetual alms all the lands of Clonmoylan, also an Alice Kerry bestowed on them two tenements and two and a half acres of land.

In 1387, Joanne Brown gave them more land. Also a James Caer, dean of the diocese of Tuam, gave them six acres of land at Cloynbiggan. (This could be the earliest reference to the present day town land of Cloonbiggen!)

15th Century

Pope Martin V in March 1426 addressed a mandate to Cormac O'Callaghan, a canon of Annaghdown, in answer to a petition almost certainly sent to him by a Claregalway friar. This mandate authorised him to grant dispensation to a friar named William Pulard from an irregularity incurred by him. The offence was: *"that William being then a priest, when playing with other clerics and laymen a game customary in those parts among both seculars and religious, accidentally struck another player, Donald O'hAschi, layman, near the ear with a sharp pointed stick, from which wound, Donald, a year later, owing to his own and his surgeon's carelessness died".* Also, *"if this poor friar was on his knees all this time over the death of this poor man, which was by accident, if the facts were as stated, then the parish priest here was to rehabilitate William Pulard and dispense him and allow him to minister again".*

In 1430, William de Burgo, with the consent of all the citizens of the town of Clare, granted them the pasturage of twenty-four cows in the common pastures of the town.

In 1433, Pope Eugene IV granted an indulgence of four years and four quarantines to all the faithful who visited the Franciscan church of Claregalway, chiefly, it would seem, to encourage the people to contribute to the renovation of the church and the completion of the steeple.

16th Century

Two great waves of destruction were responsible for the ruined state of most abbeys and churches in Ireland, including the Claregalway friary. The first was brought about by the suppression of the monasteries during the reign of Henry VIII and the second associated with the Confederate wars and the ensuing invasion by Oliver Cromwell.

On the 11th July 1538, Henry VIII sent Lord Leonard Gray to Galway. It is recorded that the abbey of friars at Claregalway was rifled by Gray's troops on their way to the western capital and *"neither chalice, cross nor bell left in it"*.

By 1541 most of the monasteries were closed, their possessions confiscated and their communities scattered into the surrounding countryside. The monasteries were scavenged for anything of value: lead, glass, timber and slates.

Queen Elizabeth I granted the abbey, with all its appurtenances (belongings) to Sir Richard de Burgo in 1570. However the friars remained in or near the place until about 1589 when Sir Richard Bingham, the English governor of Connaught, cleared the actual building of its inmates and used it as a barracks. According to undoubted tradition, he stabled his horses in the monastery chapel, while his soldiers were quartered in the cloisters.

17th Century

King James confirmed the title of local lords who obtained church lands following the confiscations of the previous century. The Earl of Clanrickard was given the *"the late monastery of Balleclare (Claregalway), with the site, church and church yard, 6 cottages and gardens, 24 acres arable, common pasture for 24 cows on the commons yearly, and a waste water-mill..."*

After the commencement of the civil war in 1641, the Franciscans made an attempt to restore the buildings, but owing to the turbulence of the times, were unable to carry out their intention.

18th Century

Edward Synge, The Anglican archbishop of Tuam, wrote on 25 November 1731: *"There is a Friary in Claregalway, where three at least are always resident"*. Stratford Eyre, the High Sheriff of the county, in submitting his report in 1732 stated: *"The friars of Claregalway live close to the Abbey and are building a large house. It is the estate of Thomas Blake."*

In 1744, Richard Croasdaile, a priest hunter, forwarding from Loughrea to Dublin Castle *"the most perfect list I could make"*, included the names of the guardian and of a friar, who he stated were then living at Claregalway.

There are several accounts given by people who travelled through the area. Pococke, the Anglican bishop of Meath, travelling in 1752 from Mayo to Galway wrote:

"In three miles I came to Baliclare (Claregalway); and near it on a rivulet saw Clare Galway Abbey, where the high tower, in the middle of the church, built on arches, is a curious piece of architecture; I saw the chapel of the church converted into a Mass house."

This use of the side chapel, or rather transept, had become necessary because of the dilapidated condition of the church of the friary.

In 1766, a report from the provincial of the friars, prepared for submission to the authorities at Rome, included the information that there were then five members, three of whom were advanced in years, in the community at Claregalway.

In 1791, Coquebert de Montbret, who was then the French consul at Dublin, recorded in his journal that at Claregalway *"The monks are settling down among the ruins."*

19th Century

Another traveller, a John Bernard Trotter who was a native of Co. Down, passed through Claregalway in September 1817, gives the following account:

"Between three and four miles on our way we reached the hamlet of Clare Galway, distinguished by a ruined castle and monastery. A handsome little river runs past them both. A neat cottage, adjoining the latter building, attracted our attention as well as the monastery. It had belonged to the Rev. Mr. Blake, a Catholic ecclesiastic of learning, benevolence, and taste. The good man was no more; but his cottage and gardens, though now neglected, evinced that a superior mind had dwelt there. A little raised spot, (planted with evergreens and other shrubs) made for pious meditation, and marked by an engraved stone, praying for the remembrance and prayers of survivors for himself, was near the cottage. The river murmured pleasingly near the garden in front. The ruined monastery immediately behind this sweet, but now melancholy cottage, is a very

fine and venerable old building. Here we saw a great quantity of skulls and bones as at Quinn (Co. Clare).

The housekeeper of the late venerable resident gave us a hospitable reception. Milk, butter, potatoes of the best kind, with household bread and eggs, were our fare, served up in the parlour of the late worthy owner. His housekeeper showed that she felt a deep and lasting sorrow.

The good ecclesiastic had a small chapel formed out of part of the old abbey, roofed in, and adorned with simple, but not inelegant taste. We learned with concern, that in the unhappy times of 1798, it had been ruined and defaced by some English militia, though Mr. Blake had given all his provisions to the soldiery. "I may live to repair it, and I pardon them", was all his remark; he had the satisfaction to leave his humble chapel in better order than it was previous to this outrage, before he died.

The housekeeper told us the fact without ceremony, but with a sort of surprise, mingled with calm forgiveness, at a transaction that must have dreadfully shocked her feelings when it happened. Doubtless it made a powerful sensation amongst Mr. Blake's flock, and nothing could be more unwise, or improper."

It was presumably, in the course of the demoralised retreat of the government forces from Castlebar, at the end of August 1798, that the chapel had been 'ruined and defaced'. The Rev. Martin Blake died on the 15th December 1816 at Waterdale in county Galway aged 63. There are two stone plaques that refer to him. (For details, go to the sections within this chapter on the Transept and the Outbuildings.)

According to a tabulated list of houses in the province, compiled by Fr. J.J. Mullock. OFM, in 1838, the community in Claregalway then numbered two preachers; neither the chapel nor residence had been constructed within the previous decade. Also according to the Complete Catholic Registry for 1845: the community in Claregalway then consisted of but two members.

The difficulty of maintaining the friary in such difficult circumstances had become a very real one for the Irish Franciscan province. Overall numbers had been decreasing steadily, from about 220 members in 1766 to about 150 in 1782, chiefly it would appear, as a result of restrictions imposed by the authorities at Rome in 1751. Of the 36 houses that were occupied in the year 1800, only 16 were still open in 1837, and these were staffed by a total of about 55 friars. It was therefore inevitable that a small foundation such as Claregalway could not continue its separate existence because it was situated in a rural area about 6 miles from Galway, which had its own community. There were just not enough personnel available to staff it.

It would appear from a newspaper report in the Galway Vindicator on November 1847 and supported by a local account that the community ceased to reside at

Claregalway friary during the month of November 1847. The account states:

"One day, one of the two friars who were the last to reside at Claregalway, having been questing for contributions for their support felt himself become ill and, instead of returning to Claregalway, asked the driver of the pony-trap to convey him to the friary at Galway. The driver complied and on his return to Claregalway, informed the other friar, who thereupon said in grief, 'That means that I too must leave here'. On the following day the driver brought him also to Galway".

The friar who took ill was Fr. James Hughes and the other friar was Fr John Francis. See the photograph of a portrait in oils, said to be of Fr. Francis, which was formerly in the friary at Galway. It measures some 28 by 21 inches and is signed 'R.O. Simmons'. Fr Francis died on 28th August 1858.

Portrait of Fr. John Francis, said to be the last friar to reside at the Friary in 1847

However on feast days, friars used to come from Galway to Claregalway to celebrate Mass, hear confessions and preach there. From the year 1860 not even these services took place. Guardians continued to be appointed up to about 1872. This however does not necessarily indicate that a community had again taken up residence there, because 'titular' or nominal guardianships were traditional, and at that time were numerous in the Irish province of the Order. They were particularly valued for the right of voting at chapter meetings that they conferred.

The Franciscans did not own the friary as such since it had been given to the Clanrickard family early in the 17th century. There is a receipt dated 16th January 1872, which records the payment by the then guardian at Galway of the sum of £9-9-8d, *"being one year's rent due to the Right Honourable Lord Clanmorris up to the first day of November 1871, out of his holdings in the Abbey, Claregalway".*

On the 21st September 1892, the building that was then in the possession of Lord Clanmorris was vested in the Commissioners of Public Works, under the provisions of the Ancient Monuments Protection Act of that year.

The Franciscan Friary

Architecture

The Claregalway friary building like most other friaries is composed of two main parts:
• the church, including the tower, and
• the living quarters, including the cloisters.
The church is the central and the most outstanding part.

A view from the southeast showing the imposing belfry tower

The church:

A cruciform church is shaped like a cross. The nave and the chancel are like the upright beam of the cross, while the transepts form the arms of the cross. The transepts run north and south from the point where the chancel joins the nave, and the tower marks this point. However, the Claregalway church does not have a south transept. The church is basically rectangular shaped and like most churches of the period was built facing due east, with the altar on the eastern end. The total internal length of the structure is 142 feet. The original church was built in the early pointed style of the thirteenth century. The tower, the east gable window and the north transept were added in the fifteenth century.

Chancel

The chancel refers to that part of the church, near the altar, which was reserved for the clergy and choir and is on the eastern end. It is 52 feet long and 23 feet

The Franciscan Friary

wide. There are six tall narrow pointed (Gothic style) windows in both the north and south walls that provide light; each window is 2 feet in width and 11 feet in height.

Also there were originally three pointed windows in the east gable, but these were replaced by the present one in the fifteenth century that reflected the elaborate ornate style of that time. This east window is the crowning glory of the church. Mullions or vertical stone shafts divide the window into five lights or sections with very gracefully proportioned patterns in the upper part of the window.

A close up view of the magnificent east window, which was inserted during the fifteenth century, with the belfry in the background

On the south wall of the chancel are the remains of a *piscina*, which is a stone basin in which the chalice used in the Eucharist is rinsed, and the *sedilla*, a group of three seats let into the wall for the clergy performing the service. The De Burgo tomb, with the arms and crest of the De Burgos, stands in the north side wall, the position in which the founder or other great benefactor's tomb is generally placed. It carries the following Latin inscription:

> *Husc Incum sibi elegit Dus Tho Burgo de Anbally, Fils Richarde de Derrymaelaghni Anno Domini 1648*

In translation: "Thomas de Burgo of Anbally, son of Richard of Derrymacloughney chose this place for himself, 1648 AD."

Nave and Aisle

The nave is the main part of the church; it is on the western end and was where the congregation and laity sat. It is 72 feet long and 23 feet wide. The word nave comes from the Latin word nave, meaning a ship, for the ship was thought to be the symbol or sign of the Christian church, which carries believers over the sea of life into the safe harbour of heaven. Almost the entire western gable end is no more.

An old 1792 sketch of the Friary shows an elaborate window with four sections interlacing with round pieces over the heads. The people's main entrance was by a large door in the western gable, of which the outline can just barely be seen. The western gable together with the door and window collapsed sometime in the 19th century. There are several sedillas on the south wall; the broken arch of one has been repaired with small red tiles.

The De Burgo tomb set in the north sidewall in the chancel area of the Friary

There was a north aisle, with a width of 11 feet, which was separated from the nave by an arcade of four pointed arches on cylindrical pillars. The Romanesque style, rounded arch, connected the aisle with the north transept. Unfortunately this aisle is now demolished.

Transept – north

This measures 25 feet long by 16 feet. There is a doorway from under the tower into the transept chapel that would have been used by the clergy. However the public had access from the then north aisle of the nave through the arch. Its north window has three shafts with interlacing heads and the two windows to the east are richly carved like some of the window heads in St. Nicholas' church in Galway. The chapel has an altar and altarpiece, and also a *piscina* near the door. The arch had been closed and the north window blocked, when the friars had earlier modified the transept to serve as a penal day chapel. Also it had been unroofed around 1915 by the Rev. PJ Moran. There is a tablet affixed to the wall of the chapel to the right of the entrance under the tower which carries the following Latin inscription:

> *Quisquis eris, qui transieris,*
> *Sta, Perlege, plora,*
> *Sum qd. eris, Fueramq. qd. es,*
> *Pro me, Precor, Ora,*
> *P.M.B. o.s.f.*

In translation: "Whosoever you may be who should pass by, stop, read thoroughly, mourn. I am what you shall be and I was what you are. I entreat that you pray for me, F(ather) M(artin) B(lake). O(rder) (of) S(t). F(rancis)". The plaque measures 28 inches by 7.5 inches is not dated and may mark Fr. Blake's burial place.

Tower

The tower or belfry was built about 200 years after the original building and within the walls of the church. It rises in three stages above the roof, to a height of 80 feet from the ground level. The insertion of this prominent tower blocked up one of the clerestory windows of the nave and an adjoining window seems to have been taken out and a larger two section window put in its place, to compensate for the loss of light. It is built on arches or a groin type vault supported by four massive piers.

The huge corbels (projecting stones) in the belfry piers were probably for the support of a roof beam. If you look very closely, you'll see four small stone heads on each pier and one in the centre of the roof vault. Also near the centre of the roof vault, you'll see two small round holes, through which ropes may have been threaded to allow the friars to ring the bells from below.

The windows in the bell storey of the tower are normally the largest to allow free egress to the sound of the bells. These windows have two sections with transoms (horizontal bars) to strengthen the mullions (vertical shafts) and perhaps to enhance the appearance. The tower roof was probably a pyramidal shaped spire crowned by an outsized iron cross.

There is an opening or little doorway in the south wall of the tower within the roof space of the church, which may have been constructed for ventilation purposes or to affect repairs. It may suggest that there was some sort of loft or attic overhead although there is no evidence of a practice of arranging living quarters over the church as that would imply a lack of reverence. This doorway was approached by way of another doorway over the northern lean to of the cloister wall, which doorway was in turn approached from the north of the east dormitory.

Today the tower looks very tall because the church is no longer roofed, thus giving it extra visibility.

An interior view with the arches of the aisle on the left and in front the piers that support the belfry tower

Living Quarters and Cloister

On the sheltered, sunny, south side of the church is the cloister. The cloister is the rectangular open green space, which is surrounded by a path – this path used to be covered with a lean-to roof. This lean-to provided shelter from the rain for those passing from one part of the friary to another. The cloister enclosure measures 57 feet by 72 feet.

The living quarters was composed of dormitories, kitchen, refectory or dining area, chapter room and a monk's day room. The building to the east of the cloister seems to have abutted against and obstructed the light of three of the church chancel windows. The upper portions of this contain the dormitories. Also this building shows signs of frequent changes. There are traces of three built up openings onto the cloister that probably formed the entrance to the chapter room. There are three stories in the monks' day room and in the south wall on the upper floor, there is a large open fireplace, at the back of which externally is a built up window. The buildings south of the cloister also show signs of frequent changes. It is possible that the friars who inhabited the monastery in the eighteenth century occupied this portion only, which was changed to suit the needs of a small community who sought refuge in the ruins.

Outbuildings

There was probably a water mill about twenty five yards to the south of the friary. Also there are some obscure remains of a building about thirty five feet south east of the friary between it and the Clare river and located on what is designated 'site of garderobes' at the lower right hand corner of the accompanying ground plan. It's reached by steps leading from the north and from the south. There is an engraved stone facing the steps from the southern, river bank side. It carries the following Latin inscription:

> IHS
> Orate Pro anima Rdi
> Patris Martini Blake
> Qui hunc Montem Fie
> Ri Fecit Anno Dom.i
> 1812

In translation: "Pray for the soul of Rev. Father Martin Blake who caused this mound to be erected in the year of the Lord, 1812"

A water channel probably flowed alongside both of these buildings.

Conclusion

The friary is undoubtedly the most notable landmark in the parish of Claregalway. For over 700 years it has withstood the ravages of time, weather and man. It provides a very visible reminder of our heritage and religious tradition. The annual cemetery Sunday maintains this religious tradition. When one walks in the cloister courtyard, with the river Clare flowing gently in the background, one can escape the hustle and bustle of modern life and the constant noise of traffic on the N17. Here one can achieve a sense of peace and tranquillity.

It is an important and unique amenity that is available to the local community and is neatly complimented by the nearby castle and nine arches bridge.

A view of the Friary from the east

The Franciscan Friary

Friary Guardians

The guardian is the name given to the superior of a Franciscan abbey. The following list of guardians has been taken from the book 'Liber Lovaniensis', editor Fr Cathaldus Giblin O.F.M. Dublin. 1956.

17th Century

15 Aug 1629:	vacant	(named "conventus Clarensis")
14 Oct 1639:	vacant	("Ballinclara")
8 Feb 1645:	Peter Tiernan, re-app.	("conventus de Clare")
5 Sept 1647:	Hugo Canavan	("conventus de Clar")
4 Feb 1648:	Hugo Keanavaine, re-app.	
17 Aug 1650:	Peter Tiernan	
9 Oct 1658:	Anthony MacDonnell	
26 Feb 1659:	Anthony MacDonnell, re-app.	
8 Sept 1661:	Hugo MacTeig	
18 Oct 1669:	Charles Osbaldeston	("Balliclare")
5 Mar 1670:	Bartholomew Skerrett	
21 Nov 1672:	Francis de Burgo (Burke)	("Ballyclare")
23 Sep 1675:	Francis Quinn	("Baileclaire")
23 Jan 1676:	Francis Quinn	("Baleclare")
24 Sep 1678:	Charles Osbaldeston	
28 Apr 1680:	Andrew Vitalis (mac an Bheatha, mcVeigh)	
14 Mar 1681:	Anthony Kelly junior	
16 June 1683:	Anthony Kelly junior,	re-app.
23 Aug 1684:	Bernard (Brian) Flaherty	
27 Jan 1685:	Francis de Burgo (Burke)	
15 Aug 1687:	Francis de Burgo	
5 May 1689:	Bonaventure Geraghty	
24 Aug 1690:	Francis Bodkin	
18 Feb 1693:	Patrick Nolan,	re-app.
25 July 1697:	Michael Osbaldeston	
26 July 1699:	Anthony Giffort (Gifford)	

The Franciscan Friary

18th Century

17 Sep 1700:	Peter Martin (John William Burke deleted)	
9 June 1702:	Michael Osbaldeston	("Balli Clare")
13 Nov 1703:	Michael Osbaldeston	
9 June 1705:	Patrick Kirevan (Kirwan)	
13 Nov 1706:	Michael Osbaldeston	
12 May 1708:	John de Burgo (Burke)	
12 Oct 1709:	John Brock	
7 June 1711:	John Cunningham	
13 Oct 1714:	Francis Madden	("Ballclare")
10 May 1716:	James Walsh	("Balliclar")
16 Oct 1717:	John Broxa	("Ballinclare")
30 May 1719:	John Broxa	("Ballenaclare")
3 Sept 1720:	Anthony Kyeghry (Keighry) (died there)	
22 July 1724:	John Kelly	
16 Aug 1727:	John Mannin STL	
17 Nov 1729:	John Mannin STL	
5 Sept 1733:	Anthony Kelly	
5 Mar 1735:	Anthony Kelly	
6 Sept 1736:	Joseph Burk(e)	
6 Mar 1738:	Joseph Burk(e)	
24 July 1739:	Bonaventure de Burgo junior	("Clare Galway")
25 May 1741:	Bonaventure de Burgo junior	("Clare")
16 Aug 1742:	Thomas Morris	("Clare")
16 Apr 1744:	Thomas Morris	("Clare Galway"- from now on)
12 Aug 1745:	Bonaventure de Burgo junior	
12 Feb 1746:	Bonaventure de Burgo junior	
22 Aug 1748:	Patrick Neilan	
16 Feb 1751:	Patrick Neilan STL	
26 Aug 1751:	Bonaventure de Burgo junior	
26 Feb 1753:	Bonaventure de Burgo junior	
26 Aug 1754:	Martin Brady	
24 Sept 1755:	Bonaventure de Burgo	
29 Aug 1757:	Bonaventure de Burgo junior	
19 Feb 1759:	Patrick Neylan STL, ex-Definitor	

The Franciscan Friary

18 Aug 1760:	Bonaventure de Burgo junior	
19 Oct 1761:	Bonaventure de Burgo junior (Burke)	
22 Aug 1763:	Patrick Neilan, ex-Definitor	
17 Apr 1765:	Bonaventure Millerius (Myler) de Burgo	
12 Nov 1767:	Patrick Neylan STL, ex-Definitor	
8 Oct 1770:	Patrick Neilan (Kiervan deleted)	
31 Aug 1772:	Francis Burke	
11 Nov 1773:	Francis Burke	
1 July 1776:	Andrew Canavan	
30 Apr 1778:	Patrick Neilan, ex-Definitor	
19 July 1779:	Patrick Neilan, ex-Definitor	
29 May 1781:	Patrick Neilan, ex-Definitor	
22 July 1782:	Anthony Hughes	
12 May 1784:	Anthony Hughes	
25 July 1785:	Patrick Neilan STL, ex-Definitor	
9 May 1787:	Joseph Joyce	
14 July 1788:	Joseph Joyce	
18 May 1790:	Martin Blake	
11 July 1791:	Martin Blake	
23 July 1793:	Martin Blake	
14 July 1794:	Martin Blake	
6 June 1796:	Martin Blake	

19th Century

22 Sept 1800:	Joseph Blake	
13 July 1801:	Joseph Blake	
13 July 1802:	Joseph Blake	
16 July 1804:	Joseph Blake	
14 July 1806:	Joseph Blake	
12 July 1815:	Martin Blake, ex-Definitor	
14 July 1819:	John Heany	
15 July 1822:	John Heaney	
14 Jan 1824:	John Magrath; Praeses: John Heaney (before Magrath arrived as Guardian)	
13 July 1825:	John Magrath	
14 July 1831:	James Hughes	
11 Nov 1832:	Patrick Burke	

The Franciscan Friary

23 July 1834:	Patrick Burke	
13 Jan 1836:	Patrick Burke	
19 July 1837:	Patrick Burke	
19 Aug 1840:	vacant	
30 Mar 1842:	Patrick Burke	
25 Oct 1843:	Patrick Burke	
29 Jan 1845:	John Francis	
26 Aug 1846:	James Hughes, ex-custos	
18 Jan 1848:	John Magrath, ex-Definitor	
18 July 1849:	John Burke	
23 Jan 1851:	John Burke	
13 Oct 1852:	John Burke (Praeses or President, not Guardian)	
21 Sept 1853:	Laurence Steen	
18 July 1855:	Laurence Steen	
14 Jan 1857:	Laurence Steen	
20 Apr 1858:	John Francis (last resident Guardian - FLK MSS 426)	
24 Jan 1860:	vacant	
28 Oct 1870:	Fr Bernard Cooney, titular Guardian ("conventus Clarensis")	
23 Apr 1872:	Fr Bernard Cooney	

August 1873, titular guardians were abolished. Since then, no friar was appointed to vacant friaries.

It is interesting to note the various names for the friary. It was first known as "conventus Clarensis" in 1629 and after many changes finally known as Claregalway in 1739.

Chapter 6: Castles in the Area

Claregalway Castle - History

Introduction: There is no information on when the Claregalway castle was built, the indications are that it is probably late 15th century and may have been built on the site of an older wooden structure. It's situated on the lowest crossing point of the Clare River before it flows through bogland into the Corrib. While commonly referred to as castles, technically there are more accurately described as tower houses. They were fortified residences that also served in a military capacity.

References to Claregalway and its castle keep cropping up because it was an important strategic point in the defence of the city of Galway itself. Some of these references are fragmented and it's difficult to get a clear picture, but nevertheless we get some idea of what life was like in those times.

The Normans built a number of castles along the Clare River. The De Burgos were the first of the Normans that came into Connacht. In 1225, King Henry III of England granted the province of Connacht to Richard de Burgo. They secured their territories by building stone castles. They later became known as Burkes and they split into two opposing families, the McWilliam Íochtar (the Mayo Burkes) and the McWilliam Uachtar (the Galway Burkes), who eventually became known as the Clanrickards.

The historic Claregalway Castle

1470: The combined forces of O'Donnell of Tirconnell and the Mayo Burkes *'encamped for a night in Claregalway and then burned it and continued for a while laying waste the country round about.'*

1504 – Battle of Knockdoe: Knockdoe is about 3 miles from Claregalway and it was where the forces of Garret Mór Fitzgerald, Earl of Kildare, who was the Lord Deputy of Ireland, fought the Clanrickard, head of the Burkes. Garret Mór Fitzgerald led his army from Leinster to thwart the ambitions of Clanrickard. The Burkes had a number of Irish chiefs fighting with them and they also had engaged Scottish mercenaries known as Gallowglasses. It was the first time that guns were used in Ireland to do battle. According to reports they were not sure how to fire them and they used them as clubs instead. Clanrickard was defeated and thousands were killed.

Claregalway is mentioned twice in connection with this battle. The night before the battle, the Burkes *'played cards in the castle 'till late hours of the following morning and they were drinking.'* After his victory, Garret Mór marched towards Galway, looting Claregalway castle en route, and taking as prisoners the two sons and a daughter of Ulick Burke.

1538: Lord Gray on behalf of King Henry VIII attacked Claregalway castle with 250 regular troops and artillery. This artillery included cannons such as a half culverin, a saker and double falcons. The following details regarding these cannons will be of interest to the military historian:

Cannon	Weight of Shot	Calibre	Weight of Gun
Half-Culverin	9 lbs.	$4^{1/2}$ inches	3,000 lbs.
Saker	5 lbs.	$3^{1/2}$ inches	1,500 lbs.
Falcon (or double falcon)	$2^{1/2}$ lbs.	$2^{1/2}$ inches	800 lbs.

Lord Gray took the castle and handed it over to Ulick Burke, it is said, for cash.

1571: Sir Edward Fitton, the President of Connacht, was camped outside Claregalway and he reported that *'we are refused at the Earl's castle by the Earl's son where the rebel is the constable of the castle and upon hearing of our coming to pass by it to Galway, he burned the town, uncovered the castle and offered plain resistance.'* This action may appear strange, but an important tactic in defending a castle was to burn the town so the army coming in would not have any shelter or food and to unroof the castle, which was made of thatch, so as to prevent archers from firing burning arrows into it. They could defend it perfectly when it was unroofed. However it was reported that Fitton captured the castle and put the garrison of sixteen men to death.

1572: The Earl of Clanrickard had two sons, John and Ulick who were wild and uncontrollable and caused a lot of turmoil and destruction around Athenry. They were described as *'the most executable evil-doers, doing destruction across Loughrea, Athenry and so on.'* The mayor of Galway wrote to the Lord Deputy complaining about the two sons.

1576: Under the English Surrender and Regrant policy, the Earl of Clanrickard surrendered the castle to Queen Elizabeth and she regranted it back to him.

1603-1625: King James I made a number of grants to local lords to hold fairs and markets in order to boost the local economies. Cattle trade became very important. The Earl of Clanrickard was granted a licence for a weekly Wednesday market at Claregalway.

1641-1651: In October 1641, rebellion against the English rule broke out in Ulster and soon spread to the rest of the country. For the next eight years, England was the scene of a fiercely fought civil war between King Charles I and the extreme Protestants or Puritans led by Oliver Cromwell. The fighting soon spread to Ireland where armies supporting both sides fought each other. The Catholic rebels, who included Old Irish and Anglo-Irish, formed the Federation of Kilkenny. The Earl of Clanrickard, who was the King's Governor of Connacht, eventually became involved but was a reluctant rebel.

In 1642, Claregalway castle was strongly garrisoned by Clanrickard and he used it as a base for operations to overcome Galway. It was there he received the proposals for the surrender of Galway as signed by the mayor Walter Lynch and delivered by Dominic Browne and others. In 1643 the castle was surprised by Captain Richard Burke of Anbally, through the treachery of a tenant, the carelessness of the warders and the collusion of a Franciscan friar. Its giving up was one of the conditions of the treaty for the surrender of Galway.

In 1648, the Papal Nuncio was in Galway and he wrote to Clanrickard about the capture of Thomas McKiernan of the Franciscans in the castle and he asked that he be released.

After the execution of King Charles I, William Cromwell landed in Ireland in 1649 with a big army with the purpose of putting down the rebellion. He quickly captured a number of towns and departed in May 1650. Sir Charles Coote, a Cromwellian, seized Claregalway castle in 1651. Galway was the last stronghold to surrender to the Cromwellians. Thus ended about ten years of warfare, which was then followed by the Cromwellian Plantation.

Architecture

Claregalway castle is a well preserved rectangular five-storey tower. Its dimensions are 12 metres in length and 9.75 metres in width. The castle entrance is by a pointed arched doorway of cut stone near the northern end of the southwest wall. The presence of opposing vertical grooves in both of its jambs indicate that it was protected by a portcullis. The portcullis is a heavy latticed iron grating in the gateway, which could slide up and down in grooves in the doorjambs and was used for protecting the ordinary wooden door of the castle. There is a small apartment above the door into which the portcullis rose and where the lifting machinery was located.

This doorway opens into a small lobby with a guardroom to the left and a spiral stone staircase to the right. This staircase ascends for the first 35 feet and then a straight narrow staircase leads from the south side of the castle to the top. Directly above the lobby is a small rectangular opening known as the 'murdering hole'. This was used to pour hot liquids down on unsuspecting attackers.

A stone vault exists between the second and third floors. Mural passages occur in the northeast wall on the first floor and in the southeast wall on the third floor. There are mural chambers in the southwest wall on the first floor and in the southeast, southwest and northwest walls on the third floor.

Garderobes (used for sanitation) survive inside the southeast wall on the second and third floors. Fireplaces are visible in the southwest wall on the first floor and in the north east wall on the second floor. Traces of the wall-walk survive as well as remains of the parapet along the southeast and southwest walls. The parapet was a low wall alongside the exterior edge of the wall-walk that protected guards as they patrolled.

Protecting corbels centrally placed on top of the walls formerly supported machicolations at parapet level. Corbels are projecting stones, firmly imbedded in the walls, which were usually intended to carry a wooden beam or in this case machicolations. A machicolation was a projecting parapet on the top of a castle wall with openings in the bottom through which missiles could be dropped or discharged on attackers. They protected defenders who were trying to attack the assailants at the base of the castle wall. There was at least one positioned directly over the castle entrance.

There is no part of the roof remaining. It was probably made of oak and thatched, as lead roofs were not common in Irish castles.

There were no windows in the lower 20 feet, only loopholes. The castle was originally designed to be defended by archery and was never modified to meet the requirements of firearms. The loopholes are narrow slits that were wider on the inside to give the defender an advantage when shooting arrows or guns. A variety of window types occur in Claregalway castle. Many display Gothic-like features including pointed arches, ogee heads, an intricate curved design and one that is mullioned and transomed (vertical and horizontal stone bars).

Cloghmoyle Castle (Cloch Mhaol)

The poorly preserved remains of this castle are located in flat open pastureland in Carnmore West. This rectangular shaped building (length 10.3m, width 7.2m)

Castles in the Area

contains two surviving storeys. There is no trace of a doorway but there are two large gaps in both the north and east walls (1.05m thick). At the southwest and northeast corners are the poorly preserved remains of what appear to be foundations for two turrets. These turrets were tower-like structures. The ground storey is divided internally by a later wall that has blocked a single-lighted window with wide internal splay.

This tower house was probably built in the 15th Century by the Normans (De Burgos). Local history also refers to it as being a convent!

Lydacan Castle

This towerhouse was sited on a natural rise overlooking Claregalway. It was originally a three storey rectangular building that was later incorporated into a 19th Century house (Greated's). Until recently traces of a spiral staircase plus a pointed arch doorway were visible. Numerous cut-stone fragments from the towerhouse were incorporated into the later addition.

Cloghmoyle Castle in Carnmore

Lydacan Castle, it was the residence of the landlord Greated.

Lissarulla Castle

Sited on slightly elevated area in a generally low-lying region. All that remains of this castle is a small portion of the south wall. This surviving part indicated that it had at least two storeys with traces of two window openings at first storey level. A number of large fragments of masonry are strewn about the site.

Lissarulla Castle

Kiltrogue Castle (Cill Torroige)

A fine five-storey towerhouse (length 10.3m, width 7.2m) built on the east bank of the Clare River with a small stream gushing out from a few yards of its walls. In fair condition except for the top portion which is in a very ruinous condition. The four walls are still standing but almost all floors are missing. The east end, which comprises the staircase and subsidiary chambers was six storeys high, while the rest of the tower is five storeys high. A lean-to shed has been built against the north wall. The main entrance is a pointed arch doorway, which is centrally placed in the east wall. Inside a guardroom and spiral staircase are evident with the latter being in a poor state of preservation. A stone vault exists between the first and second floors. This vault is arch shaped. A fireplace is visible in the north wall on the first floor. Corbels, which supported a machicolation over the doorway, are visible on top of the east wall.

The castle was probably built at the end of the 15th Century by the De Burgos and was owned by John Blake FitzRicard. Tirlagh Caragh McSwine owned it in 1574.

Kiltrogue Castle

General Attack and Defence of Castles

Most castles were taken through the doorway either by force, surprise or treachery. Castles could be escaladed but the castles were built specially against an attack by ladders. Castles were largely designed to be defended from the top.

In an attack by force, the first step was to nullify the fire from the castle. This could be done by assigning three men to fire on each loophole and window from behind cover. Then the artillery could be drawn near to effect a breach or to fire burning arrows onto the roof. Men could advance to widen or make a breach with pickaxes and crowbars. While the defenders could fire down from the top of the castle, this was not easy.

There is an account of how the Lord Deputy stormed Lissmagh castle in Longford in 1596. The assailants spent the night making fireworks. Next day, a soldier threw up a firebrand which set fire to the top of the roof, which was covered with thatch, and thereby much inconvenienced the garrison. Then the assailants lit a fire at the door and portcullis. The garrison was smothered. The soldiers made a breach, probably at the door and stormed the smothered garrison.

Chapter 7: Trades and Occupations

Claregalway Post Office

The present post office for Claregalway is situated in Hughes supermarket and is run by the Hughes family. However the post office was not always located here. The site of the original post office was formerly on the estate of the landlord AJ Holmes who resided in Rockwood. It was located between the Nine Arches Bridge and the Duggan household. Indeed remains of the old structure are still visible. It came under the Congested Districts Board. The area that went with the post office was 16 acres 0 rood 16 perches. It was registered on 23rd March 1915.

James Hession's public house about 1962. Now the Summerfield bar

Records provided by An Post show that the first post office was opened in Claregalway on 6th January 1833. Although the records do not show the exact location of this post office we presume it was at the Nine Arches. In 1903, records show Margaret Hession was the postmistress. On the 18th April 1906 James Cahill took over duties as postmaster. He was a relative of the Hessions who had been working in England with the Ordnance survey. On returning he married a lady named Nora Monaghan (her relatives still reside in Claregalway). They had two daughters Cecelia and Bridget Mary. Bridget Mary Cahill took up duties on 6th September 1926. James Cahill died shortly afterwards on 25th November 1926. The Cahill sisters ceased to run the business in 1929. They were still not twenty.

Mary Hughes became the successful applicant and she took up the running of the post office on 23rd November 1929. She was married to Michael Hughes. They were Mícheál Hughes grandparents and so the post office remains in the Hughes family to this day.

Post Men in Claregalway and Carnmore

Pat Tynan postman while he was in the Irish Guards

Claregalway – records provided by An Post (no records prior to 1900). Records show that in 1900 there were three postmen working from the Claregalway Post Office (all were walking posts)

- Hugh O Dea was on the Kiltrogue and Cregmore area
- Michael Williams was on the Claregalway / Bawnmore area - retired 1st April 1930
- Laurence Codyre was on the Rockwood, Cregboy, Cloon, and Cahergowan area

These were three part-time postmen according to the records. In order to elaborate on the information regarding the above named postmen and that era we draw on local knowledge as follows – Mike Williams was a brother of Patrick who was a cobbler who lived in the last remaining thatched house in Claregalway, now home to the Dunleaveys. He lived where Martin Noone now lives on the road to the Claregalway Community centre. He went by the name of "sixty" as this was the number on his uniform.

Laurence Codyre lived in Pollaghrevagh.

It is also recalled that another walking postman worked in the area named Pat Flaherty and it is believed he resided where Horans now stands. Dan Caulfield who lived in the Knockdoe cottages also worked as a part-time Postman.

Trades and Occupations

Guard Ryle and Pat Tynan postman

So to return to the records provided by An Post.

Name	Dates	Area Covered	Notes
Patrick Tynan	Born: 27 Jan 1879 Commenced: 13 May 1913 Ceased: 28 Jan 1944	Claregalway to Ardgaineen	Left on active service 'called to the colours' with Irish Guards on 5th Aug. 1914. Resumed P.O. duties on 14th mar 1919. Pay scale: from 15 Shillings to 21 Shillings per week. On resumption in 1919/20 from 18 Shillings to 34 Shillings.
Micheál O'Síoda (Silke)	Born: 24 Sept 1898 Commenced: 11 May 1925 Ceased: 24 Sept 1963	Claregalway to Ardgaineen and later to Currandrum (by Cycle post)	Pay scale: 18 Shillings to 34 Shillings
Patrick Reilly (O'Raghallaigh)	Born: 25 Feb 1905 Commenced: 27 Sept 1937 Ceased: 16 Oct 1951	Claregalway to Ardgaineen	Wages scale: 26 Shillings to 42s and 6d

Michael Madden (Ex Eyrecourt P.O.)	Born: 7 Nov 1910 Commenced: 13 Sept 1931 Ceased: 8 Nov 1975	Claregalway to Kiltrogue (Bicycle Post)	Pay scale: 18 Shillings to Shillings plus 1 Shilling per week for cleaning bicycle

Again to return to local knowledge it is a matter of fact that Pat Tynan served with the Irish Guards or as was said, *"was called to the colours"* on 5th August 1914 to serve in the First World War. He was a native of Mayo and lived with the Lenihans in Lakeview.

Tommy Geraghty operated the first postal van service in Claregalway. He is currently a well-known actor with the Pegasus Theatre Company. Tommy operated the van service from 21st November 1966 to 2nd November 1975 when he transferred to Headford.

Best remembered locally is Michael Madden. A very familiar figure for many years as he delivered news good and bad in all weather conditions. He was a very distinguished figure on his official bike with the mailbag slung over his shoulder. The second postal van arrived at the time of Michael Madden's retirement and was operated by Tony Gavin from 11th November 1975. The arrival of the second van marked the ending of postmen based in the Claregalway P.O. Michael Madden was the last postman based in Claregalway. A noted hurler in his youth, he is the father of the GAA stalwarts Tommy, Fergus and Gerry Madden and daughter Margaret. Mick died on the 19th August 1990.

Carnmore Post Men

On 25th October 1899 postal delivery began in Carnmore. When war began in 1916 post was only delivered on average three days per week. The present service began on 6th February 1926.

The first postman to serve in Carnmore area was Michael Dermody. He delivered from day one until 10th February 1912 when Martin McLaughlin, who came from Crusheen, Co. Clare, succeeded him. He served for 26 years until Oranmore man John O'Toole took up deliveries for 10 years until 1948.

In the next eight years three different postmen served the area. These men were Colm Boyle, Timothy Curran and Tom Lynskey. In 1956 Johnny Monaghan from Caherdrimeen delivered for 18 years until his retirement in 1974. After this date the number of postmen increased and the van came into service. Since 1974 there has only been one long surviving postman, namely Eamon Diviney who served until 1979.

Trades and Occupations

Michael Skerret carpenter working on the outer rim of a cartwheel

It can be gleaned from local knowledge and gathered from interviews with long time residents that Claregalway parish had an abundance of crafts and trades in olden times. Many of those occupations are now in decline. It must be understood that official statistics are difficult to get so we must rely on local knowledge.

We begin our compilation at the Claregalway crossroads. As we travel towards the bridge there was a row of thatched artisans cottages. First was Pat Egans, where Hughes supermarket now stands. This was a weavers/loom. Pat Egan was Michael Hughes great grandfather. Next was Skerrets. Michael Skerret was a carpenter who specialised in making horse and donkey drawn carts and wheels. His sister Maggie was a dressmaker. Hughes car park occupies the site where the Skerrets cottage and workshop once stood.

Skerret's cottage and workshop in Claregalway, now demolished

Trades and Occupations

Next to Skerrets was Donoghues where Horans house is now. Donoghues owned a small grocery shop. Next to Donoghues was James Hession's public house. It was built by Kellys and then became Longs. James Hession known as 'velvet' (because of his jacket) returned from America and married into Longs and so it became Hessions until November 1974. It is now the Summerfield bar. Next to the Summerfield bar there is the last remaining one of the thatched cottages, which is the residence of Kathleen and Bob Dunleavey. Brid and James Glynn formally occupied it, Brid was a teacher and James was a local guard. This was the residence of Pat Williams, a cobbler. Pat was the brother of Mick Williams the postman.

Next door to Pat Williams was Pat Ross who was a tailor. Nothing remains of the Ross house. After the water pump lived Mick Burke who had a pub there. He was known as a ridire chaorach because he owned 1001 sheep. No descendants now remain. Right beside the handball alley stood Lenihan's public house, which was popularly known as Binas. Binas father was Pat Lenihan and his wife was Kelly from Waterdale. It is mentioned in an interview with Kathleen Dunleavey (Binas niece) that this may have been at one time a bakery owned by the O'Reillys. In the late 1960's the business was transferred to where Dunleavys bar and grocery now stands.

Over the river towards Loughgeorge and next to the castle on the right side back in the field is Casey's cottage. Pat Casey fought in World War II. This was a herd's cottage.

On the left where the Western Irons crafts is now, stood the Hanley brothers engineering company. The Hanley brothers' father was Martin and he owned a dance hall on this site. It was known as Hanley's hall.

Michael Smyth blacksmith

Trades and Occupations

Michael Smyth in front of his forge

The Central Tavern, which is a pub and restaurant and whose proprietor's are Joe and Julie Kyne has a long history. Roddy Kelly who was Joe's uncle owned it. Roddy's father was Malachy Kelly from Drumgriffin in Corrundulla and he emigrated to America many years ago. He became wealthy in America and returned to Loughgeorge and purchased the pub along with 270 acres of land at a reputed price of £1 per acre. He purchased the property from the Ffrenchs. Joe inherited the pub in 1970. When replastering an upstairs wall the name Helen Ffrench was discovered.

Travelling towards Tuam a few hundred yards further on we find Michael Smyth's forge which is still in use. Michael and his ancestors were blacksmiths. In the townland of Peake, Tom Duffy a tailor lived. Tom's family now live in Prospect Hill beside Lohan's chemist. Also in this locality lived another tailor named Higgins and a cobbler named Commins. Moving left towards Mullacuttra/Bawnmore there lived James Keane who built many of the newer houses in the 1950's, 1960's and 1970's, including the extension to the Summerfield Bar and Cormicans in Lakeview. William Tarpey at the crossroads was a blacksmith. He was Peter Feeney's grandfather. Tim Tarpey in Cloughaun was a farrier. In Waterdale, Willie Cullinan was a stone mason, John Dolly a thatcher and Willie Keaney also known as "Coogan", was a blacksmith. The name "Coogan" derived from Fintan Coogan T.D. who was also a blacksmith. Willie worked with Martin Cannon, a blacksmith in Tonroe, Lydacan, his brother Paddy who died in November 1998 was also skilled. In Gortadubha-Cloonbiggen there was a thatcher named Seamus Loftus. Returning again to the Claregalway crossroads and into Montiagh we find Seamus (Liam) Duggan a thatcher (father of Padraig). In Cahergowan-Clogher were the brothers John and Michael Cogavin, known as gaeilge as O'Cogabhain, who were tailors.

A thatcher named Seamus O Loughlin, a weaver named Martin Duggan and a cooper named Sean McGuinness who was also a boat builder. Stephen Lynskey was a thatcher and he and his brothers Sean and William were members of the Old IRA. John (Kitty) Forde was a champion slaner (turf cutter) and Tom Forde (brother of John and Mary) was a thatcher and also a chimney builder. As we come out onto the main road and return towards Claregalway crossroads we can point out a trademan's house of old where the Concannons now live, whose name was Samways and he was a nailer. Just before that at the Clogher turnoff was Scullys. Pat Scully was a cobbler and his son Mike was a thatcher and a stone mason. On the left, down the field lived Pat Clancy a thatcher. His brother was drowned at Curraghmore bridge along with Charlie Quinn's brother and Fahy from Cregboy. There was a grocery shop owned by Clancys where Carrs is now. Pat Carr (Pat's grandfather, Matties father) lived and he drove a steamroller with Galway County Council. He was a good mechanic. Patrick Cullinan lived where Cullinans old house now stands and he was a horse doctor. He was a member of the cavalry in the USA army, hence his knowledge of horses.

Michael Skerret's tools of the trade – all hand operated

Mrs Flood, the national teacher, lived near Cullinans. Her son Peter was a bus conductor in Galway. Father Malachy Mannion lived in Cahergowan. Remains of his house are still there, also there is a road through the bog and commonage known as Clochan an tSagairt.

In Tonroe, Lydacan we have Martin Cannon a blacksmith and Andy McDonagh a builder. In Caherlea lived a stone mason named Kerrigan who was known as

Trades and Occupations

Willie Laffey former employee of Michael Skerret, sharpening his chisel

An Preabaire Ciarragain. Fahy a carpenter, lived in Kiltrogue. In Carnmore we find from local knowledge a thatcher named Flaherty and another named Rabbitt.

House builders named Kings and Kellys, Martin (Mhichil) Fox a thatcher, Rooneys were carpenters who made wheelbarrows. Lallys lived where Feeneys near the airport now live and they were weavers (fiadoiri). Sean O Bane and his son William were stone masons. Moving down to Ballymurphy there was a shop that was owned by two brothers named Murphy. And finally we conclude our journey at Morans old family residence in Lakeview (by the river) and this was originally a herd's cottage.

Martin Lally weaver

Trades and Occupations

Guards

According to James Hession, the first Gardaí to serve in Loughgeorge were: Gardaí Shannon and Donohoe and Sergeant Riordan in 1924.

Over the years since the new barracks was built the following Sergeants served there:

Sgt. Sean Gillispie, Donegal
Sgt. Con Gillispie, Donegal
Sgt. Liam Doherty, Donegal
Sgt. Tony Doherty, Donegal
Sgt. Henry
Sgt. Pat Fitzmaurice
Sgt. Dan McNulty, Donegal

The following Gardaí served in Loughgeorge:

Gárda Gerry Sugrue Kerry
Gárda Seamus Glynn, Williamstown, Co. Galway, who was married to Bríd Glynn, NT
Gárda Michael Guigheen, who came from the Blasket Islands. His daughter is Carmel Kenny from Carnmore.
Gárda Christy Glynn transferred to Galway as a detective.
Gárda Tom Ryle was married to Roddy Kelly's sister and was transferred on promotion to Loughrea. He came from Donegal.
Gárda M. Kavanagh was Kruger Kavanagh's nephew.
Gárda John Leen, Kerry, now a retired detective, lives in Renmore.
Gárda Pat Reilly, Belmullet.
Gárda J. Curtin, Loughrea.
Gárda John Buckley was married to Kathleen Dunleavy's sister, Marie Moore.
Gárda Liam Folan was stationed in the 1950's and spent years in the Tuam station.
Gárda Paddy Conroy stationed at Mill St. retired, owns Adare guesthouse, Grattan Road.
Gárda Tony Gillespie, Crossmolina.
Gárda Ned Walsh, Tralee.
Gárda Nick Gilroy, Galway.
Gárda Jim Healy.
Gárda Norman Quinn
Gárda Martin O'Malley, Mayo.
Gárda John Lowry, Carnmore, a detective in Galway for many years. Lived in Renmore.
Gárda B. Houlihan, Kerry.
Gárda O'Connell
Gárda M. Carey, Belmullet. Dave Carey's father who was married to P.J.

Hughes's sister Mary.
Gárda Pat Murphy, Ballinrobe.
Gárda J. McGee, Donegal.
Gárda P. Harlow, Galway.
Gárda W. Cosgrove, Galway.
Gárda Padraic Allen, an Irish speaker from Inverin.
Gárda M. Ward, Donegal.
Gárda Gerry Cummins, Mayo.
Gárda Pat O'Connell, Kerry.
Gárda Jim Carmody, Kerry, stationed in Carna in the 1960's.
Gárda Duffy.
Gárda John O'Donnell.
Gárda John Curran, Connemara, stationed in Salthill.
Gárda James Reidy, Tralee, brother of Gerry Reidy, ex C.I.E.
Gárda Pat Heneghan

Many of the Gárdai mentioned above were never actually stationed in Loughgeorge, but were posted there during times of local agitation or for extra security duties. Indeed the number of Gárdai who were based or resided locally would have been quite small.

The Garda station at Loughgeorge

Local newspaper - 26th July 1947:

'GUARD WHO TOOK PART IN HOWTH GUN RUNNING

Gárda Michael Carey, Loughgeorge, Claregalway and a native of Belmullet, Co. Mayo has retired from the Gárda Siochána on pension.

Trades and Occupations

He joined the D.M.P. (Dublin Metropolitan Police) in 1912 and in 1914 was one of the D.M.P. who refused to seize guns in the hands of the I.R.A. He resigned from the D.M.P. in 1917. He also took part in the Howth gun-running adventure. He was Captain of Volunteers in Mayo afterwards and was the first President of Sinn Fein in the Barony of Erris, Co. Mayo. He was reinstated in the Gárda Siochána on its formation in September 1923 with his old service in the D.M.P. added and was stationed in Cloghane, Co. Kerry for three years.

Gárda Carey was a member of the D.M.P. team that won the All-Ireland tug-of-war championship in 1914.

One of his daughters, Mrs. Hogan, wife of Captain Hogan, California, USA, won the 'George' medal during the late world war for bravery during the removal of patients in air raids to safety from St. Olive's hospital where she was nursing throughout the war.

District Justice W.P. Cahill, at Athenry District Court last week heard the last case brought by Gárda Carey. Referring to Gárda Carey's retirement, he said: "You carried out your prosecutions in a proper manner and we are all sorry to lose you. You carried out your duty properly and fairly towards the people. We wish you the best of luck and many happy days in your retirement."

Gárda Carey thanked the Justice and also Supt. Kelly and the District Court Clerk, Mr. Michael Rooney from all of whom he said he received nothing but kindness during his time in the district.'

Bina Lenihan's pub during the 1950s. Note the stacks of corn beside the handball alley

Trades and Occupations

Kelly's pub now known as Kynes Tavern. From left: Mary Qualter, Joe Kyne and Mrs. Kyne

Malachy and Mary Ellen Kelly, builder and first owner of Kynes Tavern

Chapter 8: Poems, Prayers and Recitations

1. An Marquee 'Tá i nGarraí James Hession
(Fonn: Cnocáinín Aerach Chill Mhulre)

Tá clú agus cáil ar 'The Talk of the Town',
Halla damhsa brea fairsing i nGaillimh,
Ar Seapoint, an 'Hangar' 's an Oslo cois trá
Agus Teach Furbo féin - nil aon chaill air!
Las Vegas i dTuaim is an 'Ranchhouse' ó thuaidh
Ag mealladh na sluaite ón gcathair, ón tuath
Ach mise i mbannaí gur fearr na' iad siúd
An Marquee 'tá i ngarraí James Hession.

CURFÁ

Ó molaim go hárd é is molaim le brí,
Ní fheicfeá a leithéide siúd in aon tír,
Gach rath air is beannacht, ádh mór
Is fad saoil ag an Marquee i ngarraí James Hession.

Tá sagart na háite ag obair go crua
Leis an teach pobail ársa a chóiriú,
Bhéas compóirdeach, maisiúil is álainn dá réir
Ina ndéanfar an Tiarna a ghlóiriú,
Lucht Lúthchleas Gael - go raibh acu 'fair play'
Tá siadsan ag bailliú go greathach dóibh féin
Agus sin é an t-údar atá leis an scéal
Faoin Marquee 'tá i ngarraí James Hession.

Tráthnóna breá samhraidh i gceartlár "July"
Cuireadh cuaillí is canbhás anáirde
Is urlár mór sleamhain de chuid "maple" is "ply"
Agus soillse mórthimpeall an stáitse.
Tá 'cloakroom' thar barr ann is 'mineral bar'
Le deochanna boga den chinéal is fearr.
Ni fheicfeá aon tabhairne sna tíortha thar lear
Mar an Marquee i ngarraí James Hession

Poems, Prayers and Recitations

> *Tagann ógánaigh aeracha,seandaoine gnaoíúla*
> *Cailleachaí críonna na háite;*
> *Sean-Séamas chun tosaigh is Brid lena thaobh,*
> *An Sáirsint's an Sagart Paróiste.*
> *Tagann sluaite ó Mhóinteach, as Eochaill isPéic*
> *Iad piochta is bearrtha, iad gleoite gan bhréag*
> *"Ceard a thug Seímín Lachtnáin air 'Vanity Fair'*
> *An Marquee i ngarraí James Hession!*

> *Bíonn ceoltóirí cáiliúla ann as gach ceard-*
> *Mar Joe Loss, Stanley Black is Jack Barrett,*
> *Tom Mór, na 'Mainliners' is buíonta nach iad*
> *"Ó nach iontach", deir Máirtin, "an racket"!*
> *Féach - gluaisteáin sa pháirc ann as Gailllmh's Blá*
> *Cliath,*
> *As Caisleán a Bharraigh is Baile átha 'n Ri,*
> *As Doire, Béal Feirste, is Corcaigh cois Laoi*
> *Is iad páirceáilte i ngarrai James Hession.*

> *Má tá dúil agat sa damhsa is suim a't sa spraoi,*
> *Tearra uait is beidh romhat mile fáilte,*
> *Is geallaimse duit go mbeidh oiche thar cionn*
> *Agat féin ag do ghaolta 's do chairde.*
> *Beidh bia agus deoch ann le fáil agaibh saor*
> *Is gach cinéal milseán i siopa V.G.*
> *Beidh riméad ort fanacht is filleadh aris*
> *Ar an Marquee i ngarrai James Hession.*

This song was composed about twenty five to thirty years ago by members of Cumann Éigse is Seanchas, Bhaile an Chláir. This group disbanded around 1990, following the death of some of its members. The 'garraí' of James Hession was located in the field between the Summerfield Bar and Hughes' shop. The new estate backs on to this field. By all accounts it was a great event, drawing young and old alike to meet, dance and have the 'craic' while the local sagart Paróiste and Sergeant looked on as you sipped your soft drinks. The purpose of this dance was to raise funds for the local GAA and for the church. Michéal Ó hÉidhin from Carnmore kindly supplied the words.

Poems, Prayers and Recitations

2. Mainistir Bhaile Chláir
(An Scoil éigse & seanchais, Baile Chlair)

Féach thall i an Mhainistir Arsa úd maorga
Ina seasamh cois abhainn is a dá cheann le gaoth.
A ré órga thart is na bráithre ar iarraidh,
An foirgneamh tréigthe le cúpla céad blian.

An té bheadh 'na chónai san áit seo an uair úd
Le linn ré na manach is í faoi ard réim
D'fheicfeadh sé iontais de ló is d'oiche
Deámhóid na mbráthar ag guidhe chun Dé.

An clog thuas sa gclogás ag bualadh gach maidin
Leis na bráithre a dhúiseacht le breacadh an lae,
Ag fógairt an ama don cheantar mórthimpeall
Bheith i mbun a gcuid saothar le allas a ngéag.

Bhíodh ceol binn na salam le cloisteál á gcanadh
Go binn is go ceolmhar ag trátha an lae,
Is comh-fhuaim a nglórtha mar chellifir na smólach
Ag éiri go glórmhar mar chumhran go spéir.

Ba mhinic na bráithre le feiceáil ar bhóthar
Ag comhrá le daoine faoi ghnóthai an tsaoil,
Ar cuairt sna tithe, ag comhairliú na ndaoine,
Ag leigheas a n-easaontas 's ag cothú dea-chroí.

Ba mhinic an t-ord úd faoi chruatan is ancró
Braithre á gcailleadh is á gcur os cionn cláir,
A gcairde ina dtimpeall á dtóramh go maidin
Ach séidfear an trumpa ag Michéal ar ball.

Bhi an cluiche go dian ag na bráithre go minic:
Ag saothrú a mbeatha ag obair gan scíth,
Ag lorg na déirce ón bpobal thart timpeall
Nó ag iascadh san abhainn thíos le slat agus líon.

Ach is é mo chrá géar go raibh mi-ádh i ndán dóibh
Bhi Cromaill is a chúnamh ag réabadh go crua,
Ag scrios is ag dóghadh is ag marú na ndaoine,
Ni raibh saoirse i ndán dóibh mo léan is mo thrua.

Poems, Prayers and Recitations

Tháinig na saighdiúir le gunnaí is airm,
Gur loisc is gur scrios siad gan taise gan trua,
Gur bearnaíodh na ballaí is gur scaipeadh na manaigh
'S nár fágadh sa deireadh ann ach fothrach fuar.

Go ndéana Dia trócaire ar an gcomhluadar uile
A d'fhullaing an fuar sléacht san am úd fadó,
I bhflalitheas na nGrást go raibh siad le chéile,
I measc na bhfíreann 's na n-Aingeal gan scaradh go deo.

Inniu seasann na ballai is an túr mór go láidir
Ainneoin gach gála,gach síon is gach slad,
A h-Ealaíon go buacach ansiúd do na sluaite
Séod luachmhar don tír seo is don domhain mór ar fad.

This poem was written about the monks who lived hundreds of years ago in the friary in Claregalway. It praises this fine monument which has survived the pillage of Cromwell. It seems the monks sought alms from the locals and in return provided good humour, daily chats, problem solving and even counselling! One can almost imagine the monks fishing in the Clare River, the peaceful psalm singing, the tower bell tolling and the workers toiling in the surrounding fields. Though life was tough it was slower-paced - the friary stands proudly as a testament to by-gone days.

3. The Old Chapel of Claregalway

This really refers to the old chapel that was sited near Henry Duggan's house, on the Galway side of the Nine Arches, which is presently under re-construction. It was written in the last century, possibly pre 1838 by a stone mason cum poet called Padhraicin Ó Ciaragdin from Caherlea or An Preabaire as he was known. It would seem that the church had fallen into disrepair and the priest was seeking funds to build a new one on the site of the present one. Some of the more affluent locals disagreed as they weren't 'great' with the priest anyway and refused to hand over any money. The priest commissioned the Preabaire to compose a 'dán', which might encourage the said locals to respond favourably. However the Preabaire composed two verses which greatly insulted and angered the locals. The following verses clearly show a powerful picture of the bad state of the church but also of the meanness of the congregation. The truth can be bitter! I have left it in its original version, as its message is more potent:

Poems, Prayers and Recitations

Nach mór an chúis náire don phobal
Is a liachtaí fear maith i mBaile an Chláir
An bháisteach bheith anuas ar an sagart
An fhad 's bhionn an t-Aifreann dá rá.

Nuair a thosaíonn an phobal ag cruinniú
Bionn an leacóigín cloiche ina láimh
Le cur faoina nglúíní sa ngreallach
Is go deimhin bíonn drab ar na mná.

The Preabaire had to make changes to the poem (see 'Amhráin Mhuighe Seola'). He encouraged the people to help the priest by finishing the new church and that they would be blessed for it. Work went ahead as planned until the night of the Big Wind on January 6th 1839. Almost every house in the country had its roof blown off including the partially erected roof of the church. The next morning the Preabaire was back up on the roof fixing and mending. (Séan Ó Ceallaigh, Craughwell supplied some of this information). The following is a translation of the original, Mainistir, Bhaile Chláir:

Is it not a hard saying? Is not death cruel and heart-rending,
That would not give me a half-hour, or a moment of time? That
the body is not worth
A red halfpenny, nor the corpse, when it is stretched above
boards?
And may the Son of Mary assist our souls if we are creatures
who will be put astray.

But I firmly and solemnly declare,
That if I were a priest in the place,
I would not put any judgement of penance,
On any man in Claregalway.

For they are renouncing sin,
And following the best rules of life:
And as long as Peter is in the Chair,
Our friends will be found in Heaven.

That which you have already begun,
Let us see that it is brought to a finish,
For you will have a blessing from the priest,
And a twelve-fold reward from the Son of God.

Poems, Prayers and Recitations

You will rise up from the bare gravel,
And will go (to kneel) on boards of pine,
And it is not for himself he collected the tax,
But for the benefit of the people forever.

And is it not a great shame for the people,
Seeing the number of good men in Clare (Galway?),
That the rain is falling down on the priest,
During the time that he offers the Mass?

And when the people begin to assemble,
Everyone has a little flag in his hand,
To put under his knees on the gravel,
And assuredly there is mud on the women's (clothes).

Do not say aught to the priest,
You have no right to say anything,
For he comes to the head of the bed to you,
Putting the holy oils on you at death.

And thus writing a 'pass' for our souls,
Up to the bright King of Grace,
And, O Mary, what shall we do,
Considering how often we offended him?

The man who walked Dublin and Galway,
Past Aran and Ballinamore,
Gave the palm to the work a week ago,
Saying he didn't see its equal so far.

How terrible for him who would not say that prayer,
As well as the twelve decades (prescribed)
In honour of the angels in Heaven,
And also of the grace of God's Son.

4. *Memory by Tom Greally (New Zealand)*

The summer evenings of my youth
So gleefully did I play
With hurley, ball and fishing rod
To pass the time away.

Poems, Prayers and Recitations

The cuckoo, corncrake are on my mind
The fleeting swallows too
Leaping salmon a treat to watch
And trout rolling over too.

The croaking frogs, frightening at times they were
But then I didn't care
As I strolled along, singing a song
Down by the river Clare.

Tom Greally composed the above poem for his sister Mary, Montaigh.

5. *Caoineadh an Chapaill le Michéal Ó'Sioda*

Mike Silke composed this in the early sixties when tractors were replacing workhorses. He lived near the schoolhouse in Carnmore. The horse speaks through the poem, lamenting and talking about the past and the changes that were on the way.

Nach doilíosach is nach brónach an scéal
Tá anois agam le n'airis daoibh.
Go bhfuil mo chroí bocht briste agus leónta
Ó thús m'óige go deireadh mo shaol.

Go bhfuil mé anois caite le fána
Agus sé is dóigh liom go mbeidh agus chaoin
Mile buíochas le rí gheall na glóire.
Is nach iomaí sin athrú ar an saol.

Is mise an capaillín gleoite
Bhi clúthuil is cailiúil ariamh.
Bhi mise luafar is láidir
Is chuir mise barr glas ar shliabh.

Ag treabhadh is ag fuirseadh na mbánta
Mé fhéin is mo chomrádaí liom.
Muid ag tarraingt mar -sheisreach le chéile
Is nach deas cothrom do choiníoch muid anonn.

Muid ag treabhadh leis an gcéachta gearr geancach
A bhiodh go santach ag iompú an fhóid.
Is an treabhadóir inár ndiaidh go síoraí ag caint linn.
Is muid ag tarraingt le chéile gan stró.

- 98 -

A reabhadh na dtaltaí ó chéile
Idir ardán is isleán is gleann.
Do chuireadh muid aris pór is grainne ann.
Is bhiodh an ithir 'ainn saoraigh go glan.

Dá bhiodh muid ag obair sa ngarraidh
Ó ar maidin go dul faoi don ghréin
Nuair a tugtaidh muid isteach ins na stáblai
Agus d'fhágladh muid togha coirce agus féar.

Do théitigh an t-uisce le h-aigh ól 'ainn
Bhiodh sé measca le min, choirce is bran
Agus nuair a bhíodh an deoch sin 'ainn ólta
Nach muid a chaitheadh an oiche go teann

Bhiodh leaba dheas ghlan 'ainn le luidheadh uirthi
Is an mainséar is é lionta le féar.
Is nach buacach a bhiodh muid go maidin
Go mbiodh an ghrian neó go h-ard ins an spéir.

Nuair a thiocfadh an máistir ar maidin
Le bricfeasta coirce glan deas
Do bhíodh sé dá slíocadh is dá gcóiriú
Go mbíodh dealramh na gréine inár gnéas

Dhéanadh sé muid a fheistiú is a réiteach
Le gléas treabhadh nó sin le gléas cairt.
Is thabharfadh sé neart uisce le n-ól dúinn
Mar bhi greada fionn uisce sa gclais.

Do bhíodh muid ag obair le chéile
Ar an bhfeilm go mall is go luath.
Is nach iomai sin allas a chuir muid
Mar bhiodh muid ag obair fíor chrua.

Do bhaineadh muid an féar deireadh an t-samhraidh
Do bhaineadh muid é go deas glan
Do bhaineadh muid an t-arbhar sa bhfómhair
Is bhailiodh muid é go deas cruinn.

Poems, Prayers and Recitations

Muise nach iomai sin uallaigh breá móra
Do thug muid isteach ins an gcró
Idir coirce, cruinneacht is eoirne
Idir fataí, féar agus móin.

Ach anois tá mise ar thóir máistir
Is a thuairisc ni fhéadaimse a fháil
Ach tá faitios mo chroi go han mhór orm
Go bhfuil an 'tractor' dhá thógáil im áit.

Ach anois a thalamhaigh dílis,
Seo comhairle a bheirimse díobh
Má leanann sibh an sean-tractor gránna
Go bhfaighfidh sibh gorta agus gantan sa saol.

Mar é fhéin is a chráigeanna móra
Déanann sé bouta do ithir is dríb
Is ní fhásfaidh ina dhiaidh pór nó gráinne
Is go mbeidh sibh gan cuid nó gan maoin.

Ach seo é anois deireadh mo chomhrá
Ach go bhfuil focal beag eile 'am le rá.
Go géar daineach a caoineas sibh fós mé
Nuair nach mbeidh mo thuairisc le fáil

6. Oiche na Gaoithe Moire

(Words kindly supplied by Michéal Ó hEidhin, Carnmore. It was said that sea-spray was felt as far inland as Carnmore.) This was the storm that blew the roof off the newly built church on 6th January 1839.

Ar Oiche Chinn an dá lá déag
Beidh cuimhne grinn go h-éag
Mar is iomaí mílte a d-éag
I mbaile, muir a's tír.
Oiche na gaoithe móire
Oiche stoirme a's dóghadhí
A rinne coillte is crainnte stróice
Is obair ghlan na saor.

Oíche uailleach sgréachach
Fuaimeach stoirmúil gaétheach
Is duine dall nach léighfeach

- 100 -

Cumhacht an Ard Rí thuas.
An domhain ar fad ag géimneach
Is an mhuir le gealt ag léimneach
Ainmhithe dúil is éanlaith
Faoi eagla agus uafás.

An talamh ag crith le buaireamh
Peacaidh ag scread 's ag uailleadh
Ar feadh na mbeagán uaire
Dhár thionnscail Dia a gnúis
Thug ordú uaidh don ghaéth seo
Séideadh láidir léithe
Carraig is aill do réabadh
Agus tithe a thabhairt anuas.

Ní túisce a dúirt na briartha
Ná tagann ar ball aniar í
Fuillteach cúrmhar fraochmhar
Ag briseadh in aghaidh na trá
An mhuir fheargach thréitheach
Ag ciapáil leis na néalta
Taréis na mílte céadta
Ins na duibheagáin do bháth.

Míle is ocht de chéadta
Trí 'gus naoi na déagtha
Siúd é an dáta dréachtaí
Anuas go dtí an bhliain.
Ó thuirling Críost ó Mháire
I mBeitlehem sa stábla
Nó gur eirigh an ghaoithe anáirde
Ag a leathuair taréis a naoi.

7. An Mharthain Phádraig (A Prayer)

Nellie Mullen (nee Greally) who died on March 31st 1985 gave this prayer to her sister Mary Newell. It was found in the grave of our Lord in the year 100 and was sent for safety by the then Pope to the emperor Charles as he was going to battle.

'Whoever shall repeat it everyday or hear it read, or keep it about them shall not die a sudden death, nor be drowned, nor shall not fall into the hands of his enemies in battle, nor shall poison take effect on him and it being read to

Poems, Prayers and Recitations

anybody in great pain - he shall get instant relief. If you see anyone in fits, lay this prayer on his or her right side and he (she) shall stand up and be blessed by the Lord. He who will laugh at it will suffer. Believe this to be certain, as it is true as the Evangelists have written it. They who keep it always with them shall not fear thunder or lightening and they who will repeat it everyday shall receive three days warning before their death'. (According to Mary Newell)

Oh adorable Lord and Saviour Jesus Christ dying on the gallows tree, save me.
Oh Holy cross of Christ, see me safe true.
Oh Holy cross of Christ, ward off from me all weapons of danger.
Oh Holy cross of Christ, ward off from me all things that are evil.
Oh Holy cross of Christ, protect me from my enemies.
Oh Holy cross of Christ, guide me the right way to happiness.
Oh Holy cross of Christ, ward off from me all dangerous deaths and give me life always.
Oh crucified Jesus of Nazareth, have mercy on me now and forever more.
Oh blessed Mother of God, intercede for us poor sinners. AMEN.

In Honour of Our Lord Jesus Christ,
In Honour of His Glorious Resurrection and God like Ascension
To which he wished to bring me the right way to Heaven.
True as Jesus was born on Christmas Day
True as Jesus died to save sinners
True as the Three Wise Men brought gifts to Jesus true as He ascended into Heaven
So in honour of Jesus will keep me from my enemies visible and invisible now and forever more. AMEN.

Oh Lord Jesus Christ have mercy on me,
Mary and Joseph pray for me.
Through thy sufferings on the Cross, this soul was flattering out of this world.
Give me grace that I may carry thy Cross,
And keep me from suffering and dangerous death now and forever more. AMEN.

- 102 -

Poems, Prayers and Recitations

8. Seanráteanna

Oíche inide gan feoil
Oíche an Nollaig Mhóir gan im
Oiche Mhicil gan brochán
Trí chomhartha an bhotháin a bheith lom.

Feast of St. Michael and St. Martin,
Oiche Mhicíl/ Oiche Mhartán.

A Mhairéad Ni Chionnaigh a bhfuil tú istigh?
Tá's a deir Mairéad hé sin amuigh.?
Máirtin Mhicil cothrom an oiche anocht
Mar mharaigh tú an mhuc bhreac dhubh
Beidh tú os cionn cláir seachtain ón oíche anocht.

CULLINAN ÓG:
Ag dul soir Baile Chláir dom sea chonaic mé an t-iontas.
Bhí mná óga na tíre ag na croisbhóithre romham.
Ba é ráiteas gach duine as béal a chéile
Go mba deas an áit cónaithe a bhí ag Cullinan Óg.

Ceathar sagart gan a bheith santach.
Ceathar Francach gan a bheith buí.
Ceathar gréasaí gan a bheith bréagach.
Sin dáréag nach gheobhfá i dtír.

Nádúr an tsaoil

Bliain ar láir capaill	(mare)
Naoi mí ar bhó	(cow)
Seachtain is fiche ar chaora	(ewe)
Se seachtain déag ar chráin	(sow)
Naoi seachtain ar mhadra	(bitch)
Sé seachtainí ar chat	(cat)
Oiche agus lá ar luch.	(mouse)
Iompú an t-sop ar dreancáid	(flea)

Amhrán gearr ó fear siúil:

Shiúil mé thart agus siar le fána
Agus trasna go dti Gort Cloon Mór
Ach ni bhfuair mé tada ar feadh an ama sin
Ach leathphingin ó Séamus an tsróin mhóir.
(S. Ó Coineannain)

- 103 -

10. Prayers and Sayings:

The following were given by Michéal Ó hEidhin, Carnmore:

STATIONS OF THE CROSS:

Canon Moran would say at each station:

Adhraím thú a Íosa, molaim thú.

The people would respond:

Le do chrois naofa a tháirthail thú an domhain. He would continue:
Adhraím thú a Íosa, molaim thú agus adhmhaím gur tú mac Rí na Glóire agus graíním méid agus meáchan mo pheacaí do chráidh thú chomh mór sin. Ceil mé in do chroí Íosa, falluigh mé in do chréachtaí, ná lig dom scaradh leat go h-éag aríst. Déan mo chroí do réir do chroí is déan mé dílis d' ód chrois chaoin.

At the station where Jesus is laid on the cross he would pray:

A Íosa a ciapadh is a goineadh le sleá is a stialadh le iarain ó mhulach go sáil.A Íosa a fuair spící do chos i do Iáimh, a Íosa ag iarraidh do choimrí atáim.

At the station where Jesus is hanging on the cross he would pray:

A Íosa a céasadh ar do chrois, is a d'fhualaing táírní cos is láimh, iompaigh liom is iompóchad leat, is nár iompuighead uait aríst go bráth.

A PRAYER TO THE BLESSED VIRGIN

(Canon Moran would say this with the children after Holy Communion)

A Mhaighdean ghlórmhar, mhórmhar mhaiseach. Is tá mo stór, mo lón is mo thaisce. Is tú mo réalt eolais rómhaim sa mbealach. I ngleann seo na ndeor seol an peacach. Is ar shliabh an bhróin fóir ar m'anam.

His version of 'Soul of Christ be my sanctification' was:

A anam Chríosta naomhuigh mé. A chorp Chríosta slánuigh mé. A fhuil Chriosta meanamnuigh mé. A uisce thaobh Chríosta unluigh mé. A pháis Chríosta neartuigh mé. A Íosa ró-mhaith deónaim éisteacht. Falluigh mé istigh do chréachta.Leatsa fhéin ná lig dom dealú. Cosain mé ar an namhaid mhallaithe. Ar uair mo bháis deónaigh mé a ghlaoch. Chugat dordaigh mé do thígeacht mé do mholadh imeasc na Naomh, tré saol na saol, ÁMÉAN a Chríost.

A PRAYER FOR RAKING THE FIRE:

Coiglím fhéin an tine seo mar a choiglíns Críost cách. Bríd ina bun agus Muire ina barr. Dhá aingeal déag agus Athair na nGrást. Ag cumhadach an tighe seo is na daoine go lá.

A PRAYER FOR SETTING OUT ON A JOURNEY:

In ainm an Athar le bua,
In ainm an Mhic a d'fhulaing an phian,
In ainm an Spiorad Naomh le neart,
Muire is a Mac linn in ár dtriall.

PRAYERS WHEN GOING TO BED:

A Mhuire dhilis is a mháthair Iosa, go raibh tú ag mo cheann. A Eoghain Baiste
agus Ard Easpail, go raibh tú ag mo bhun. Teachtaire Iosa le ola Chríosta go
raibh 'gam in am a chuirfheas scáladh ar manam dilis. In ainm Iosa a céasadh
ar an gcrann.

Ceithre choirnéal ar mo leaba.
Ceithre aingle ortha scartha
A's má fhaim bás as seo go maidin
Go Flaitheas Dé go rachaidh m'anam.

AFTER EACH DECADE OF THE ROSARY:

Ó Iosa maith dhúinn ár bpeacaí. Slánuigh muid ó thinteacha Ifrinn. Treóir gach
anam chun na Flaithis, go h-áirid iad seo is mó gá le do thrócaire.

GRACE BEFORE MEALS:

Baill na g-cúig 'ráin's an dá iasc, a roinn Dia ar an gcúig mhíle fear. Rath ón
Rí a rinne an roinn ar ár gcuid agus ar ár gcómh-roinn Áméan.

GRACE AFTER MEALS:

An té a thug an bheatha seo dhúinn go dtabhairidh sé an bheatha Shioraí agus
glóire na bhFlaithis dár n-anamnaí agus anamnaí bochta Phurgadóra.
Beannacht dhílis Dé le h-anamnaí na marbh, Áméan.

Chapter 9: Schools and Education

Claregalway National School
Early History

At the beginning of the nineteenth century schools in Ireland were run by individuals and voluntary societies, e.g. the Kildare Place Society, the London Hibernian Society and the Irish Society. The largest category of schools was the 'pay' schools where payments by the children supported the teacher. Many of these schools corresponded to hedge schools and it was estimated by an official commission in 1824 that they numbered about 9,000 and catered for almost 400,000 children.

The old Claregalway School that was situated at the church car park   *Replacement school built in 1929 which is now incorporated into the present building*

The earliest written record of education in the parish of Claregalway is contained in a document entitled "The Grievances of the Parishioners of Clare Galway" in the Galway Diocesan Archives. Referring to the Parish Priest, the document states: *"He has shut the chapel contrary to the custom heretofore established, of having the young children instructed and their catechism taught them there although the parishioners have largely contributed to the repairs of it, and they feel very indignant at such treatment."* It is thought that this document dates from around 1808/9 and that the Parish Priest in question was Fr. Malachy Mannion. A second document, dated 29th October 1811, seems to confirm this. In this second document the parishioners complain once again about the situation in Claregalway: *"That Memorialists have seen, and still see with inexpressible concern the youth of this Parish destitute of an eligible person to superintend their education nearly these three years back, in consequence of no teacher having been allowed in the Parish Chapel, which keeps them in an absolute and deplorable state of ignorance."*

The twelve signatories request the Warden to rectify the situation *"by asserting your right and that of the Parishioners to the chapel on which they have at various times expended considerable sums and which was the purpose of your Exhortation when last you visited the chapel"*

Claregalway School girls – early 1920s
Front Row (L to R): ?, Forde – Cahergowan, Mary Beatty – Lydacan, ?, ?, Nora Moran (Glynn) – Clogher, ?, W. Forde – Cahergowan. **Middle Row (L to R):** ?, Greally – Cloonbiggen, Maggie Clancy – Cregboy, B. Hanley – Cloon, Molly Fahy – Cregboy, May Hession (Liston) – Claregalway, May Morris – Cregboy, Fahy – Cregboy. **Back Row (L to R):** ?, ?, ?, Greally – Cloonbiggen, Margaret Moran – Lakeview, ?, ?, Nellie Fahy – Cregboy

The chapel in question is marked as Old R.C. Chapel and School House on the Ordinance Survey Map of 1840 (County Galway, Sheet 70). It was located a short distance south of the river, just off the main road, on a road leading south-eastward (behind where Duggans house is now situated). This was beside a place referred to locally as *An Geata Mór*. The chapel is also marked on a 'Map of part of the Bogs in the District of Lough Corrib in the County of Galway (1814)'

In the Second Report of the Irish Education Inquiry of 1826 the school is referred to as being "held in the chapel", which suggests that the differences of 1808 and 1811 had been overcome. It is described as a 'pay' school with an attendance of 50 boys and 30 girls. The master, who received an annual income of £12 to £15 per annum (paid by the children), was named as William Loftus. A school is also listed in Carnmore where the master, John Hanly, received from 2s 6d per quarter

Schools and Education

from each pupil. It is described as 'a small hut' with an attendance of 18 boys and 12 girls.

A third school, at Brannamore, is listed in the parish of Claregalway. The mistress, Mrs. Haverty, taught twelve girls. The school is described as 'a room' and the income of the mistress is 'not stated'. We have been unable to establish the existence of a townland called Brannamore in the parish, through local people or through Ordinance Survey maps. Could it possibly be Bawnmore? The Ordinance Survey map of 1840 has a schoolhouse marked just a few yards north of Kynes Central Tavern, directly across from the road leading to Corrandulla.

Claregalway School boys – 1923
Front Row (L to R): Willie Lenihan, 'Bull' Feeney, ?, James Hession (Velvet), PJ Hughes, Frank Duggan (Val), Mattie Flesk and Mick Kelly (Cloon). **Middle Row (L to R):** ?, John Scully (Cregboy), Charly Duggan (Kelly Montiagh), Eddie Morris, Peter Kelly (Cloon), Billy Morris, Willie Duggan (Val), Jimmy Moran (Lakeview), Henry Duggan (Peadar), ?, ? and ? **Back Row (L to R):** Thomas O'Connor N.T., ?, Jimmy Noone, ?, Moran (Cregboy), ?, Patrick Moran (Clogher), Bodkin, Michael Murphy (Paddy - Ballymurphy), ?, Christy Morris, ? and ?

A detailed record of education in the Parish of Claregalway is contained in the Report of the Commissioners of Public Instruction (1835) which gives details of the membership of different religious denominations and of the schools in each parish. The report states that there were two schools in the parish. The first school, which had been established for one year, was "in the chapel of Claregalway, and kept by John Duggan", and was supported by "payments by the children, from 1s 6d to 5s per quarter, producing from £5 to £6 per annum". The children who attended, 46 boys and 30 girls, were taught "reading, writing,

Schools and Education

arithmetic, book-keeping and Roman Catholic catechism". The second school is recorded at "Clash, kept by Patrick Carr" and this also was supported by "payments by the children, from 1s 3d to 2s 6d per quarter, producing about £6 per annum". This school, which had been established for two years, had an enrolment of 36 boys and 20 girls who were taught "reading, writing, arithmetic, and Roman Catholic catechism".

Local folklore (Ciarán Bairéad, Irish Folklore Commission, Notes on the Ecclesiastical History of Claregalway Parish, 1963, Galway Diocesan Archives) refers to two hedge schools in the parish. One, which was said to have been located in Ballinacregg, was run by a man called Grimes who had the reputation of being very harsh. Could this be the school referred to in the Education Inquiry of 1826?

The second school, which was said to have been situated beside the pump in Montiagh, was run by a man called Tomáisín Bacach, who was, as the name suggests, lame. It was said that he was a great penman who wrote books containing Irish songs, etc. one of which is in the Irish Folklore Commission in Dublin (not verified). The books were known as 'Leabhraí Thomáisín Bacach' or 'Leabhraí Thomáisín'. It is possible that this is the school listed at Clash in the 1835 Report of the Commissioners of Public Instruction. Local people say that Clash was the name given to a field behind Mike Hessions but there was also a place in Montiagh called Clash na dTincéirí.

In 1831 the Irish national school system was established through the agency of Lord Stanley, Chief Secretary of Ireland. Schools already in existence before 1831 became affiliated to or absorbed into the national system under the authority of a Board of Commissioners for National Education appointed by the government. Some schools received support for building and it was hoped that these schools would be vested in the Board though many were subsequently vested in local trustees. Non-vested schools (schools built without the aid of the Commissioners) benefited from grants for teachers' salaries and books.

The 1851 Commissioners Report on National Education records a boys' school (with an enrolment of 78) and a girls' school (enrolment of 54) in Claregalway. (There is no local record as to the exact location of these schools). It is worth noting that the average attendance in schools around this time would have been around 30% of enrolment. The boys' school, which is listed as temporary, received allowances of £2 0s 7d for school requisites, £10 0s 0d for teacher's salary and £5 10s 0d as a local contribution in aid of teacher's salary. Allowances for the girls' school are shown as £8 15s 0d for teacher's salary and £2 10s 0d as the local contribution to it. An appendix to the report which, gives particulars of the examinations of teachers of National Schools, lists Mr. Michael Carrick as the Principal of the boys' school. There is no record of the teacher in the girls' school.

Schools and Education

Claregalway School girls – about 1949

In 1855 a National School was built in the townland of Cregboy in the Barony of Dunkellin (where the Telecom Eireann station and church car park are now situated). There were two schools within the building – boys and girls were separated. A Daily Report Book (1911 – 1919) from the girls' school, printed for His Majesty's Stationary Office by John Adams, Belfast, records that the school was non-vested and "built by the people of the parish" with the dimensions of each school room 35ft long, $18^{1/2}$ ft wide and 20ft high.

According to notes by Canon P. Moran, P.P., Claregalway (1915-1946) held in the Diocesan Archives, dated 1st July 1920, 'these schools, together with the plot of ground, were leased on the 10th July 1888 by the owners, Mary Commins and John Commins to the trust of Rev. Dr. MacCormack and the Rev. Martin Commins P.P., for 99 years at the yearly rent of one penny and vested in fee simple in Bishop MacCormack and Rev. Martin Commins by order of the Irish Land Commission of 7th April 1902.'

Payment by Results

The oldest records available from the girls' school are a number of Examination Rolls from 1895 to 1899. The rolls contain the names of pupils who had made 100 or more attendances within the previous year and were thereby eligible for promotion if they passed examinations in reading, writing and arithmetic. The rolls were signed by the teacher, Bedelia Daly (probably the Principal). In 1899 they were signed by Margaret Brady and we assume that she married around the turn of the century as the Principal from 1905 to 1931 is recorded as Mrs Margaret Flood.

Schools and Education

Claregalway School boys – about 1935

These Examination Rolls were of extreme importance to the teachers because the period in Irish education from 1872 to 1899 was known as the 'pay by results' period when, as the name suggests, teachers were paid on the basis of results of pupils' examinations in the 3Rs. Precise programmes were set for each subject from Infants to Sixth Class with Reading, Writing, Spelling and Arithmetic as the obligatory subjects up to Second Class and Grammar, Geography, Needlework (girls) and Agriculture (boys) being added from Third Class upwards. Two extra optional subjects could be taken in the senior classes from a long optional list. A scale of fees was devised for each subject in each grade and a pupil at sixth grade, who was successful in all subjects including two extra subjects, could earn 18 shillings for his teacher. Children were examined by the inspector annually and teachers were paid on the basis of the results.

An accompanying inspector's report from 1898 states that there were 101 girls enrolled in the school, 37 of whom had made the qualifying number of attendances but on examination of school accounts he had found the names of ten other pupils who had made over 99 attendances but whose names had been suppressed from the Roll!

In his 1899 Report to the Board of Commissioners, District Inspector for Galway, Mr. W.H. Welply expresses concern regarding the practice of suppressing eligible names from the examination rolls and gives the obvious reason for same:

"... one or more pupils may be unlikely to pass creditably and so lest their probable bad marks should detract from the appearance of efficiency of the school, such pupils' names are sometimes omitted, and the risk taken, that, in the hurry of the examination, the accounts may escape the often long and wearisome

Schools and Education

check that enables an Inspector to detect these omissions."

He was also worried about the practice of allotting incorrect ages to children when they were enrolled. He gives an example of "a child of six years on admission. As often as not, his age in the register will be put down as four, and he will, in all probability, remain in the Infant classes until he attains the official age of eight. He arrives in the 1st class at the real age of ten and in 4th at 13."

The 'pay by results' system was scrapped in September 1900 when a revised programme was introduced. As well as the 3Rs, kindergarten, manual instruction, drawing, singing, object lessons and elementary science, P.E., cookery and laundry were added as obligatory subjects.

20th Century

A Roll Book from 1927 contains an extract, regarding school attendance, from the Irish Education Act of 1892. The extract states that *"the parent of every child not less than six nor more than fourteen years of age shall cause the child to attend school during such number of days in the year and for such time on each*

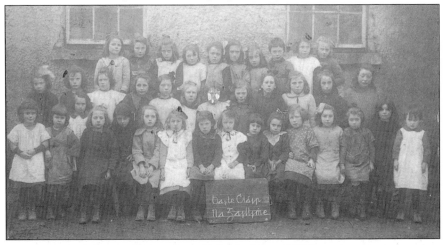

Claregalway School girls – 1923?

Front Row (L to R): *?, Baby Quinn, ?, Maureen Kelly-Murphy, Mary Hession (James' sister), Mary Duggan (Val, Montiagh), Lena Donaghue, Sarah Duggan (Val, Montiagh), Mary Casserly (Kiniska), Cissie Hughes, Bridget Hanley (Cloon), Julia Carr (Gortatleva), Baby Long (Kiniska), Eva Morris (Cregboy) and Sally Glynn-Fahy.* ***Middle Row (L to R):*** *Maggie Fahy (Lydacan, nun), Celia Fahy-Keesham, Mary Connell-Kerrigan, Bridie Moran-Small, Nelly Greally-Breac, Evelyn Fahy (Cregboy), Mary Duggan (Thomais), Mary Donaghue (Lena's sister), ?, Flesk (Cloon), ?, Nora Lenihan (Mick's sister) and ?* ***Back Row (L to R):*** *?, Nonie Long (Kiniska), Nellie Bodkin, Long (Kiniska), Nellie McDonagh (Gortatleva), Mary Carr-Duggan, Carr (Gortatleva), Greally, Mary Duggan-Greally and Julie Murphy-Flesk.*

Schools and Education

day of attendance as are prescribed in the First Schedule of this act." The First Schedule notes that ".... The number of attendances shall be 75 complete attendances in each half year". Among the reasons regarded as reasonable for non-attendance were "... sickness, domestic necessity, or by reason of being engaged in necessary operations of husbandry and the in-gathering of crops or giving assistance in the fisheries...".

Mr. Welply's Report of 1899 notes that "...the Compulsory Attendance Act has been very recently put into force in Galway but beyond casually learning that the unaccustomed scarcity of 'caddies' upon the local golf links is attributable to this cause, I have not had an opportunity of judging its effects."

He also notes that *".... as a general rule fuel is provided by the pupils, and it is not uncommon to see them of a morning carrying along with their books their daily contribution of peat."*

Records from the old boy's school are not as plentiful but a Register of teachers shows that Mr. George Carter was Principal from 1878 to 1915. Mary J. Carter, who acted as assistant teacher in the school from 1906 to 1912, was probably his daughter. Mr. Carter was succeeded by Thomas O' Reilly (1915- 1920) and he in turn was followed by James P. Donnellan (1920-22). In 1922 Tomás Ó'Conchubhair, a native of Kerry, was appointed Principal, a position he held until 1962. His assistant for most of this term (1915-1954) was Mary Cullinan (nee Moran), grandmother of Gerry, Cahergowan. Miss Greally succeeded her.

Inspectors' reports from that period laud their diligence, teaching ability and commitment to the Irish language. Conditions in the old school left a lot to be desired as we can gauge from the following portions of inspectors' reports:

Claregalway School boys – late 1940s

Girls

1909 - The roof is unceilinged. There is not sufficient accommodation for shawls, hats, etc. of the pupils. The room is insufficiently heated by one fireplace.

1910 - The school is inadequately heated and needs many repairs to floor, walls and windows. Eave shoots are also required.

1921 - A map of the British Isles and a scale map of the locality are required.

Boys

1916 - A fireguard is needed. Desks for small children are not suitable.

1919 - The boundary wall requires repair at the back. Stones should be cleared off the playground. Distempering is required. The school has been seriously affected by closing for epidemics, changes of teachers (through the absence of the Principal at a University course for the Diploma in Education) and an occasional absence owing to illness.

Work began on the building of a new school in the townland of Lakeview in 1929 (the oldest section of the present school). This was completed in 1930 with the official opening on October 6th as shown in an entry on the Daily Report Book (girls) of that month:

6 adh Deireadh Foghmhair 1930
Fosgluígheas an teach scoile nua seo inniu.
Bhí 52 i láthair. P.S. Ó Móráin S.P.

It is reported that the building cost £3,000 - the parish contributed £150 and the remainder came from government funds. Boys and girls were separated once again. In 1931 a new principal was appointed to the girl's school. Eibhlin Bn Mhic Suibhne (Ní Mhuirghuis) – Helena Mc Sweeney – who had acted as assistant teacher since 1919 was the new principal, a post she held until 1940 when Eibhlin Bn. Uí Dhuibhghiolla (Eibhlin Divilly) succeeded her. Assistants during this period were Bríd Nic An Iomaire (Bríd Ridge) (1932-36) and Polín Ní Lorcáin (Pauline Larkin) (1936–43). Bn. Uí Dhuibhghiolla remained as Principal until 1963 when she was succeeded by Máire Bn.Uí Lochlainn (Maire O'Loughlin).

In 1943 Bríd Bn. Uí Aodh (Bríd Hughes) from Oileáin Árann was appointed as assistant teacher, a position she held until her retirement in 1984 – a remarkable forty one years of service to the parish.

The boys and girls' schools were amalgamated in 1970 under the principalship of Seán Mac Gloinn (Séan Glynn), Woodquay, who had succeeded Tómas Ó

Conchúbhair (Thomas O'Connor) as Principal of the boys' school in 1962. He retired in 1978 and was succeeded, as Principal, by Máire Bn. Uí Lochlainn, who had acted as Principal of the girls' school before the amalgamation. She in turn retired in 1991 to be succeeded by the present Principal, Pádraig Ó Comhghain (Pat Coen).

Claregalway School girls – mid 1950s

Enrolment figures from the old Claregalway girls' school show that there were approximately 100 girls enrolled around the turn of the century. This number decreased gradually during the 1920s and 1930s and was in fact halved by the 1940s when the enrolment was 50 girls. By 1955 the number had risen to 74 only to start a downward trend again to an all time low of 43 in 1968. Around the time of the amalgamation of the boys and girls' schools in 1970, sixty nine boys and fifty four girls were enrolled but the following twenty years were to see an enrolment explosion due to a house building boom and the popularity of Claregalway as a place of residence for young families. The phenomenal increase in enrolment can be seen from the following figures:

Enrolment:
1971 123 (Total – boys and girls)
1974 130
1976 150
1978 178
1980 192
1983 244
1987 292
1993 300

As enrolment almost trebled in twenty years, extra teachers were appointed and a major extension of five classrooms, staff room, general purpose room, etc. was added in the 1980s. Far from the turf fires, cold rooms, substandard toilet facilities and lack of proper water supply in the old schools the children now had the comfort of central heating, en suite toilets, modern furniture and running water in all classrooms. A further extension of two classrooms and a staff room was added in the mid 1990s. The appointment of a remedial teacher brought the number of teachers to twelve.

The introduction of free school education in the 1960s led to an increase in the number of pupils going on to second level education. School records from the 1920s to the 1960s show that only a small number of pupils went on to second level. In the 1990s we see all children going on to second level with a large percentage continuing on to third level.

1975 saw a big change in the management of schools when teachers and parents were granted positions on the new Boards of Management. The Boards, comprised of Bishop's nominees, teachers and parents' representatives, now had the responsibility of managing finance, maintenance, appointment of teachers and the overall running of the school.

The members of the first Board of Management were:

Canon Gerard Callanan, P.P., Chairperson
Kathleen Dunleavy, Secretary
Séan Walsh, Treasurer
Parents' representatives: Paddy Joe Hughes and Martin Commins
Bishop's nominees and Mary O'Loughlin representing the teachers.
(In 1997, Kathleen Dunleavy was appointed as Bishop's nominee to the latest Board of Management of the school. This means that she will have completed 25 years of unbroken service to the school when the Board finishes its term)

The Irish Language

The position of the Irish language in schools has seen many changes over the years. History from the hedge schools tells us that children wore 'tally sticks' around their necks and each time they used the Irish language a notch was placed on the stick. They were then punished after a certain number of notches appeared on the stick.

The Irish language was not acknowledged as a national school subject until 1922 when it became an obligatory subject for at least one hour per day. All school records up to 1923 are in English. The language flourished during the 1940s and 1950s and families received a 'deontas' (grant) for speaking the language. An inspector visited the school and examined the children orally to ascertain if Irish was the *'teanga an teaghlaigh'* (the language of the home). The deontas was originally £2 per child but was increased to £5 and later still to £10. Families that received the 'deontas' were entitled to Gaeltacht grants for house building, repairs, etc. The use of the Irish language was widespread in Claregalway with the village of Montiagh being renowned for its beautiful Irish. Acht na Gaeltachta was passed in 1955 and this defined the boundaries of the Gaeltacht areas.

Tomás O'Connor, principal teacher in Claregalway, on his retirement in 1962. Also are Fr. Forde, parish priest and Mrs. O'Connor

The large influx of people, mostly non native Irish speakers, into Claregalway from the 1970s through to the 1990s meant that only a small percentage of children coming into school were from homes where Irish was the *'teanga an teaghlaigh'*. This led to a dilution of the use of the language, particularly in the playground. Recent trends show that the language is making a comeback and a large increase in the amount of the 'deontas' encourages families to have Gaeilge as *'teanga an teaghlaigh'*.

Carnmore National School

The old school in Carnmore opened on June 16th 1885. The 1886 Report on National Education shows that the school was vested in Trustees with an enrolment of 98 boys and 80 girls. In that year a total of £91 16s 10d was paid to the school in salary, result fees and gratuities while £9 6s 0d was listed as having been paid locally towards school fees. A further £3 10s 0d was received in voluntary local contributions. The Parish Priest at that time was Fr. Martin

Schools and Education

The old Carnmore School. The commemorative stone plaque over the door reads: 'Scoil an Cairn Móir, Scoil Náisiúnta, 1935'

Commins – he also oversaw the building of the parochial house in Claregalway. (According to the notes of Canon P. Moran (Diocesan Archives 1st July 1920) the school was vested in the trust of the Most Rev. Dr. O'Dea, Bishop of Galway, Rev. Antony J. Considine, C.C., Galway, Rev. Peter Davis, C.C., Galway and Rev. Redmond McHugh, P.P., Claregalway.)

Carnmore School boys and girls – 1965/67

Schools and Education

SCOLÁIRÍ AN CHADHNAIGH

Carnmore School boys and girls – c 1938

Back Row (L to R): *Stephen Walsh, Peter Grealish (Michael), Mick Grealish (Baile Nua), Martin Grealish (James), Eddie Fox, Jimmie Collins, John (Jodie) Fox, anon, Martin Grealish (Sean), anon., Seamus Grealish (Baile Nua), anon. anon. and anon.* **Fourth Row (L to R):** *Maureen Commins, Theresa Carr, Peggy Girvan, Mary Theresa Higgins, Annie Carr, Mary Killilea and Girvan.* ***Third Row (L to R):*** *Eileen Fox, anon, Una Grealish (Baile Nua), Sally Hanley, Bridgie Collins, Bina Girvan, anon. Martin Hanley (Tom) and anon.* ***Second Row (L to R):*** *Kitty Girvan, Kathleen Grealish (Cross Roads), Julia Grealish (Sean), Annie Joyce, anon., , Tommie Killilea, Mickey Grealish (Sean), Eamon Grealish (Cross) and Michael Fox.* ***Front Row (L to R):*** *Nonie Higgins, Mary Walsh, Margaret Costello, Paddy Walsh, Michael Hynes, William Hynes and anon.*

Many of the children had already been attending school in Claregalway, Oranmore and Lackagh. An old report book gives the dimensions of the schoolroom as 33ft. in length, 18ft. in width and 10ft. in height. This room was divided in two with infants to second class on one side and the senior classes in the other half. A turf fire provided heating, as was the case with nearly all schools at that time. Furniture consisted of the usual long desks of approximately 10ft. long, forms of similar length, a teacher's table and a rostrum.

As this was in the middle of the 'pay by results' period in Irish education, the emphasis was on the 3Rs with annual inspections and examinations by the inspector. The introduction of a wider curriculum in 1900 made for more interesting and varied education for pupils and teachers. One of the new obligatory subjects was Cookery and Laundry. Children learned about cleaning, washing, starching, ironing and folding various items of clothing, including silk handkerchiefs. They were also educated in the use of various cooking utensils and the preparation of a wide variety of dishes.

A Corporal Punishment Book was kept in every school. Corporal punishment, which was administered by the Principal, was recommended only for grave transgressions, never for failure in lessons. The book was regularly checked and

Schools and Education

signed by the inspector.

Details of the earlier teachers in Carnmore are very sketchy. Mrs. Kelly was appointed in 1887 and there is a record of a Mrs. Gaffney being appointed in 1917. Mrs. Kelly was still there in 1928 when she was joined by Miss M. Casserly. Mrs. O Kane and Mr. McDonagh, Principal, also taught in the school and the latter was succeeded by the renowned poet and writer, Máirtín Ó Cadhain. Many people commented on the fact that he was a great teacher but a disagreement with Canon Moran P.P. led to his dismissal as Principal. He was succeeded by Seamus Ó Marranáin (in 1937) who suffered from the fall-out of his predecessor's sacking to such an extent that he required police protection both in coming to and going from school and even in the school yard. He weathered the storm, however, and remained in Carnmore until 1975 when he retired and was replaced by the present Principal, Pilib Ó Cadhain. Carnmore School was renovated and enlarged in 1935.

Máiréad Nic Dhiarmada was appointed as assistant teacher in 1949 and she was later succeeded by Úna Breathnach who came from Cill Ainnín in 1968. Carnmore remained a two–teacher school until 1977 when Bairbre Ní Iarnáin –

Carnmore School boys of 1926.
Front Row (L to R): *Mickey Grealish, Murty McGrath, Willie Collins, Patrick Killilea, Tommy Murphy, Peter Grealish, Jimmy Grealish, Tommy Holland, Paddy Carr and Paddy 'Bawn' Grealish.* ***Second Row (L to R):*** *Martin Duggan, Tommy Lardner, Paddy Lardner, Peter Kelly, Stephen Ruane, Thomas Fahy, John Bane, Martin Cooney, Thady Carr, ?, Michael Collins, Paddy Hanley and Denis Lardner.* ***Third Row (L to R):*** *John Kelly, Jimmie Leonard, Michael McGrath, Larry Fox, Roger McGrath, Michael Cooney, Martin Beatty, Paddy Collins, Patrick Collins, Michael Beatty and Paddy Grealish.* ***Fourth Row (L to R):*** *Michael Carr, Paddy Fahy, Johnny McGrath, Johnny Clarke, Michael Carr and Johnny Collins.*

later Bairbre Bn. Mhic Dhonncha – joined the staff as second assistant. The old school was now almost 100 years old and conditions were obviously substandard. A new school was built and officially opened on December 14th 1983. Shortly afterwards, in January 1984, Bn. Mhic Dhonncha left for An Cheathrú Rua and was replaced by Nóirín Bn. Uí Eidhin. Enrolment figures were rising and Carnmore soon became a four-teacher school with the appointment of Máire Ní Chuilleanáin from Claregalway. Máire took a career break in 1989 and headed for Australia where she married and settled down. Áine Bn. Uí Mhóráin was appointed in her place and shortly afterwards, in September 1990, Seán Ó Raghallaigh was appointed as a fourth assistant. Úna Breathnach retired in 1991 and was replaced by Gina Bn. Uí Mhainnín.

Almost two hundred years on from the earliest written record of education in the parish of Claregalway it can be safely said that the parish is well served with two modern, growing schools. Most of the credit for this goes to Canon Gerard Callanan P.P. who oversaw the building, extending and staffing of the schools during the 1970s, 80s and 90s. He has left a splendid legacy to the people of the parish who must also be credited for their financial support during that period.

Bawnmore National School

Though situated in the parish of Lackagh, Bawnmore N.S. has provided primary school education for many people at that end of Claregalway parish. The history of the school has been documented in a beautifully presented booklet, which was

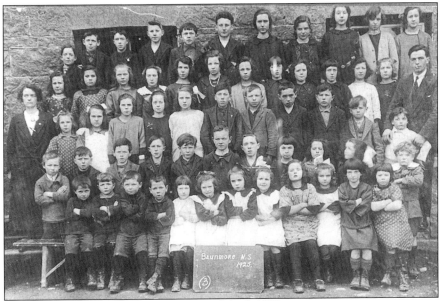

Bawnmore School, 1925

Schools and Education

produced for a school reunion in summer 1998.

The old school was established by Richard Kirwan of Bawnmore House in 1863 to educate the children of his tenants. At first there were two separate schools – one for boys and one for girls – with Mr. Patrick Heavey being the first Principal of the boys' school and his wife, Bridget, Principal of the girls' school. In 1875 the two schools amalgamated. Peter Brennan took over as Principal in 1864 and he in turn was succeeded by James O Brennan in 1898. In 1935 Bill Mannion was appointed Principal and he was later succeeded by his wife, Maura.

Plans by the Department of Education to have the old school closed and the children from the area transported to a central school in Lackagh were opposed by parents in the sixties. As a result of this strong local opposition the plans were scrapped and it was decided to build a new three -classroom school instead. The new school was opened on October 1971 and shortly afterwards Mrs. Mannion retired to be replaced by the present Principal, Mr. Pat Duddy. Bríd Glynn who resided in Claregalway taught for most of her teaching career in Bawnmore. She started in Bawnmore in May 1939 and retired 36 years later in July 1975.

Chapter 10: Irish

Seán Ó Ceallaigh

Ar an gCluain i mBaile Chláir na Gaillimhe, a rugadh Seán Ó Ceallaigh (sa bhliain 1916). Bhí an Ghaeilge aige ón gcliabhán. Chuaigh sé ar scoil sa Scoil Náisiúnta i mBaile Chláir agus i Meánscoil Naomh Seosamh i nGaillimh. hOileadh ina mhúinteoir é i gColáiste Naomh Pádraig i nDroim Conrach, Baile Átha Cliath (1934-36). Chaith sé ceithre bliana ag múineadh scoile ar an Oileán Iarthach i Ros Muc, seacht mbliana eile i nDoire Uí Bhriain i ndeisceart na Gaillimhe, agus le hocht mbliana déag, bhí sé ina phríomhoide sa bhunscoil i gCreachmhaoil, i gCo. na Gaillimhe.

Bhain sé amach céim B.A. i gColáiste na hOllscoile, Gaillimh, sa bhliain 1955, agus bhí sé ina chúntóir i Roinn na Gaeilge i gColáiste na nOllscoile, Gaillimh, ón mbliain 1956 ar aghaidh. Bronnadh céim M.A. air i gColáiste na hOllscoile, Gaillimh, sa bhliain 1966 de thoradh a thráchtais *Filíocht na gCallanán* a chuir sé le chéile sa leabhar den ainm ceánna.

Seán Ó Ceallaigh

Micheál Ó Síoda, Scéalaí agus Seanchaí (1888-1966)

Rugadh Micheál Ó Síoda ar an bPáirc Gharbh, Carn Mór, i bparáiste Bhaile Chláir ar an deichiú lá fichead de mhí na Bealtaine, 1888. Tá an Pháirc Gharbh tuairim a's sé mhíle Éireannach soir ó Ghaillimh, an taobh ó thua den bhóthar atá ag dul go Muine Mheadha.

Micheál a bhí ar a athair freisin - Micil Ó Síoda mar a tugtaí air - agus feilméaraí a raibh tuairim a's fiche acra aige ab ea é. Máire Williams a bhí ar a mháthair, agus rugadh ise freisin ar an bPáirc Gharbh i dteach nach raibh mórán le dhá scór slat ón teach ar phós sí isteach ann. Deir an dream a raibh aithne acu uirthi gur bean í a raibh éirim agus meabhair thar an gcoitiantacht inti, agus ina theannta sin go raibh sí ina scoláire mhaith. Dúirt Micheál héin liom go raibh sí ar ghearr-scoil le linn a hóige a bhí i mBaile na Creige, tuairim a's míle ón bPáirc Gharbh, ag fear den ainm Grimes. Bhí gaol aici le gréasaí i mBaile Chláir a raibh Tom Williams air. Bhí a mhac, Tom eile, ag gréasaíocht ann ina dhiaidh, agus mac eile Mike, ina bhuachaill posta ar fea blianta fada sa gceanntar. Cailleadh Máire Williams i 1909, agus Micil Ó Síoda i 1912.

Ba dh-é Micheál seo againne an duine ab óige de mhuirín fhada. Éamon a bhí ar an duine ba sine den chlann, agus cailleadh é sa mbaile nuair a bhí sé ocht mbliana fichead. Ansin bhí Jude (Julia), an iníon ba sine. Níor phós sí ariamh, ach d'fhan sí sa teach, agus is í a bhí ina bean-tí acu gur cailleadh í i 1952. Bhí sí trí nó ceathair de bhlianta os cionn ceithre scór an t-am sin. Ansin bhí Searlaí a chuaigh go dtí an Astráil ina óige agus a chaith blianta ann. Bhí sé ag obair sna gold diggings i Kalgoorlie. Thainic sé abhaile roint bhlianta os cionn dhá scór ó shin agus 'pínneachaí aige', agus d'fhan sé cúpla bliain nó trí sa sean-áit. Ansin cheannaigh sé gabhaltas thalúna i Monach Thaidhg, i n-aice le Creach Mhaoil agus chuaigh sé 'un cónaí ann. Phós sé bean de mhuintir Ghrállaigh as Mearaí i bparáiste Óráin Mhóir. Níor mhair sé ann ach achar gearr gur cailleadh é. Ní raibh aon duine clainne acu. Tá sé ráite gurb é deannach an óir a chuaigh i bhfastódh ins na scamhógaí aige sa Astráil ba siocair báis dó.

Bhí cúigear iníon eile ann, Bríd a cailleadh in aois a bliain a's fiche, agus Máire a cailleadh nuair a bhí sí in aois chúig bliana a's dá fhichead Níor fhág an bheirt an baile ariamh, agus cailleadh gan phósadh iad. Ansin bhí Neilí agus Katie agus Liz. Chuaigh an triúr acu go dtí an Astráil - is é Searlaí a chuir fios orthu agus a d'íoc a mbealach amach. Phós an triúr acu ann, agus tá a gclann ann ina ndiaidh.

Nuair a thosaigh mise ag dul ag an teach, ag déana ar shé bliana déag ó shin anois, ní raibh ann ach Jude agus Patch agus Mike. Bhí Jude ag breathnú chomh sean an uair sin thar an mbeirt dritheár agus go gceapfá gurb í a máthair í. Bean chiúin lách a bhí inti gan mórán le rádh, agus bean 'nár dhúirt focal le aon duine ariamh' (i.e., a bhí cóir múinte le chuile dhuine). Bheadh Mike an uair sin dhá bhliain os cionn na trí scóir, agus Patch seacht mbliana eile. Fear caol éadrom, agus tuairim agus mean-airde ann a bhí i Mike, agus ceann-aghaidh laethúil air, agus taréis gur chaith sé a shaol ag obair ar an bhfeilm, ní lámha sclábhaí ná fir oibre a bhí air. Bhí siad caol fíneáilte. Bhí sé uasal in a intinn freisin. Níl tabhairt amach ar bith sa gcondae i rith na bliana, nó dhá ndéarfainn é, i gConnacht ar fad, is mó ná Rástaí na Gaillimhe. Bíonn an Domhan Mór agus a mháthair bailí' ann, ach dúirt Mike liom nach raibh sé ann ariamh. Nuair a rinne mé íontas dhó

Irish

sin agus gan páirc an rása ach ceithre mhíle ón teach, dúirt sé liom:

'A, níor mhaith liom ariamh a bheith in aon áit a mbeadh troid ná achrann ná droch-chainteannaí ar bun, agus 'chuile chineál tincéaraí baili' ann!'

Chuaigh sé ar an scoil náisiúnta ar a' gCarn Mór, scoil nach bhfuil ach dó nó trí chéadta slat ón teach. Beirt bhan a bhí ag múnadh ann an t-am sin, Bean Uí Cheallaí, Cúig-Ulach as Dromore, agus an cúntóir a bhí aici, Bean Mhic Ghamhna. Bhí an bheirt acu pósta le póilíní, agus ní raibh focal Gaeilge ag ceachtar acu ná aon mheas acu uirthi, rud nár fhág aon mheas ag Mike orthu héin. D'fhan Mike ar scoil go raibh sé ins an rang ab airde, agus chaith sé bliain eile ar scoil Bhaile Chláir. Dúirt sé liom gurb é an fáth a ndeacha sé go scoil Bhaile Chláir, go raibh an Ghaeilge ghá múnadh inti. Gaeilgeoir dúchasach as na Forbacha, toabh thiar de Ghaillimh, Seoirse Mac Artúir, a bhí ina phríomh-oide inti ag an am sin.

Fear mórán ar an airde chéanna ab ea Patch, ach bhí sé níos téagaraí agus níos láidre. Dúirt sé liom uair amháin nach ndeacha sé ar scoil ariamh ach ceithre lá, ach bhí an fhíneáilteacht chéanna ag roint leis a bhí le Mike. Fear tuisceanach stuama a bhí ann, agus é deaslámhach. Bhí sé in ann claidhe maith cloch a dhéana, agus cuid de úirlisí an tsiúinéara a láimhseáil le mar bheadh gádh leis, agus go leor rudaí eile.

Bhí foghlaim mhaith ar Mhike nuair a bhí sé réidh le scoil Bhaile Chláir, agus shílfeá go mbeadh rún aige anois 'posta a chuir roimhe héin', sin nó dul thar sáile mar rinne cuid eile den mhuirín, ach má smuintigh sé ar a leithid, níor chuir sé i gcrích é. Níorbh fhurasta dhó mar bhí a chúnamh ag teastáil sa mbaile. Bhí an t-athair ag eirí sean anois, agus ní raibh sa mbaile ach é héin agus Patch le obair na feilme a dhéana. Ina theannta sin fuair siad méadú mór ar an bhfeilm nuair a roinneadh dúiche an Charn Mhóir, agus bhí cuid den tala nua a fuair siad dhá mhíle ón teach, rud a chuir stróbh mór orthu.

Dúirt Mike liom uair amháin nach Síodach ó cheart é héin chor ar bith, go mba Ó'Dúgáin an sloinne ba dual dó. Ar na Croisíní, áit atá dhá mhíle nó mar sin ó thua don Pháirc Gharbh, a rugadh a athair, agus Ó'Dúgáin a bhí air. Nuair a bhí sé ina pháiste chuaigh sé 'un cónaí le uncail dhó a bhí gan pósadh ar an bPáirc Gharbh - sean-Mhicheál Ó 'Síoda - agus ón am sin thug chuile dhuine Micil Ó 'Síoda air, agus lean an t-ainm sin ar uaidh sin amach agus ar a chlann ina dhiaidh.

Ní raibh teora ar bith leis an stór seanchais agus scéalta a bhí ag Mike, agus bhínn ag cuir tuairisc leis cé uaidh nó cé'n chaoi ar eirigh leis é ar fad a chruinniú. Dúirt sé go mbíodh go leor daoine bochta - 'bochtáin Dé,' mar thugtaí orthu - ar na bóithre an t-am sin, agus bhíodh siad ag fáil lóistín ins na tithe, cúpla oíche nó trí anseo, agus cúpla oíche nó trí ansiúd. Bhí cuid acu ag teacht mar sin, uair no dhó sa mbliain ar fea blianta, agus bhí meas agus ómós rómpu. Bhí leabaí le na

Irish

n-aghaidh sa teach acu héin, agus shocráití an leabaí sa gcúinne cois teallaigh dhaofa. Bhí scéalta fada agus gearr acu, agus 'chuile chineál seanchais, tairgín agus eile acu, agus ní bhíodh tuirse ar Mhike ag éisteacht leofa, agus ó bhí cuimne cinn ar leith aige, ní dhearna sé dearmad ar aon cheo a chuala sé uatha. Bhí fear acu a rugadh i gceanntar an Ghoirt, agus bhí go leor eolais aige ar Bhriseadh Eachroma. Bhí fear eile ag dul thart leath-chéad bliain ó shin, 'Brother Michael' a thugadh siad air, bráthair a briseadh as ord eicínt, agus is uaidh sin chuala sé go leor den tairgín a bhí aige. Dúirt sé liom freisin go riabh uncail lena mháthair ina chónaí i bhFuarchoill (Coldwood) in aice le Creachmhaoil - sílim gur Búrcach a thug sé air - agus go mbíodh sé ar cuairt aige go minic. Chuala sé go leor uaidh sin freisin, agus chuala mé ráite é, cuid mhaith den eolas a bhí aige gur ó Shean-Mhicheál Ó'Síoda, ar labhair mé thuas air a tháinic sé. Bhí sé fiosrach i gcónaí i gcúrsaí mar sin, agus rud ar bith a chloisfeadh sé ní bheadh sé sásta go dtuigfeadh sé thríd a's thríd é. Nuair a thugainn héin cuairt air taréis a bheith imí' tamall in Árainn nó i gConomara nó in áit eicínt eile, ní fhéadfainn blas a dhéana an oíche sin ach ag cur síos ar mo chuid imeachta agus ag freagairt ceisteanna ar gach a bhfaca mé agus na daoine a casadh orm, agus bhí Patch 'chuile phioc chomh fiosrach leis.

Bhí eolas mór aige ar luibheanna agus planndaí, agus bhí sé in ann ainm Ghaelige a chur ar os cionn leath-chéad acu dhom a bhailigh muid, agus muid ag siúl thrí na páirceanna. Cá bhfuil an fear eile le fáil a dhéanfadh é?

Le peann agus páipéar a bhínn ag scríobh ó Mhike i dtosach. Níor thaithnigh an t-Eidifón leis donn ná dath, ach bhain sé ceart maith don tape-recorder nuair a fuair mé ceann acu. Is ar éigin a bhí fear ariamh ab fhusa scríobh uaidh ná é. Labhaireadh sé go mall agus go soiléir, agus thiubhradh sé greadadh ama dhuit. Dhá mba scéal fada é nach bhféadfaí a inseacht i n-aon oíche amháin, an chéad oíche eile a rachthá aige, dhá mbeadh sé cúpla lá nó seachtain, nó fiú mí, thosódh sé ar an scéal aríst go díreach san áit ar stop sé chomh maith agus mara mbeadh ann ach sos chúig nóiméad. Bhíodh Patch ag éisteach, agus déarfainn go raibh an oiread eolais aige ar na scéalta agus a bhí ag an bhfear eile, mar dhá ndéanfadh, Mike dearmad beag ar bith, is beag ag baol go ligfí leis é! Scríobh mé píosa seanchais ó Phatch anois agus aríst, ach sin nuair nach mbeadh Mike sa mbaile. Oíche ar bith a mbeadh Mike ann, d'fhágadh sé an obair faoi.

Is minic a theighinn acu taréis mo dhinnéir, agus d'fhanainn go mbeadh sé deireannach. Thugadh siad mo chuid tae dhom, agus ansin nuair a thuitfeadh an oíche lasadh siad coinneall i gcoinnleoir práise, agus leagadh siad ar chathaoir le mo thaoibh í. Ní raibh acu an t-am sin ach lampa ola, agus bhí siad ag déana amach nach raibh an solas uaidh sách láidir dhom. Go gcúití Dia a gcineáltas leofa anois!

Amannta nuair a bhíodh scéal dhá inseacht a mbeadh eactraí íontacha draíochta ann nó eachtraí faoi fhathaigh agus mar sin, bhínn ag iarraidh a dhéana amach ar chreid siad iad. Tá mé cinnte gur chreid Patch 'chuile fhocal. D'aithneá sin ó rudaí adéarfadh sé. Cuimním uair amháin go raibh Mike ag inseacht scéil faoi dhá bhuachaill beag a sciob fathach leis i gcoill, agus dúirt Patch:

'Á, na créatúir! Nach dhaofa a d'eirigh an mí-ádh! A, a Chiaráin, dheamhan suim a bheadh aige sin iad a chuir síos sa bpota agus iad a bhruith le h-aghaidh n-a dhinnéir ach an oiread a's dhá mbar péire lachain a bheadh iontu!'

Níl mé chomh cinnte sin i dtaobh Mike, ach déarfainn mar' chreid sé ar fad iad gur chreid sé cuid mhaith acu. Scríobh mé leagan den scéal coitianta sin faoi bhás Chromaill uaidh, agus nuair a bhí sé scríofa dúirt mé leis nach mar sin a bhí tabhartha síos sa history.

'Ó, a Chiaráin,' a deir sé, 'níl an history ceart. Ní mar tá sé sa history a thárla sé chor a' bith!'

Ní thaithneodh leis go gcaithfeá aimhreas ar bith ar aon scéal dhá n-inseodh sé.

Bhí go leor eolais aige faoi Bhriseadh Eachroma. Bhí cuid dá shinnsir ag troid sa gcath sin, triúr dritheár. Maraíodh beirt acu, bhí sé ag rádh liom, agus thainic duine acu as. Ba dh-é an tríomha duine seo sinnsear Sean-Mhicheál Ó Síoda a thóig a athair isteach mar oighre. Is air a bhí an rímhéad Domhnach dhár thug mé soir go h-Eachroim é agus shiúil muid páirc an áir le chéile, agus chonaic muid sean-iarsmaí den chath atá bailí i dteach na scoile ann. Domhnach eile, achar gearr shal má fuair sé bás, thug mé suas ar an nGort é, agus nuair a bhí muid míle nó dhó taobh thuas go Cill Cholgain - ní raibh sé ann ariamh cheana - dúirt sé liom go mba cheart go mbeadh loch a raibh 'Loch na bhFranncach' air in áit eicínt ar thaoibh na láimhe deise dhúinn, mar gur ionsaíodh dream de na Franncaigh ann nuair a bhí siad ag déana ar Luimneach taréis Briseadh Eachroma. Ceart go leor, nuair a chuaigh muid scathamh eile, chonaic muid an loch. Dúirt sé liom gurbh ó'n seanfhear siúil ón nGort a mbíodh siad ag tabhairt lóistín dó fadó a chuala sé an scéal sin.

Cailleadh Mike ar an 29 Deire Foghmhair, 1966. Cailleadh Patch roint blianta roimhe sin ar an 10 Márta, 1962. Tá siad curtha i roilic Leacaigh, buil a sinnsir. Beannacht dhílis Dé agus na hEaglaise lena n-anam!

Ciarán Bairéad 1967

"An Rud atá le d'aghaidh, Ní feidir leat dul thairis"

Seo mar leanas scéal a d'inis Séamus Ó Mórain dhom as Cathair Ghabhain, ar imeachtaí an t-sean t-saoil agus an cruatan oibre a bhí ann fadó. Níl tuiscint ar bith ag an dream óg atá ag eirí aníos anois ar an saoil sin.

"B'as Mointeach mo mhathair, bhínn féin ag dul isteach ann i mo leath-ghasúr ag tabhairt cúnamh do m'uncail leis an obair.

San am sin, nuair a thagadh an bhaisteach i ndeire an tsamhridh, sceitheadh an abhainn ina thuillte, ba gheall leis an bhfarraige mhór siar go Loch Corribhe í. Leis an mbád a chaithí an féar agus an mhóin a bhailiú agus a thabhairt abhaile. Go h-iondiúl beirt a bhíodh sa mbád, an fear deire le cleithe leis an mbád a stuiriú agus an fear i dtús an bháid le sluasad, le í a choinneal amach as an tanaí. An lá seo, ar chuma ar bith, bhí muid ag bailiú an féar as na cocaí on mbád, séard a bhíodh muid ag deanamh, na an féar i mbarr uisce a bhailuí agus an bun a fhagháil ansin. Bhí an lucht féir lionta againn agus muid ag deanamh ár mbealach ar an mbaile, mise i dtosadh an bháid ag cartadh leis an sluasad. Bhí an abhainn mhór taobh amuigh dhuinn.

Bhí an oiread sin féar sa mbád nach raibh mé in ann an fear taobh thiar díom a fheiceaíl. Bhí seiseann ag fanacht le comhartha uaimse leis an gcleith a oibriú ar an domhain. Mise ba chionn t-siocair leis mar nár thug mé an fógra don fhear deire. Thanaig sineán gaoithe i ndeas, rug sé ar an bhféar agus chuir sé glan as an áit a bhíomar siar thar Gort Chluain Mór muid go dtí an áit a bhfuil an choill anois. Ní raibh muid in ann an bád a smachtú. I ndeire na dála, thainig muid ar chor san abhainn agus seídeadh isteach muid ar an tanaí arís ar an taobh thall.

Shíl mé go raibh mo phórt seinte. Mise i mbannaí dhuit ! Bhí mo cheacht foghlamtha agam. Bhíos níos airdeallaí ar mo ghnó as sin amach agus thugas mo shean-bheic don fhear i ndeire an bháíd i am tráth."

"An Rud atá le d'aghaidh, ni féidir leat dul thairis"

Micheál Ó Conaill

Scoil Éigse

Thart ar an mblian míle, naoí gcead agus trí scór (1960), a thánaig fear darbh ainm Liam Ó Donnachú go dtí an paróiste seo. Bhí sé ina oifigeach Gaeilge le Coiste Oideachais Ghairm Beatha Chondae na Gaillimhe. Thánaig sé go Carn Mór ar dtús agus thosaigh sé ag plé le dramaí gearra agus le roinnt ceoil a mhúnadh. Bhíodh na ranganna i dteach na scoile agus d'eirí leis sathach maith.

Bhí saol difriúil ann an uair sin le hais anois agus bhain cuid mhaith daoine spraoí agus taitneamh as na dramaí go háirid ar feadh roinnt blianta. Comh maith leis sin chuir sé roimhe craobh de'n Scoil Éigse agus seanachais a bhunú agus bhí rath ar sin freisin.

Thagadh daoine a bhí sean go maith agus fir a bhí níos óige isteach sna céad blianta. Fir mar Mhichéal Ó Síoda (seanachaí cailiúl), Micheál Ó Ciarrgain, Seán Ó Cleirí, Micheál Ó hEidhin, Eamonn Ó hAinlí agus cuid mhaith eile. Bá ag cumadh píosaí is mó a bhí i gceist - filíocht agus dánta agallamh beirte agus scéalta. Blianta beaga ina dhiadh sin, chuir sé craobh de'n rud céanna ar bun i mBaile Chláir. Thagadh daoine mar Sonny Ó Ceallaigh, Seán Conceannan, Seán

Ó Casarlaigh, Seámus Conceannan, "Rocky" Ó Moraín agus go leór eile isteach le freastal air. Thart ar chuile thrí seactainí ar an méan a bhíodh tíocht le chéile ann.

Thainig bainistíocht nua i réim ins na scoileanna tar éis na chead blianta, nach raibh sásta na cruinneachaí a bheith ionta agus i dtighe conaí a bhíodh siad ansin. Is iomaí teach a caiteadh geimhreadh nó dhó ann, ach tigh Leacaí agus Tom Mac Bhailtéar (Qualter) i n'Gort Chluain Mór a thagadh na baill le chéile ar feadh blianta fada sa deire.

Gach samhradh bhíodh Oll Chruinniú na Scoileanna Éigse ann, in áit éicint i gConamara agus thagadh thart ar bheirt ionadaí as gach Scoil Éigse eile le chéile chuig an gcruinniú agus bhíodh siad in iomaíocht le chéile agus thanaig cor dhuais go dtí an paróiste ó h-am go h-am. Bfiú go mór an rud ar fad. Bhí taobh maith soísialta leis, bhí spraoi agus spóirt ann, cuireadh aithne ar dhaoine agus cruithíodh cáirdeas. Chuaigh ceann Charn Mór i leíg do réir a cheíle agus scoireadh ar fad é sa deire ach lean ceann Bhaile Chláir ar aghaidh cé go raibh sé lagtha go mór nó gur eirigh Liam é fhéin as obair go luath ins na naochadaí. Ceád Slán leis an Scoil Éigse agus Beannacht Dé le h-anamacha na Mairbh.

Gaeilge agus gaelachas pharóiste Bhaile Chláir na Gaillimhe

Ba i an Ghaelige gnáth-theanga mhuintir Bhaile Chláir i dtús na fichiú aoise agus is feidir liom fein fiannaise a thabhairt go raibh an Ghaeilge á húsáid go forleathan suas do dtí na blíanta thart ar 1950. Bhí sé de nós ag an am sin ag fir an pharóiste tamall a chaitheamh ag comhrá agus ag inseacht nuachta dhá cheile taobh amuigh den seipéil tar éis aifreann an Dhomnaigh. Bhíodh na buachaillí óga, mar mé féin, ag seasamh in aice leis na fir, agus is cuimhin liom gurbh í an Ghaeilge a bhí dhá labhairt ag cuid mhaith doibh cé go raibh Béarla dhá labhairt ag cuid eile. Is e mó bhariúl go raibh tuiscint mhaith ar Ghaelige ag 90% do mhuintir na pharóiste agus go raibh liofíocht sa Ghaelige ag 50% ar a laghad.

Bhí aithne go pearsanta agam ar gaeilgeoiri líofa ó Eocaill, Mullacurtra, Leacht Seoirse, Bothar Bhaile Chláir, Cluain Biggin, Móinteach, Ceathar Gabhann, Clochar, Cluain agus ar an taobh eile den bothar mhór: Creag Bhuí (Baile Fánach), Radharc Locha (Turlach Bréige), Gort an tSléibhe, Baile Ui Mhurchú, Bhaile na Creige, Cinn Uisce agus Chill Tróg. Chomh maith le sin bhí an Ghaeilge a labhairt go forleathan in san gceantar thart timpeall ar Scoil Cairn Mór.

San am sin freisin bhí an Ghaeilge go coitianta in sna tighe Ósta, go h-airthe i dtigh Ósta Ó Leanachan agus is gaeilgeoir líofa a bhí sa bhean tí, Bina agus a dearthaír Tómas.

I rith na mblianta sin bhí Tomás Ó Conchubair ina mháistir scoile i mBaile Chláir, fear a raibh sar-mheas ar an teanga aige agus rinne se obair dhían ar son

irish

na teangan.

Tar éis na g-caogadaí bhí athrú mór ag teacht ar an saol agus bhí damáiste mór déanta ag an imirce ó thaobh teanga agus chultúir de, agus nuair a fuair glúin tús na h-aoise seo bás, faraoír, fuair an teanga nadúrtha bás leo.

Padraic Ó Conceanainn, Eanair 1999

Tobar an Chúilín	The well on the back road
An bhearna bhui	The yellow gap
Boirin na bláthai	Buttermilk lane
An tsúilin	The gulley
An droichid beag	The small bridge
An ché	Quays (where boats are held)
An scairbh	Where the river turns
An scraith	Strip of land
Caladh bád	Boat slipway
Mullach na nGort	The highest point in the fields
Poll an challa mhór	The deepest point in the river
An sraith buí	Strip of land with yellow clay

(Paidir)

Art an Chreide Cré

Art an creide cré a bhionn againn ar uair ar mbáis
Tháinig an t-aingeal anuas le sonas i gluais na mná
Trí ráithe a bhi mac Dé faoi na broinn nuair a thurling sé air an saol
Nach maith an sagairt e mac Dé agus
nach maith an baiste a rinne sé
nuair a bhaist sé Eoin agus bhaist Eoin é.
Nuair ba mhian leis an gcon seo bheith ré,
mac Rí Neamh ag dul sa gcrann in
aghaidh gach ball da bhfuil sa gcré.
Níl aon duine a dheireann Art an Chreide
Cré uair gach lá nach bhfeicfidh
sé Mhuire Mháthair tri uair roimh a bhás.

Sorcha Ní Choinceannain
Sean Ra (old sayings)

Móinteach

Baile beag socair in ascal abhainn an Chláir is ea Mointeach. Ta sé suite míle éireannach díreach siar ó Bhaile Chláir. Áit stairiúl é ina bealach féin a bhfuil cáil

Irish

fé leith sa dúiche mar gheall ar an iascaireacht mhaith atá le fáil gar don bhaile.

San meán aois bhí mainistir agus manaí ar an mbaile agus tá an áit ar a raibh an mhainistir tógtha le feiceál fós. Tugtar an lisín ar an áit agus bhí muintir an bhaile dá úsáid mar chillín nó roillig do pháistí beaga a fuair bás anuas go dtí 1932.

I dtús an octhú aois déag bhi scoil ar an mbaile (cineál hedge school is dócha) agus d'fhoghlaim cuid mhaith de mhuintir an bhaile léitheoireacht agus scríobhneoireacht. Príomh ghné don scoil sin nach raibh cead ag na páistí Gaeilge a labhairt agus uair ar bith a chuala sé páistí ag labairt Gaeilge sa scoil chuir se píonós orthú. B'fhéidir gurb é sin an fá gurbh é Mointeach an áit deire i bparóiste Bhaile Chláir in a raibh Gaeilge mar gnáth theanga.

I dtus an chéid seo bhí dhá scór teaghlach ar an mbaile. San mblian 1908 tré scéim Coimisúin na Talun fuair roint teaglaigh feirmeacha i gCill Tróig agus ar an gCroisín. Ba iad sinn muintir ó Dúbhagáin, Ó Móráin, Ó Murchú agus O Nuadhain. Chomh maith le sinn chuir imirce isteach go mór ar an mbaile agus thart ar an mblian 1950 ní raibh ach 17 teaglach fágtha agus daoine sean a bhi i gcuid maith dóibh sinn.

Ba cheart a rá go raibh an gaelachas agus an náisiúntas go láidir i gcónaí agus nuair a tháinig tacaí Liam Mellows ar an mbaile i 1916 chuaigh seisear amach leo cun seasamh ar son óglaigh na Cásca. Ba iad sin Séan Ó Conceanainn, Domhnaill Ó Dubhagáin, Annraoi Ó Dubhagáin (Liam), Tadg Ó'Dubhagáin, Tadg Ó Corcaid agus Annraoi Ó Dubhagáin (Seán). Buíochas le Dia tháinig siad ar fad abhaile slán. Mar gheall ar sin is dócha tháinig na Dubh Chrónai (Black & Tans) chuig an mbaile trí huaire ach bhí an "Bush Telegraph" ag obair go maith agus dá bhrí sin bhí fir óga an bhaile imigh "Fé thalamh".

Le gairid anuas sa mblian 1960 d'fhág cúig teaghlach eile an baile faoi scéim eile Coimisúin na Talún agus bhain sin an croí agus an gaelachus amach as an mbaile. Mar sin féin le blianta anuas tháinig ceithre teaghlach nua isteach agus tá fáilte rómpa agus tá súil againn go bhfuil siad ag baint taithneamh as.

Le focal scoir ba bhaith liom 'Baile o Dhia oraibh' a rá le muintir

Mhóinteach ar fad agus go háirithe iad sin atá i Meiriceá (Na Dúbhagáin agus na Corcaid), atá i Sasana (Na Conceanainn agus na Dúbhagáin) agus sa tSéalainn Nua (Na Gralaigh).

Slán agus Beanacht.

Padraic Ó'Conceanainn Marta '92

Craobh an Achréidh de Chonradh na Gaeilge

Bunaíodh Craobh an Achréidh deich mbliana ó shoin sa cheantar leis an gcuspóir an Ghaeilge agus an cultúr a chur chun cinn. Ciallaíonn 'an Achréidh' talamh cothrom. Is sin le rá an réigiún soir ó Chathair na Gaillimhe. Tá Baile Chláir na Gaillimhe i gceartlár an cheantair seo.

Tá go leor imeachtaí ó shoin i leith a raibh baint mhór ag an gcraobh lena bhforbairt agus a gcur chun cinn. Tá dhá naíonra bunaithe sa cheantar ar thug an Chraobh cuidiú dóibh tosnú agus dul chun cinn a déanamh. Tá moladh ag dul do na stiúrthóirí atá i gceannas faoi láthair agus atá ag déanamh dul chun cinn chomh mór le forbairt na ngasúr sa chultúr agus sa teanga.

Bíonn ranganna Gaeilge agus damhsa bliantiúl ar siúl sa cheantar ó cuireadh an Chraobh ar bun. Tá an Chraobh freagrach as an dá Champa Samhraidh atá ar siúl sa cheantar le deich mbliana anuas. Freastalaíonn leanaí ó 8 mbliana go dtí 14 bliana ar na campaí samhraidh seo. Tugann na himeachtaí seo cabhair an-mhór do na leanaí smacht a chur ar labhairt agus úsáid na Gaeilge. Mar sin tá moladh mór ag dul do na múinteoirí agus na daoine go léir a mbíonn baint acu le reáchtáil na gCampaí Samhraidh.

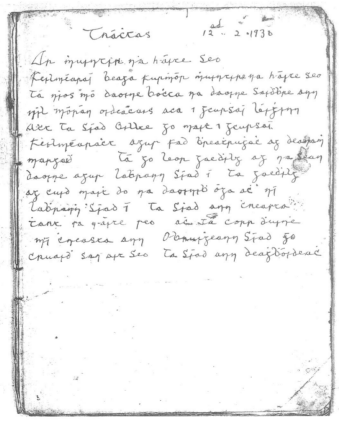

Sample of the old style of Irish handwriting by Tim Feeney from Mullacuttra

Irish

Ó am go chéile thug grúpaí drámaíochta agus scoraíochta cuairt ar an cheantar le taispeántas a thabhairt. D'éirigh thar barr leis an himeachtaí seo. Thug muintir an Achréidh cuairt arais ar na ceantair éagsúla a ba'as na grúpaí sin. Le cúnamh ón gCraobh tá cúrsaí Gaeilge ag dul ar aghaidh sa Ghaeltacht do dhaoine atá ag iarraidh feabhas a chur ar a gcuid Gaeilge. Tugann an Chraobh cúnamh le hAifreann Gaeilge a chraoladh ar Raidió na Gaeltachta ó ionad S.M.A. Baile Chláir na Gaillimhe. Le linn bunú Gaelscoil de hÍde in Órán Mór thug an Chraobh cabhair airgid agus chomh maith leis sin thug baill den Chraobh cúnamh le gach bailiúchán leis an scoil nua lánGhaelach a chur ar a cosa. Thug baill na Craoibhe a gcuid ama saorinaisce agus doibridear go deónach chun an obair fhorbartha a dhéanamh ar an fhoirgneamh ina bhfuil an scoil nua lonnaithe.

Bá mhaith leis an gcraobh ar an ocáid speisialta seo ár mbúiochas a glacadh leis na daoine ar fad a thug a gcuid ama agus saothair in aisce ó bhunaíodh an chraobh.

Ba mhaith le coiste Craobh an Achréidh fáilte a chur roimbh bhaill nua le cabhrú forbairt agus dul chun cinn a dhéanamh ar labhairt ár dteanga.

Mícéal Ó hEidhin	Úachtarán
Áine Nic Ghloinn	Cathaoirleach
Paraic Ó Conghaile	Leas Cathaoirleach
Colette Ní Chonghaile	Rúnaí
Máiréad Geraghty	Leas Rúnaí
Seosamháin Ní Núadhain	Cisteoir
Bríd Ní Chonghaile	Leas Cisteoir
Paraic Ó Núadhain	Oifigeach Caidreamh Poiblí

Chapter 11: Local Folklore and Superstitions

Now it still goes on, you can still catch them telling stories. They love to talk. They draw their tales from the figures that flame up and fade in the big open fire under the black crane. They bring you back under thatch, sitting on the edge of a hard hob with the wind whistling into you from the chimney corners. These tales really happened to them or were told to them by someone who knew who it happened to. So this chapter begins with a collection of open-fire tales told in the very words of the people from whom they were taken and put down on paper.

Bean Sí heard but not seen

Many people tell or have heard stories about the Bean Sí. John Casserley, Cahergowan, remembers her. She frequently featured in stories told to him in childhood. Also Michéal Ó'Heidhin, Carnmore, tells us:

"There was a lot of people very much afraid of her. I heard that she combed her hair. She had long black hair and wore a white gown. It was said that there were certain families she would appear to."

The O'Brien's were one such family. Nora O'Brien (nee Egan, Casla) shares with us her experience of the Bean Sí:

"I did not see the Bean Sí. I heard her. I heard my grandmother saying long ago that she would be washing clothes, and that she used to spread the clothes out on a sloe bush, and that she had a lace cap on."

Next Nora describes a close encounter she had with the Bean Sí:

"This night (there was an outing to Connemara) for the altar servers and the choir. And they were to be home at nine o'clock Sunday evening. And I had hay and a box of matches so we would have a fire for the bus. It was a summer's evening and I was out there. It went on to the stroke of twelve, and when I say twelve I really mean one o'clock. I heard this terrible cry. I heard the cry coming up on top, along the wall, up towards me. And when Daniel (a neighbour) heard the crying he ran into his mother. And asked was she trying to frighten Nora about in the road crying like the Bean Sí. So the crying was coming up, up all along till it was within ten yards of me. And a car pulled up. And I went into the house. And I called 'Daddy', my husband, and he came. 'Do you hear that crying?' he said. 'I do', I said, 'What is it?' 'Ah! I do not know', he said, 'it must be someone, a child.' But no, it was the Bean Sí. When the car pulled off and

- 134 -

wasn't the Bean Sí gone. But the bus did not come until four o'clock in the morning. I heard the Bean Sí in Barnaby. It was over forty years ago anyway."*

Nora also tells us about another incident about the Bean Sí when her children were out playing:

"They went back to the cross-roads hurling. And I said, 'Be back before it is dark'. After an hour or so didn't I hear this crying. And I said that one of the lads must have had it, one of their friends or the other way around. When they came back I said, 'Which one of you was crying?' As that was where the crying was coming from, where they were playing. That very night Daniel (a neighbour) was coming from a funeral. And just a short piece from our house, he was struck down by a lorry. It was one-thirty. I was lying in bed and Tom (Daniel's son) came to the window. 'My father was hit by a car', he said. My husband did not move with the shock. So I got up and I prepared the body. A Loughgeorge Garda came. I heard the Bean Sí crying the night before. I heard it as plain as noon day. I remember there was a man near us. His name was O'Brien. He was a mixer. He said, 'The Cáilín was at it last night'. This was the Bean Sí, I said: 'Did you hear her often?' 'I did, (he said) she cries after certain people'".

Should you wish to meet the Bean Sí, Michael Walsh, Gortatleva, gives us direction on where to find her:

"The people of this parish used to go to a village called Crusheen over there. There was a well there. It was there they saw the Bean Sí. Michael gives a short account of what he heard: What they say: the banshee was a woman that wasn't churched. That she was after giving birth to a child She was young because she had a child. And he recalls that: There she was anyway washing herself in this well. This fella said something to her. And she followed him. And she nearly got him at the door. I heard talk of that now, that she nearly grabbed him by the head."

Telling Ghost Stories

As well as stories about the Bean Sí, stories are told about other strange encounters. Frequently encountered in the Cregboy area, up the hill from the Community Centre, was a large horse drawn coach. Michael Walsh, Gortatleva, heard of this ghostly *Cóiste Bodhair* in Cregboy: *"It was a kind of hearse drawn by horses and bells."* The name Cóiste Bodhair suggests either a deafening sound or silence accompanying this coach. There is no doubt in Michael's mind that it exists:

"The only thing I will ever know and never forget till the day I die is the story I'm going to tell you now. My father was going to the fair one morning. He said: 'come with me'. I would say now that it would be anything up 'till six o'clock. It was down there before you. Come down the hill to the Centre. The damnedest

Local Folklore and Superstitions

thing came down the road. I heard the bells and the horses coming. And I could see nothing. I'm not saying that it was that now or not."

And if you have any remaining doubt, Tom Flaherty, Cahergowan tells a collaborating story:

"Well, there was an evening I was cycling up by Ballymurphy, this car supposed to have been seen at the back of this house. I was coming along one night at four o'clock in the morning. There are two bends there. And I thought I would have that bend taken before he came down, whoever he was. When I came to the second bend, it went out of sight altogether; until I came below Gortatleva where I thought the car was. I got afraid all right. At the corner there are two gates. And in it on that side of the road at one or the other. And that is where the fairies used to call. Geata na gCeann, they used to call it. That is halfway between Gillespie's house and Gortatleva."

Stories are told of dead people seen walking the roads at night *"Now, I'm only saying what I heard"* is how Michael Walsh, Gortatleva, begins telling us about such a happening to a man from Loughgeorge. This man went to the wedding of a man from Lackagh and a girl from Kiniska.

"And he said that while he was coming home that morning from the wedding he saw that woman (the girl from Kiniska) at the head of the road. And he could swear that it was she that was in it. And didn't she die about three days after the wedding. And there was nothing wrong with her."

Michael goes on to tell us of a similar happening to another man in the Carnmore area. *"The devil was shook on him long ago. Johnny used to get up for Mass in Claregalway. And his wife was not long dead when this happened to him. The night before, he put the clock out. And he woke up. And he got ready for Mass thinking that it was Mass time. In fact, it was three o'clock in the morning. When he was setting off for Mass, he heard the talk coming back the road. And he seen two women who were long dead at that time. He knew that it was his wife, and the other woman was (also dead). They were like if they were alive, chatting away to themselves. But he couldn't know what they were saying to themselves. He knew his wife and her voice. And he never went to First Mass after that."*

Similar stories are told of the ghosts of dead people being seen in the locality, until such a time as masses were said for their souls. Whether or not such sightings are linked to the fairies is not clear. The fairies are however linked to other strange happenings.

Being had by the Fairies

Some happenings are strange. They are difficult to explain. We are told of strange happenings that cannot be explained. Maybe we can put such happenings down to the fairies. In these days of the 'X-Files' on television, it is less easy to imagine that a story is true. In the open-fire days, many people truly imagined that what they heard about the fairies was true. These are some of the stories about the fairies that everyone told in the open-fire days.

Mícheál Ó'Heidhin, Carnmore, tells of an encounter with the fairies at the turn of the last century:

"Well, it was a moonlight night and the two men were coming home. They were very fond of the dancing. They stood in the middle of the road and one man began to dance. And it happened to be opposite a fairy fort. He was only dancing a short while when music started to play inside. And, he continued dancing and dancing. And after a while, Seán, who heard the music as well, was afraid he was doing too much. So he caught him and the man was nearly dead. He was jaded out, so he had to be helped to walk. When he recovered a bit, he said: 'you saved my life. Only for you stopped me, the fairies would have had me'".

Tom Flaherty, Cahergowan retells a story he heard about a man from Clogher who met the fairies:

"There was a man from Clogher and he was card playing in Montiagh and used to bring his own cards with him. One time he was coming back across Páirc na Reithe and a table was left down in front of him. He was mad for card playing, it was about two o'clock in the morning and he was coming and the table was left out in the middle of the field for him to play. Yeah, that is what he said anyway. I do not know. A man from Clogher. He was totally convinced it was fairies. That is what he said anyway. A lot of it could be lies."

While you might not meet the fairies, you could stray into enchanted places. Stories are told of places that would cause you to lose your sense of direction or become confused. Sarah Moran, Lakeview explains what she refers to as the Fóidín Mearbhaill:

"It was in some field. Something would come on you and you couldn't find your way out. Down near Sadie's, (Noone's, Cahergowan) there's a big field next to her. And they say if you went in there at night now that it would surely come on you. Late at night and you just couldn't get out of it. I know this woman that was going around and around for an hour before she got out."

Should you stray into such a place, John Casserley, Cahergowan, explains how to get out:

"We'll say at night when you're going across a field. It could even happen to you on the road. You could stay going all night. To get out of this situation, the true cure to get out is turn your coat inside out"

Sadie Noone, Cahergowan, tells us about how her father came under a similar spell and the cure for what she calls the *Píobaire Marbh*:

"It never happened to me. But I remember my father telling me at the time about

him going to the shop. And on his way back if he died he couldn't make out the stile. He went around and around the field. And when he was just about to give up all hope, he remembered the older folk telling stories about the Píobaire Marbh. And the cure for it was turn your coat inside out and that's what he did and wasn't he home in no time after that."

People seem to frequently come under such spells. Micheál Ó'Heidhin, Carnmore, gives us several accounts of this happening, the *Fóidin Mearbhaill*:

"I heard that people used to take short cuts. They could come under the spell at day or night. It can happen day or night. At that time, they would cross fields a lot. People got confused and even places they knew all the time would look different when this would come upon them. Everything was opposite. It happened to a friend of mine. He was near the railway in Oranmore. He went to go home, he lost his direction, but he was lucky because he was not on his own. He had friends who brought him home."

Micheál Ó'Heidhin, Carnmore, tells of a second such happening:

"I remember my father saying that it happened him in town in Galway one day. When he was a young man, he could not know one street or direction from the other. He met a shopkeeper that he dealt with and he told him what was on him. So, the shopkeeper put the horse under the cart, sat my father up in the cart and told my father that the horse knew its way home. And only when he was a few miles from home, the spell left him. There is no explanation for that."

In case you doubt such spells, Michael heard of a third similar happening:

"I heard of another man, when we were children, that it happened to him at night time. Outside our place was an awkward place with shrubs and a sink of water and hen house and so on. Didn't my mother open the back door. And she heard this man talking, complaining and wailing. There was someone outside. My father went out of course. There was no electricity at that time. He called out asking who was there. The man outside turned out to be a good friend of my fathers. He told my father that he went astray but he could not make out our house, nothing. He did not know the road when my father went with him to bring him home. They were as far as Ballymurphy when the man said he knew where he was. It comes back all of a sudden. To cure it, I heard that you turn your coat inside out."

James Hession, Cahergowan, remembers a similar enchantment:

"A man went down to his farm in Lakeview and into the field to feed the cattle. Then when he was ready to make his way home, he could not find the big stile. He had to wait till morning as he didn't know how to break the spell."

Indeed, James experienced it first hand:

"Sure it happened to my sister and I. We went visiting friends and going home we

decided to take a short cut. Well we were in this field and we could not get out. I noticed after a while that how I got out was due to the wind being at my side and back. If I kept the wind at my back I would have been there to this day."

Another place where this happened is about four hundred metres north of Tommy Murphy's house, Ballymurphy, as he tells us:

"There was an old turlough there one time; it is all drained now. There would be cows from every house. It was not divided that time. But it divided now. Be God, it is often people went astray in it. If you turned your cap or coat inside out was the only way you would come back.

Some places had other strange effects. Mícheál Ó'Heidhin, Carnmore, explains the Féar Gortach:

"That comes on you even if you have had a big meal and all. They make out that happened when you stood on this piece of sod and you would get the effect. To cure it, you would have to take some food. Well, people maintained that where the sod lay, people died there during the famine from starvation."

Adding his own experience of this, John Casserley, Cahergowan describes the Féar Gortach as:

"when you get hungry after you step out onto this piece of grass. It's a very true fact. It has happened to myself many's of a time".

There were also strange sightings. A red light was often seen moving slowly over the bog. Sometimes it was accompanied by a voice. Though called Jack the Lantern, generally Claregalway people did not imagine it to be a person. Sarah Moran, Lakeview, offers her explanation of Jack the Lantern:

"Well, he was a bird that used to be in the bog at Summertime and he had a shiny tail and we used to think it was a person but we found out it wasn't that - it was a bird".

John Casserley, Cahergowan heard a different explanation:

"What I was told of Jack the Lantern is that at night you could see a kind of a red light crossing over the bog and one could hear him saying Mah, Mah and Mah."

While explanations might differ, there are many stories of strange happenings. So it is no surprise that some elaborate schemes and practices were devised to avoid such frightful happenings.

Pisreoga or Superstitious Practises

To avoid mishap or cure mishaps in life, there are many pisreoga offered in advice. As you would expect, there is plenty of advice given on the weather. If a cock crew then it was a sign that the rain was clearing. A lot more signs were given for rain coming:

Soot falling down the chimney.
Hens picking their feathers.
Birds flying low.
Clouds looking low.
Cormorants coming in from the sea shore.
Black snails creeping on the grass.

Seeing a red sky in the morning is a shepherd's warning of rain or poor weather. Seeing a red-haired woman first thing in the morning is a warning of mishap or bad luck. There is a story told about an ex-policeman living in Claregalway who met three girls one morning, one of whom had red-hair. Instead of going home, he went about his business for the day. On his return home that evening, the heavy rain had wet the floor and he slipped putting out his shoulder. Most people who met a red-haired woman on the way to a fair would immediately turn believing that they would have no luck.

Death, wakes and burial involved a lot of ritual practises and pisreoga. Mícheál Ó'Heidhin, Carnmore, gives a detailed account:

"In the past, coffins were carried a lot on men's shoulders unless the journey would be very long, as there were few hearses then. I understand that there would be six men carrying the coffin. All the dead person's relatives and sometimes near neighbours would want to carry it in turn. The rule was that two fresh men would go under it in front and the others would fall back a step and the two at the back would fall out. That would happen frequently all the way to the graveyard. Where the pisreog came in was that those that went under the coffin once, felt they had to go under it three times in order to avoid bad luck, sickness or maybe death. And if their left shoulder was under it first it had to be the right shoulder next time. All this meant that often when nearing the cemetery that they would have to stop and change every few yards in order to give everyone his three turns.

I heard that you had to open the windows to let the soul out and up until recently, they turned off the clock the moment the person died in a house and it would not be put on again until the person was buried. I heard that it was bad luck to put ashes out on a Monday, but I do not know why and up until recently, they never dug a grave on a Monday and no one would get a haircut on a Monday. They said: 'Lomadh luain ort'" if they wanted to wish you ill.

Wakes allowed for a mix of emotions. From the crying induced by the keening women to the fun and games. Luke, Seán and Pádraic Concannon, Montiagh recall a story about a wake:

"A man died. And they had to tie him down with a rope to the bed, because he died in a sitting up way. Anyway at the wake everybody was there. Some were

crying and more were laughing. And whatever way the coffin was moved, the rope around the corpse came free. And the corpse sat up in the coffin. He was so stiff that when the rope was loosened the body rose up so fast that the people at the wake nearly lost their lives."

While we are told this happened in Claregalway, similar tales are told in other parts of Ireland. Generally the coffin was taken for burial on a horse cart. Three keening women would sit up on the coffin, two married and one single, facing in different directions. Micheál Ó'Heidhin, Carnmore, describes the funeral practise:

"There was another story; the horse that would be bringing the coffin to the graveyard. They did not go to the chapel that time. Instead of the night in the chapel, there was a wake in the house. The horse would be taken out three times from under the cart and brought around the cart. They would put the horse under the shafts of the cart twice from the left and once from the right or vice versa. I remember when they would be burying a child, they would not dig the grave until the coffin arrived at the graveyard."

Also the coffin had to be brought in feet foremost. There were also signs for ill health and death. If a hen crowed in or near a house, then sickness would fall on someone in that house. If a bird strayed into a house, then death would fall on someone in that house. Also if you were unfortunate enough to be deservedly cursed by a widow, then you knew that the curse would come true.

There were *pisreoga* for other occasions too. Micheál Ó'Heidhin, Carnmore, tells us a pisreog about cows after calving:

"The cow would not be let out after calving without performing a certain ritual. There would be a red rag put on her tail and inside that red rag would be a few stumps of horse shoe nails and some hens dirt and Holy Water. This would be tied on to her tail, so she would be lucky".

Another *pisreog* applies to milking a cow. You were not to milk a cow on the first of May. Also if you entered a house where somebody was making butter, you had to put your hand on the churn or dasher for luck.

To restore health, home remedies and old cures were used. Micheál Ó'Heidhin, Carnmore, explains how people were cured using charms when he was young:

"Well, they were too poor. The doctors would be too dear. They did not really believe in doctors. I remember them using charms. A person had a large boil. I remember them bringing in an old woman and she had a number of irons, old irons, some of them would be horse shoes and all those kind of things and she would say some prayers in Irish, making crosses with the irons and signs and so on. It was only once I ever saw that and I was quite small. The people of the house knelt on their knees and prayed."

Also there were people who had a cure or special gifts of healing. Mícheál Ó'Heidhin, Carnmore, tells us:

"They cured boils and ringworm. Another used to cure Craos Galar, *which is Thrush. He used blow into the mouth. It used to work. There used to be herb cures. There used to be a herb called splineworth for Kidney trouble. It used to be boiled in water and drunk."*

For minor illnesses or flu, a person would take a hot drink and stay in bed to fight it off. Such hot drinks would be made up of pepper, onions, buttermilk, sugar, vinegar, and honey. Some cures were quite strange. If you had a sore throat, you had to put a stocking worn by you that day around your throat.

Life, matchmaking and marriage also involved a lot of ritual practises and *pisreoga*. Matchmaking was a popular practise in open-fire days. There was more than one Matchmaker in the Claregalway area. The Matchmaker acted as a negotiator on behalf of the man who was seeking a wife. Stories are most often told about a middle-aged man who is seeking a younger woman to provide him with an heir.

One ingredient in the negotiation was a "dowry". The dowry was a settlement of money, stock, possessions or land to be given by the woman's family to the prospective husband. It was generally expected that the dowry would be substantial enough to convince the man that this woman should be his wife. The Matchmaker met with both the prospective husband and his potential parents-in-law. More often than not the woman was told nothing about the arrangement. When the deal had been done, the girl was told. The woman was expected to marry the man chosen by her parents.

Generally, another ingredient in matchmaking was whiskey. Whiskey was often used by the interested man to get on "the good side" of the woman's father. There is a story told by a man about how his sister was matched and how whiskey was involved. To him the matching of his sister, who was only eighteen years, seemed like the buying of a cow. The parents met the suitor over potatoes, ham and of course the drink and bargained away. The young man received one hundred pounds as the dowry, which was a fortune in those times.

Another story is told about a match that fell through, because the girl had no money. The husband-to-be wanted the money to help in the settling down. Later on the girl overheard this man tell someone else why he wouldn't marry her. He said, it was because, "she had spent the last ten years feeding pigs and she hadn't a copper". A lot more matches survived into marriage. The marriage day itself brought with it other superstitious practises or *pisreoga*.

Marriages generally took place in the evenings, unlike today. When the bride-to-be was going to the church, an odd number of girls accompanied her. If necessary one girl would be sent home. Candles were lit in neighbouring houses, though

Local Folklore and Superstitions

not in her parents' house.

When the couple left the church after the ceremony, people used to push the girl out first as superstition said that 'first out the door would die first'. The new bride also was not allowed back to her parents' house for a whole month after the wedding. The couple went to live with the husband's family, often passing bonfires on the way. A similar tradition of lighting bonfires at times of celebration has survived in the Claregalway area up to today. When the couple arrived in the house, an oatmeal cake was broken over their heads to bring good luck.

These are some of the 'pisreoga' and open-fire tales of Claregalway people. They flame up in this chapter, and fade again. They are the conversations in memory of storytellers. They rekindle the hearth of story telling in Claregalway at its enchanting best.

Chapter 12: Well Known People

Thomas Kerrigan (An Preabaire)

Thomas Kerrigan was a local poet who was born in Caherlea, Claregalway. A good many of his poems were known to the generation that has now almost passed away and fragments of them may still be found. He had not the music of Raftery or his easy fluency but his poems are valuable for the insight they gave of the local conditions in his time. His best known poem is *'Mainistir Bhaile Chláir'* – Claregalway Friary.

An Preabaire was a stone mason by trade and was said to have worked as such at the building of the previous parish church. He was said to have been a tall man, much taller than the average and a good hurler and athlete. A long distance jump, which he made, is said not to have been equalled or exceeded since. The spot at which it was made, in the fields called an *Turloch Iseal* to the east of the road from Carnmore crossroads to the Oranmore railway station, is still pointed out.

An Preabaire died in the village of Caherlea. He carved stone bedposts for himself which still survive. He was also engaged in carving a stone to be placed on his grave, but died before completing it. It is still pointed out in Caherlea.

The story of how he came to be called Preabaire, which means a lively active person, is interesting. There was a family of the ubiquitous Blakes in Summerfield near Cahergowan village who were of the gentry class. On this occasion there was some celebration there and the Preabaire was amongst those present. He asked one of the Blake ladies to dance with him and she did so. It was a daring thing for a man in his station to do but the lady was highly pleased with his audacity and no doubt skill as a dancer and in thanking him she said *'Baistim se Preabaire fir ort'* and the name remained with him while he lived.

He is also remembered for his humour and jokes as when one day himself and John Fox from Caherlea were in Galway and some of the British soldiers were playing soccer in Eyre Square. They had never seen soccer before and when the ball came out over the wall they got it and thus brought the first soccer ball to Claregalway. It is said that the football was being kicked around in Fox's turlough until the great famine.

Thomas Kerrigan died between 1920 and 1930. After his death ten ballads were attributed to him, best known of which is "The Abbey of Claregalway" which was published in 1919 by Mrs Eileen Costello, Tuam.

Well Known People

Alderman Tarpey

Alderman Tarpey was one of the most famous men in Dublin in the early 1900's. He was Lord Mayor of Dublin and owned the Tarpey Hotel in Nassau Street, a fashionable resort for years. The Alderman was born in Loughgeorge, Claregalway and was educated at a Galway School. He left school *'with nothing but his brain and his own honest hands'*. He also wrote plays and newspaper articles.

Michael Davitt

Founder of the Land League, Michael Davitt, visited Claregalway and made a speech in the graveyard and was helpful to many local small farmers.

Ciaran Bairead

Ciaran Bairead was born on the 17th February 1905 in 4 Blessington Street, Dublin. His father Stephen Barrett was from Frenchpark in Roscommon and was involved in the formation of the Gaelic League with Eoghan McNeill and Douglas Hyde and became its first treasurer. When he died his paper was donated to UCG. His mother was Murphy from Ballymurphy, Claregalway, where he spent most of his youth. He lived with his mother, who supported him, until she died in the late 40's or early 50's. Then he spent a short time with his relatives, the Morans in Lackaghbeg. He stayed 21 years, 1 month, 1 week, and 1 day lodging with the Kearneys in Turloughmore.

He qualified with a B.A. degree in University College Galway and taught for a short time in a National School in Tullamore, Co Offaly. Ciaran Bairead went working for the Irish Folklore commission in 1952. He travelled around the west but mainly in Co. Galway by bike and used an early type of tape-recorder called an ediphone to collect folklore. He also collected items for the National Museum. He later had an Anglia car and brought local children on trips around Ireland and taught some of them to swim. He was very involved in Macra Na Feirme.

He was a very religious man and disapproved strongly of foul language especially before children. He always wore a long dark coat even on a very sunny day and many thought he was planning to enter the priesthood or a religious order. Ciaran Bairead died on 16th August 1976 in Merlin Park from a tumour on the brain and following his wishes was buried in Claregalway Cemetery.

Mairtin O'Cadhain

Mairtin O'Cadhain was born on 1906 in An Cnocan Glas, a few hundred yards west of Spiddal. He trained as a teacher in Dublin during 1924-26. Both his mother Brid Og Ni Chonsola and his father Sean O'Cadhain were traditional

- 145 -

Well Known People

Mairtin O'Cadhain, a well-known Irish writer who taught in Carnmore School

storytellers, as well as many of his relatives. A brilliant linguist, he was fluent in Russian, Spanish as well as Irish, English, German and French. Nowadays Mairtin O'Cadhain is remembered mainly for his writing.

His first published work *"Idir Shugradh agus Dairire"* appeared in 1939; this was followed by An Braon Broghach (1948) and Cois Caolaoire (1967), these books were short stories. He also wrote some novels such as Cre na Cille (1949), Aithnuachan and other books. He won the Butler Award of the Irish American Cultural Institute. Before his death he had another book published: Paipear Bhana Paipear Bhreaca (1970). He claimed that he had three times as much written as what was published.

Mairtin O'Cadhain taught in Carnmore School in the 30's. This was a 2-teacher school at the time and he taught children from 3rd to 8th classes. He was dismissed from his teaching post in 1937 by Canon Moran because of his IRA activities and he moved to Dublin. He was jailed for 5 years for his involvement with the IRA and he taught Irish to his co-prisoners. He started writing there and studied other languages. He later worked in Dail Eireann as a translator and was appointed Professor of Irish in Trinity College, Dublin in 1967. He died in 1970.

Micheál Ó'Síoda

Michael Ó Síoda (Mike Silke) died at his home in Carnmore when he was almost 80 years of age. An unmarried farmer, he was an outstanding

Micheál Ó'Síoda (Silke), a well known seanachai from Carnmore

seanachai with an enormous store of folklore, tales, local seanachais, old customs and old farming methods. He had the reputation for having an inexhaustible fount of knowledge on olden times, which he could recount with great accuracy and detail. Much information from him is on file in the Irish Folklore Commission. He was also visited by many overseas scholars, among whom were Professor Heinrich Wagner from Queen's University, Belfast, and Professor Myles Dillon of the Dublin Institute of Advanced Studies. He had a life-long interest in the poet Raftery. He wrote a long poem called Caoineadh an Chapaill.

Paddy Ruane from an election pamphlet

Paddy Ruane

Paddy Ruane was a son of the late Tom Ruane who was deeply involved in the fight for Irish freedom. Paddy was also involved in Irish politics and was a member of the Galway County Council for almost thirty years since 1955 and one of the longest serving members. For one who belonged only to a tiny party, Sinn Féin, this was a remarkable achievement that required a huge personality vote to bring it about. It was more remarkable still when one considers that due to the Northern Ireland troubles he was denied access to the airways for much of this time when all the other candidates were not. Shortly before his death he went close to being elected for a further term when he lost his seat by less than a dozen votes as a direct result of another local man entering the race on that occasion.

Paddy Ruane also had a lifelong involvement with the GAA as a player, club official, district board officer and a member of the County Board. He was Treasurer of the County Board for fifteen years. Most remarkable also is the fact that he achieved all this without ever owning or driving a car.

Born in Carnmore in 1920. He was married with four children.

Well Known People

Paddy Ruane counting the money after a GAA match

Chapter 13: Sports, Recreation and Pastimes

Pastimes

During the Middle Ages, leisure time was not quite so plentiful as it is today. Work was more manual. People did not have the benefit of automatic machinery and labour saving devices. The working day began at 5 in the morning and ended at 7 or 8 in the evening, with a half-hour for breakfast and an hour and a half for dinner. Saturday was usually a half-day. Thus leaving little time for leisure.

The Authorities encouraged only those sports which would be regarded as martial in nature and which would help make a good soldier. Games that encouraged gambling were prohibited. Needless to say, it was the sports that involved gambling which outlived the others.

In mediaeval times, archery was a much-favoured sport. The Statute of Winchester, which was enforced in Galway in 1308, stated that every man between the ages of sixteen and sixty should be encouraged to practice the use of a long bow on all holidays.

In 1517, the private sale of handguns, calibres, etc., was banned. The crossbow still was used well into the sixteenth century. With Henry VIII, he encouraged sports like hunting and shooting. Hurling, football and the throwing of darts or spears were also commendable games. Handball however, was not so greatly appreciated as this also encouraged gambling. A game of quoits or casting of stones was also practised, which resembles the modern day discus. It was played in teams of four, eight or more

Bowls and royal tennis were also sports that were practised by the middle class. Besides these sports, other outdoor activities that proved to be popular were falconry and the hunting of deer, swimming, sailing, rowing, boat jousts, fishing, poaching and skating. Whilst indoors, the activities include music, which women favoured more than men. The harp was popular and favoured by all classes. This would be joined by some singing and dancing. Chess was regarded as a noble game. Card games included "primera", "trump" which resembles whist, "gresco" and "gleek". In 1528, people were fined if they were found in a gambling shop, as was the owner, unless it was for meat or drink.

Gambling has become a part of modern day living. With the introduction of the National Lottery by the Government, people who might never have placed a bet in their lives, were turned into gamblers overnight. While in Galway, plenty of

Sports, Recreation and Pastimes

big gaily-coloured shops tempt people in to have a bet on anything that takes their fancy. This is a long way from the few men (never women, they had no money) who gathered at various places throughout the parish to play pitch and toss in the evenings and cards by night.

Pitch and toss was played by different people throwing their coins at a marker usually a stone. Whoever's coin was nearest the marker then placed all the coins thrown on a comb, and tossed them in the air while calling head or tails (or heads and harps when we got our own currency). He then held onto the coins, which faced upwards as called.

The next nearest man to the marker then tossed the remainder and so on. Pitch and toss was probably played for as long as coins existed but it died out in this area around the sixties although it has been played in other places.

"The way we spent Sunday's was playing hurling in Hessions field, pitch and toss, we would have to wait until 9:00 P.M. on Sunday evening before we would get in a game of handball. Another gang would play pitch and toss all day on Sunday" (Patrick Monaghan, Claregalway)

Card Games

Cards were a popular and widespread form of entertainment over the centuries, here as in other places. Most villages had popular card houses in which 25, 30 and 110 were the most popular games. Prizes were mostly money but some houses organised their own geese or turkeys as prizes, laying on tea and sandwiches and ensuring a marathon night of playing. Hughes shop in Claregalway was one of the most popular houses. Prizes there might include cakes, tins of biscuits, bottles of sherry or whiskey. In the sixties, card playing tended to move into the pubs where hampers and bottles of whiskey were the prizes organised by the hosts. Three people playing together with two more teams of three playing 25 was the most popular game here, and still continues to be a popular and sociable game. In the eighties, another form of 25 called progressive 25 proved popular in neighbouring parishes but it never really caught on here although it has proved to be a very lucrative fundraising method for clubs. Cards were always played by both sexes.

Very few people played whist, solo and bridge, although a popular bridge club was formed a few years ago and is played regularly in Kyne's pub in Loughgeorge.

Drinking and Dancing

"I would say the local pastimes for us young lads was an hour in the pubs of James Hession, Roddy Kelly, Mary McHugh, and Bina Lenihan. The women could go to the pubs but they never did. Then after our session in the pubs we

Sports, Recreation and Pastimes

would go to the local dance hall which was in Hanley's hall in Claregalway at the time. There was no storyteller in our area at the time but there was a few locals who would tell a story or a yarn now and then but that was all. There were dances at the crossroads in Carnmore. A lot of people would walk to it, as they did not have many bicycles in those days."

(Johnny Casserley, Cahergowan)

Drinking was and is a very popular pastime in Claregalway. The pub was a great meeting place for the local people where stories were told, information exchanged, cards were played, victories celebrated, defeats were drowned in sorrow and the dead were honoured. All the above pubs are still going today, some under different management. Grealishs in Carnmore is a new addition having opened its doors in the late seventies. Malachy Hession's shop in Claregalway, while it retains the bar counter and shelves, has not sold drink since the twenties. It was not until the sixties arrived, bringing with it a new prosperity that the "lounge bars" took off. They were more comfortable, warm and welcoming, provided a greater selection of drink, laid on entertainment, and now women started to come to them on a regular basis. The "visiting houses" in each area were not frequented as often. Apart from a few people in Kiltrogue, there is no tradition of poitin being made in the area.

Dancing at the crossroads took place at nearly every crossroad in the place at sometime or another. The best known were at Carnmore, Mullacuttra and Caraun cross. Local musicians provided music and the crowds either walked or cycled to them. They probably did not need to worry too much about passing traffic apart from the odd car, also they did not have to pay a hefty insurance premium before they started to play.

"The women were not going in to the pubs because they had not the money to go in. They would be standing outside the door looking in to see would he bring out a glass of wine or something to them. There were dances back in the road there in Mullacuttra. They would be scrapping the road there, and bringing up the small stones." (Mrs Kate Glynn, Mullacuttra)

The end of the crossroads dancing came with the opening of the dancehalls. There were a good few within easy reach of a bicycle ride. Keaveneys in Cummer, Carrolls in Cregmore, Lisheen town hall in Lisheenavalla, Greaneys in Liscananaun and Hanleys in Claregalway. While these were very basic they were an improvement on barns. These had their best days from the thirties to the fifties. From then on with the increasing use of motor transport, the crowds mostly went to the bigger halls and the big bands in Galway who played in the Astaire, the Commercial, Seapoint and the Hangar.

"Hanleys hall! Oh yes there were ICA dances and hurling dances and so on, all on Sunday night. I remember it more for the films. During Lent, fellas would

come out from the town and show us pictures. They would show cowboy ones, Roy Rogers, every night the film would break down at least three times. McFaddens came also I remember they put on plays. The one I remember is Noreen Bawn. There was a very good one about the McCormack brothers when they were shot in Tipperary during the Troubles. They'd make a play about an Irish theme, they were very good, very professional. Going back to the dances, there would be a fight sometimes. That would be the best night. It could be between people of different parishes. Some times it would be between Claregalway and Oranmore. Over hurling or something. I think the dancehall closed in 1958. They had a shop where they sold hardware etc, and bicycles. About 1967 I think the engineering business started." (Paraic Concannon, Montiagh)

For a time between the sixties and eighties the Carnivals were big dance attractions. They were held initially at Kennys Cross, then in Claregalway and finally Loughgeorge. They consisted of a large canvas tent with between three and five main poles down the middle and could hold crowds of up to 2,000 people. This was during the height of the Showband era in Ireland and all the top acts of the day: Joe Dolan and the Drifters, Joe Mac and the Dixies, Dickie Rock and the Miami and on one occasion Marianne Faithful would have played locally at one time or another. They were held only in summer and usually lasted for two to four weeks at a time, with a dance on Sunday, Wednesday, Friday and Saturday. They were hugely popular despite the primitive conditions (no flushed toilets or running water) and they were a most lucrative source of revenue for the local hurling and football clubs. The present Claregalway football field was purchased and the pitch and dressing rooms in Carnmore were developed by funds brought in by the Carnival.

Claregalway Temperance Fife and Drum Band

A tradition that didn't die in Claregalway was music. The then parish priest, Fr. McHugh, founded the Claregalway Fife Band in 1909. It was composed of 24-30 flutes, four kettledrums, a big drum, two cymbals and a triangle.

There were twenty four members in all; William Hession, William Skerritt, Martin Quinn, Tom Lenihan, Martin Samways, Patrick Boyle, Patrick Hughes, Charlie Quinn, William Kearns, John Monaghan, Martin Concannon, Tim Feeney, Patrick Greally, John Concannon, John Quinn, Martin Noone, James Moran, Nicholas Kyne, Martin Fox, Patrick Concannon, Martin Hughes, Andy Quinn, Peter Feeney, Peter Fox and Peter Mooney. It was led by Martin Samways, who was their bandmaster.

The band had its own banner on which was a picture of the parish's outstanding relic of the past, the ruins of the old Franciscan Friary. The parish sponsored their uniforms and instruments and they practised regularly in the school. They played

Sports, Recreation and Pastimes

The Claregalway Temperance Fife and Drum band 17th March 1910
Seated (L to R): W Hession, W Skerritt, Martin Quinn and Tom Lenihan. *Second Row (L to R):* M Samways, P Boyle, P Hughes, Charlie Quinn and W Kearns *Third Row (L to R):* John Monaghan, M Concannon, Tim Feeney, P Greally, John Concannon, J Quinn, M Noone, J Moran and N Kyne. *Back Row (L to R):* M Fox, P Concannon, Martin Hughes, Andy Quinn, P Feeney, P Fox and Peter Mooney.

The big drum and two kettledrums from the old Claregalway Temperance Fife and Drum Band

Sports, Recreation and Pastimes

on sports days and festival days also for the public, such as hurling tournaments and on St. Patrick's day.

Fr. McHugh's successor, Fr. Griffin, continued the band in which he took great pride and he often led it on horseback. However Canon Moran put a stop to them, as he disliked the idea of their using the school for their practice.

Claregalway Bilingual Concert

(Extract from the Connacht Tribune 15 of January 1910)

"This concert was held on St.Stephen's night in the Claregalway School. Long before the hour appointed for the opening the schoolyard was filled with people anxious to be admitted. M.P. Mooney whiled away the time by giving a selection of Irish airs. At 6.30 the concert proper began, and was started with a selection of airs on the violin and piano by Messrs. Gleeson and Rabbitte, which was highly applauded.

The next item on the program was Mr. P. Hurney's Irish recitation in which he exceeded his previous famous effort. Then Mr. Mulvein gave "The last rose of summer", and was loudly encored. Mr. O Flaherty followed with a comic song, "Years and Years". Then Master P. Moran, a little boy of nine years, sang most sweetly in the old strain "An Gabha Cearthan". The next item was Mr. Mulvein's "Wearing of the Green", which was equally appreciated with his latest effort. After that came Mr. O Flaherty's comic song, "McSorley Twins", which kept the audience in roars the whole time. A gramophone performance followed. Next came a jig and reel by the Misses Lydon and Scott. Mr. John Moran sang "Caitlean Ní Neil" and was loudly applauded. Mr. Mulvein rendered "Alice where art thou" and was heartily encored. Mr. T. Carthy gave a comic song, "My own little Johnnie, the height of my knee", which fairly brought down the house, and in response to an arís he gave "Nancy Knight" and "Eochaill", which were followed by a four-hand-reel by the Misses Lydon and Scott.

Mr. Noone bringing the program to a close with "Mullachmor", to which he did ample justice. Mr. Carter, who acted as Master of Ceremonies, thanked the audience for their appreciation of the entertainment."

Horses

There seems to have been a big interest in horses as sport, as opposed to work in Claregalway. While all the farm work was usually done by horse, many people have also kept horses for sport. These were mostly for hunting and racing while in recent years show jumping has become very popular. There are two indoor arenas in Rockwood, Moores and Duffys, where people can rideout or learn to ride. There was also races held for many years around the turn of the century at Loughgeorge.

Sports, Recreation and Pastimes

"They had races in Loughgeorge on St. Stephen's Day. Tom Ruane from Carnmore used to have horses running and his sons used to ride them. They were common horses but they were able to race. Tim Feeney had another, and a good few from around Claregalway and Carnmore, They had a great day altogether. They had a dance then that night in a loft in a big shed in Loughgeorge. They would have accordions and violins. Accordions were cheap and every house had two or three. There was not one fellow around here who was not able to play the accordion. The races died out in the 1920's, I think." (Mrs Fox, Mullacuttra)

"It was mostly workhorses that raced in the races in Loughgeorge. My father used to have horses that raced in flapper meetings in Swinford, Oughterard and Scariff in Clare. They would be trained half-bred horses and he had two. Rebel and Cowboy were their names. Cowboy was a great horse...he won the Swinford Plate. They used to have to walk to Oughterard for that meeting. He used to have greyhounds afterwards. He called one of them Windsor Green because he was in Windsor Green prison. He had another one called Scrubs after Wormwood scrubs prison." (Paddy Ruane, Carnmore)

The Galway Races (which at one stage for a brief period were held in Kiltulla before moving to Ballybrit) were a popular place to visit for many local people and in most cases were the only days holidays taken all year.

"In Eyre Square, during race week, there used to be a wheel of fortune, marquee and a dance and all that. It was called a Bazaar. Sure we would pick up a bird at that time. It would be on a fortnight maybe and Canon Moran hated the sight of it. The Sunday before the races he would give a sermon about it; 'I don't mind anyone going to the Galway Races, but do not go into that Bazaar in Galway. In nine months time there will be mothers coming up to me and their daughters going to have a bastard' he would say from the altar." (Patrick Giles)

There was also a tradition of horseracing in Carnmore.

"The field beside us here is called Pairc na Rasa because there used to be races there. My father told me when he was very young there was an old man living back there – and it must be 150 years ago since that old man was young because my father would be 100 years now, God rest him, and when he was young this man was old. Well he said he remembered looking at the races in that field over there and the stables were there. He was standing up on a leacht of stones when he was only 12 or 14 years of age looking at the races – the leachts were the stands. The stables closed here in 1840. I can't think of the man that owned the land and my great-grandfather got the land. The stables were here originally. This old man said that they closed down the races in 1840, and changed back to Kiltulla turlough and then in the history of the Galway Plate and the Galway races it was never stated that way – it was stated wrongly. It said Kiltulla, Athenry, but there were races here as well. And my father said that there were races outside Tuam as well, not Parkmore but somewhere else and they made the

Sports, Recreation and Pastimes

three of them into one big race meeting in Galway. The land here was stony for racing- they were here before 1840. It was only a couple of years in Kiltulla because I suppose it was too soft there. Three big fields for Pairc na Rasa, just there near Sunshine Aluminium. They were not big enough any way. I remember when the leachts of stones were there and the lorries came in and took all the stones about twenty years ago." (Mr and Mrs Eddie Hanley, Carnmore)

Eddie and Mickie Hanley are well known breeders of horses, while Eddie's son Frank is an amateur jockey. Mr Martin Higgins, Carnmore has trained winners under the I.N.H.R. rules of racing. Mr John Cullinan, Cahergowan, is a successful trainer in England. His biggest win was in the Stewards Cup in Goodwood with 'Shikari's Son'.

Gunsports

A gunclub was formed in the early sixties by among others, Kevin Glynn, Michael Allen, John Scully, Mick Duggan, Pat Concannon, Michael Moloney, Tom Flaherty, Jimmy Moran, Tom Hughes, Seamus O'Connell and Michael Giles. They got permission from the local farmers to shoot their lands. In return they organised a regular vermin shoot every Sunday mostly against foxes. These shoots were very enjoyable and were useful in that they kept under control fox numbers, who at the time were a real nuisance. This was at a time when all farmers kept hens and chickens, both to feed themselves and to sell. The foxes were also partial to new-born lambs.

A wide variety of game was available for the gunman: pheasant, woodcock, wood pigeon, snipe and frequently partridge. Claregalway, which runs right down to Lough Corrib, could also be shot for duck and geese. The club's biggest threat in recent years has been the loss of ground because of land being reclaimed and all the houses that have been built. They have also organised clay pigeon shooting and have released pheasant and duck over the years.

GAA

The most predominant pastime for the past hundred years has been the GAA. Many men in that period would have known only their work and the GAA. Their free day being on a Sunday, "the match" be it club or county, dominated their leisure time. While the GAA also sought to promote athletics in tandem with the native games, it was not as successful in that area, but it did help to break down the barriers that heretofore existed. Now the "mechanic, artisan and labourer" could compete with the "gentlemen athletes" who competed only among themselves up to this. When the GAA was founded in 1884, it transformed the country.

"Though still quite young at the time, I still remember the great change that came over the country and the vivid and lasting impression that it made on me. Until

Sports, Recreation and Pastimes

then everything was lonely and stagnant in the land and the young men in their idle hours loitered in dull fashion by the street and fence corners. In a few months how different things became! The country was soon humming with interest and activity, the ambitions of the young men were aroused, every parish had its newly-formed football or hurling team, prepared to do or die for the honour of the little village." (J.B. Dollard. Writer, who was in his early teens in 1884)

If we look at the following notice that appeared in the Tuam Herald on Saturday 21st May 1892, we see that Claregalway was one of the earliest clubs organised and ready to go.

Gaelic Athletic Association:

On Sunday next, 22nd May, a hurling and football tournament will be held on Turloughmore fairgreen. The following clubs have intimated their intention of sending teams to encourage the revival of the pastimes of ancient Erin: Athenry, Craughwell, Clarinbridge, Oranmore, Claregalway, Galway (Rahoon), Gurteen and the home club (hurler)."

A list of winners of the Galway Senior hurling championship showed the following:

Winners	Runners-up
1893 College Road	*Claregalway*
1894 Ardrahan	*Claregalway*

Above from Fr. Padraic O Laoi's book "Annals of the GAA in Galway 1902-1934" which differs slightly from "Gaiscígh an Achréidh".

We are nothing if not inconsistent because 100 years later, in the County Finals of 1992 and 1993, Carnmore lost to Sarsfields.

That first team to reach the County Final was as follows:

Peter Ross	Pat Ross		Sean Glynn	S. Duggan
W. Giles	B. Stephen	S. Carr	H. Walsh	J. Bodkin
P. Moran		P. Mulryan		I. Smyth
G. McDonagh		T. Keaney		J. Fox
M. Rooney				J. Walsh

Of this team, the two Ross brothers and I. Smyth were all inter-county players. Sadly, this team met and lost to a very good Ardrahan side and when the sides met again in 1901, the final went to a replay but Lady Luck still refused to shine, on the "green and gold" and they went down.

The Galway Observer reported on the 15th of June 1901:

"On Sunday last a hurling tournament of the County Galway championship for the final tie was brought off at Kilcolgan between Claregalway Shamrocks and Ardrahan. It was a most favourable day for outdoor amusement that attracted an immense crowd of people to witness the play and especially, as it was supposed, it would be a lively and tight match. It proved as was anticipated, for it was a drawn match the scores being – Claregalway Shamrocks 2 goals 2 points against Ardrahan 1 goal and 5 points. There was a disputed point which was doubtful, but the referee B. Cawley (Craughwell) gave the Ardrahan team the benefit of the doubt and which therefore left it to be a drawn match.

The game was played with great spirit and determination and camans were flying through the air, and it is a mystery how the men escaped unhurt. There was one case most regrettable to relate, that of P. Ross, captain of the Claregalway team, whose hand was broken from a fall, and who had occasion to hurl owing to his team being a man short. Ardrahan won the replay".

1898

Claregalway GAA: Saturday, July 16th 1898

A hurling tournament was held in Claregalway on Sunday last. The day proved favourable for the occasion, and therefore attracted contingents from all the surrounding parishes to witness the grand display by the young blood of the above parish since the pastime was first promoted. It was principally due to the energetic efforts of their captain, Peter Ross, who kept his men up and going.

The first teams to compete for play were Claregalway and Craughwell and was refereed by Michael J. Burke, captain of the 1898 Galway team, to whom much credit is due owing to his strenuous efforts to maintain order and to compel the various teams to abide by the rules. The score was: Claregalway 2 goals and 3 points, Craughwell no score.

The next teams to play were Athenry and College Road, Galway. The score here being: Athenry 4 goals and 1 point, College Road 3 goals and 2 points.

The Castlegar and Oranmore teams next played. This was almost an even match. Castlegar winning by one point. There was no team to play Turloughmore, but in order to show sport, Athenry played a second time against Turloughmore. The Athenry men deserve great praise by doing so as the day was very sultry and most trying to players; but they could not lack courage and perseverance owing to the spirited mind of their young but manly captain. The score was Athenry 1 goal and 4 points, Turloughmore 1 point.

1902

P. Ross, Claregalway played for Galway in the All-Ireland home final versus Tipperary. Score was: Tipperary 6-13, Galway 1-5

The Claregalway hurling team – 1930s

1903

Galway S.H.C. Semi-final: Ardrahan 2-12, Claregalway 0-2

1909

T. Ruane represented Claregalway at the Annual Convention. Claregalway enter J.H.C.
Notes and News. The Connacht Tribune, Saturday the 20th November 1909.

Great hurling tournament at Claregalway.

On next Sunday week, a great hurling tournament will be held at Claregalway in aid of the Craughwell Prisoners 'Defence fund'. The Galway St. Patricks will meet Turloughmore Sarsfields and subsequently the Craughwell Shamrocks will field a team against the Castlegar Ninety Eights. It is anticipated that both matches will be interesting and exciting and it is expected that the gate will be a record one. The Forster Street, Rahoon and Maree Fife and Drum bands will be in attendance and the price of admission to the matches will be 6d. Mr. Jas. Delaney of Castlegar has left no stone unturned to make the day a record one.

GAA: Saturday December 11TH 1909

A very interesting and well-contested match in connection with the County Championships was played at Kiltulla on Sunday last, the rivals being Claregalway and Derrydonnell. The latter won by a large margin. The match was very exciting and was it not for the defective scoring line, the win would not have been such an easy one. There were some very fine exhibitions of the game shown on both sides, especially by some of the winning team and very few fouls were committed. Derrydonnell is a fine team, and should render a good account of itself for the final honours. The brothers' Henihan played excellently on behalf of the Derrydonnell team, as did also Lally and Rowan on behalf of Claregalway. When the final whistle sounded the score was as follows: Derrydonnell 4-4, Claregalway 0-1.

Mr. Michael Connolly, Captain of the Claregalway team, refereed the match in an impartial and efficient manner.

1910

Claregalway Tournament: Saturday, 30th July 1910
A Record Day

A large and representative tournament was held in Claregalway on Sunday last. The tournament, which was organised in aid of the Castlegar Prisoners' Fund, was patronised by all the hurling and football teams for miles around. Immediately after last Mass crowds began to muster from all parts of the county. The first contingents to arrive were the Craughwell hurling team commanded by Mr. Tom Kenny, vice-president GAA, closely followed by members of the Clarinbridge teams and Mr. Thomas Hynes, ex-prisoner, who received a hearty cead mile failte, as he drove along the crowded street. Shortly afterwards the Maree Fife and Drum band arrived playing the National Anthem "God Save Ireland". They received a great ovation on their arrival. The Derrydonnell hurling club next arrived with a large following. Also came the Annaghdown football club, the Cregmore hurling club and the Galway City hurling and football clubs.

The Claregalway junior hurling team. Westboard finalists in 1959

Sports, Recreation and Pastimes

At two o'clock the Claregalway Fife and Drum band marched to the field playing national airs, followed by the Maree Band and a crowd upwards of 700 people, who gave the gate officials a busy time of it for fully two hours. Craughwell and Cregmore hurling teams were the first arranged to play and were quickly on the field. Mr. M. Mulryan, Castlegar, was in charge of the whistle, and gave the utmost satisfaction to all concerned. Cregmore won the toss and agreed to play with the wind. Play was fast and furious from the start. Cregmore made a determined rush for a score and secured a point. After the puck-out play remained in midfield for some time. The Cregmore territory was soon placed in danger. McEvoy, who was doing splendid work for Craughwell, sent into Morrissey who easily scored a goal, which was followed by a point. The score at half time was: Craughwell 1 goal 1 point, Cregmore 1 point.

On resuming play the Craughwell boys soon added another point to their credit. Greaney scored nicely from midfield for Cregmore. The Cregmore backs did not prove active enough for the Craughwell forwards who shot in two goals in quick succession, which left the final score: -

Craughwell 3 goals 1 point, Cregmore 1 point.

The match between Annaghdown and Galway did not prove very interesting, as both teams seemed to have very little knowledge of the game. The Annaghdown team was a strong combination but was not scientific. The score at full-time was: -

Annaghdown 7 points, Galway 4 points

The Galway League Tie had offered a splendid medal for the best kick of football. The medal was awarded to Mr. P. Brougham of Craughwell and Mr. J. Burke of Annaghdown taking second place.

The Claregalway hurling club also offered a medal for the best puck of the hurling ball and after a well-contested struggle, first prize was awarded to Mr. P. Greaney of Turloughmore. Mr. M. Mulroyan of Castlegar and Mr. T. Burke of Galway tied for second place.

Thomas Hession and T. Ruane represented Claregalway at the Annual Convention.

The newspapers reported that 12 hurlers from Loughgeorge were summoned for *"shouting and cheering at the police"* on August 14th between Castlegar and Claregalway. The defendants' plea was that they were members of the Claregalway team returning victoriously from a match. The hurlers were: James Conway, Thos. Mulraine, John Mulraine, Thos. Hession, A. Hession, Jas Fahy, M. Lally, John Collins, Thos Ruane, Pat Coyne, Thos. Conroy and Bartley O'Donnell.

The following motion was handed in from Castlegar – "that the following

- 161 -

Sports, Recreation and Pastimes

members of the Claregalway Hurling Club be suspended for assaulting Ml. Mulryan on 15 August. viz Michael Grealish, W. Carr, Mtn. Grealish, Mtn. Grealish Jnr. and J. Walsh.

In the Galway S.H.C. Ballindereen 1-0, Claregalway 0-1. The Claregalway team was: T. Ruane, M. Grealish, M. Carr, J. Higgins, M. Grealish, M. Murphy, M. Greaney, T. Murphy, M. Samways, P. Walsh, P. Raftery, J. Collins, J. Lardner, A. Hession, T. Lally and M. Coen.

1911

T. Ruane and M. Grealish represented Claregalway at the Annual Convention in Athenry.

Claregalway enter the Senior and Junior Championship.

T. Ruane and M. Samways represented Claregalway at the AGM of the Galway Board.´

Samways, Grealish, Walsh, all Claregalway, were selected to play for Galway against Roscommon on 13th of October.

County S.H.C. Semi-final: Claregalway 6-1, Gurteen 0-0. Prominent for Claregalway were: Michael and Martin Grealish, Walsh, Murphy, Lardner, Fahy and Ruane.

Claregalway team for final: W. Corcoran (goal), T. Ruane, T. Murphy, Martin Grealish, W. Carr, P. Duggan, M. Grealish, M. Murphy, P. Fahy, P. Walsh, M. Samways, J. Higgins, J. Lardner, J. Collins, T. Lally, J. Walsh and A. Hession. Subs: M. Lally and M. Fahy.

Having won the county league in 1911, a certain amount of optimism followed the Claregalway Shamrocks, as they were known, when they reached the final. In a year in which the Board was split, Derrydonnell beat Claregalway in the "official final".

It was recorded on 30th March that a meeting of the Claregalway Hurling Club took place at Carnmore Cross to condemn the outrage perpetrated on Patrick Lally, father of three playing members of the Claregalway team. The outrage was attributed to (i) the split in the GAA and (ii) agrarian trouble.

T. Hession and M. Samways represented Claregalway at the City of the Tribes meeting.

Sports, Recreation and Pastimes

The Claregalway hurling team. 1952 County junior champions

1915

The Connacht Tribune, January 20th 1915

Final of Western Division at Athenry:

On Sunday last at Athenry, the final of the Western division of the county was decided. Galway City and Claregalway were the contestants. Fine weather favoured the occasion and there was a large number of people present to witness the match. At 2 o'clock, the referee Mr. S. Jordan, had the teams lined up. Claregalway, having won the toss, elected to play with the incline of the field in their favour. After the throw-in, the City got away to their opponent's goal, but the Claregalway backs returned to mid-field. Keeping up the pressure, the City forwards scored a point, per McInerney, after 4 minutes of play. From the puck out, the Claregalway men quickly transferred the play to the other end but King and Hurney, the city backs, again and again broke up the rushes of the Claregalway forwards. The latter, however, were not to be denied, and Walsh getting possession, equalised for Claregalway. Both teams now settled down to play with great determination and the referee had to caution a Claregalway man for rough play.

Some fine exchanges were now witnessed. The City players showing up prominently, burst through their opponents goal, Connor sending up the red flag for his side. This put the Claregalway men on their mettle, and play was quickly transferred to the other end and Murphy scored the 2nd point for Claregalway. King pucked out for the City but Casserly returned and Hession nipping in, shot

Sports, Recreation and Pastimes

a goal for Claregalway. Shortly before the half-time whistle, the City forwards stormed their opponents' goal, Dillion sending up the red flag for the City. At half time, the score was: - Galway City 2-2, Claregalway 1-2.

After the throw-in, play was fast and exciting, the ball travelling from end to end with great rapidity. Claregalway showing a better stamina than their opponents forced the pace and added a goal and a point to their credit. The City men retaliated with a point per Whelan. During the closing stage of the contest, both sides struggled hard for supremacy but Claregalway had the verdict in safe keeping and added another goal before the final whistle sounded, leaving the score:- Galway City 3-3, Claregalway 2-3.

The following are the names of the team:

Claregalway: P. Hughes (captain), M. Grealish, D. Duggan, J. Duggan, M. Murphy, P. Casserly, S. Casserly, J. Keaney, W. Corcoran and Hession

Galway City: P. Elwood (captain), P. O'Connor, M. Connor, J. Dillion, T. Burke, J. King, T. King, P. Curley, M. Fahy, D. McInerney, J. Ruffey, P. Duggan and P. Whelan

West Board Senior Championship Final:

Claregalway 3-3, Galway City 2-3.

The Claregalway Team was: P. Hughes (capt), M. Grealish, D. Duggan, J. Duggan, M. Murphy, P. Murphy, P. Casserly, M. Casserly, J Keaney, W. Corcoran and A. Hession.

P. Casserly represented Claregalway at the County Convention.

1916

West Board Senior Hurling Championship Final:

Claregalway 1-4, Craughwell 1-2.

1917

Hurling at Athenry: Saturday, April 28th 1917

At Athenry on Sunday last, Craughwell met Claregalway in the senior hurling final for the West District Championship. The game was well contested throughout and some splendid hurling was witnessed. Craughwell fielded a light team and during the game one of their players sustained an injury and had to retire. They had nevertheless hard luck in losing, as it was only in the last few minutes that Claregalway succeeded in scoring a goal, which gave them a lead of 2 points, which they held until the end. Results: - Claregalway 1-4, Craughwell 1-2.

Sports, Recreation and Pastimes

At this point political factors that were ever present overtook the great Claregalway Shamrocks team of this era. Practically all of the men took up arms during the rising of 1916 and many suffered great hardship and imprisonment as a result. Mike Lally and Tom Ruane spent long periods in British jails including the Frongoch internment camp. I will repeat here the pen pictures of those great men from "Gaiscígh an Achréidh"

- **Tom and Martin Lally**, Carnmore, both speedy and skilful. They lived where their niece, Mrs. Rita Feeney, now resides.
- **Martin Samways**, Cregboy, a wonderful club and county servant. Lived in later years in Monivea.
- **John Lardner**, an excellent hurler like his sons, Denis, Hubert and Mick.
- **Tom "Tailliur" Hession**, Cregboy, brother of Arthur. Many years of service as club Treasurer.
- **Paddy Raftery**, Cahergowan, a rugged and reliable hurler like this son "Raf".
- **Tom Murphy**, Gortatleva, brother of Philip and Michael, a speedy attacker.
- **Mairtin Paddy Grealish**, Carnmore, the outstanding forward and free taker of the side. Father of Martin and Paddy Sean.
- **William Corcoran**, Lydacan, an outstanding goalkeeper about whom de Valera enquired in the fifties.
- **Peter Fahy**, Tonroe, a giant in defence and also very effective in midfield. Father of Johnny and Paddy
- **John Collins**, Carnmore, father of Jimmy and Mick, a solid defender himself with the reds
- **Michael Murphy**, Gortatleva, father of Jack, who was a wonderful club servant as treasurer, and Martin, perhaps our best player, and Paddy our full back in the fifties.
- **John Higgins**, Carnmore, father of Paraic and Martin. An outstanding hurler and hurley maker.
- **Willie Carr**, Carnmore village, a durable defender.
- **Arthur Hession**, Cregboy, a star midfielder of club and county.
- **Paddy and Stephen Walsh**, Carnmore, both outstanding players as was their nephew Michael in the sixties

Sports, Recreation and Pastimes

Carnmore 1946 County Junior Champions
Back Row (L to R): M. Fox, MJ Hanley, M O'Brien, P. Kenny, M Grealish (ML), W. Killilea, P. Grealish (P), J. Grealish (ML), P. Carr, M. Grealish (P) and L. Fox. *Middle Row (L to R):* P. Fox, M. Bodkin, D. Lardner, M. Commins, M. Lardner, J. Commins, P. Hanley, T. Hanley, J. Murphy and J. Clarke. *Front Row (L to R):* M. Hanley, M. McDonagh, M. Commins, P. Beatty, V. Grealish, P. Grealish, T. Hanley and J. McDonagh.

1921

Claregalway represented by P. Feeney at the County Convention.

1926

P. and J. Casserly represented Claregalway at the West Board Convention.

Wm. Mannion elected Secretary of County Board.

1927

J. Hession and J. Noone represented Claregalway at the West Board Convention.

T. Ruane and T.O Connor represented Claregalway at the County Board Convention.

Wm. Mannion elected Secretary of the County Board.

1928

Wm. Mannion (Claregalway) elected Secretary of the County Board.

Claregalway 3-1, Clifden 3-0 in the West Board Junior Semi-final.

Claregalway 2-4, Galway City 2-6 in the West Board Senior hurling semi-final.

Claregalway Senior Team: T. Duggan, S O'Brien, T. O' Connor (capt), John

Keane, P. Keane, P. Carr, John Nonne, M. Duggan, W. Walsh, P. Cloherty, Ml. Bernard, Ml. Skerrit, Pat Skerrit and Dan Duggan.

1929

Claregalway 14-5, Fairhill Stars 2-3, Junior Hurling

Claregalway 5-1, Derrydonnell 3-2, Intermediate Championship

1932

Claregalway 2-1, Oranmore 3-1, Co. Junior Championship Final.

With three minutes to go the referee ordered off a Claregalway player. He refused to go and attempted to play on, so the referee awarded the match to Oranmore.

1933

Claregalway 0-0, Castlegar 6-6, Minor hurling.

Claregalway 1-0, Castlegar 5-4, Intermediate Hurling.

Minor Team: M. Morris, P. Morris, M. J. Hughes, J. Sheridan, M. Sheridan, J. Sheridan, M. Glynn, T. Healy, J. Scully, J. Glennon, J.J. Duggan and P. Sheridan.

Intermediate team: J. Hession, S. Hession, J. Flaherty, M. Flaherty, W. Walshe, M. Duggan, T. Duggan, M. Duggan, M. Madden, P.J. Hughes, P. Carr, P. Kelly, W. Duggan, P. Cloherty, T. Noone, W. Duggan, F. Duggan and J. Kane.

In the 30's the game of hurling really took off in the parish and many of the games of this era have earned the title "classics". One such game was a terrific

1984 Minor Team – County Champions

Sports, Recreation and Pastimes

struggle between Oranmore and Claregalway, where we were unfortunately on the wrong end of the scoreline. The Claregalway team at this time were sporting new jerseys which, had been purchased from the proceeds of a dance in Scully's Barn, Cahergowan. Each person was charged 1 shilling and over 70 shillings was raised, which was more than enough for the kit. Inter-county stars of this era were the much acclaimed duo of Mattie Healy and P.J. Hughes and in the minor grade Matty "Butty" Duggan kept goal for Galway in the years up to 1940.

Proof that the game was becoming increasingly popular can be gleaned from the fact that in 1935 there were actually 3 clubs in the parish. There was at this time a loss of players from Claregalway while hurling in Carnmore progressed in leaps and bounds. The third team in the parish, was only a temporary and short-lived one, but nonetheless earned a lot of admiration in their brief lifetime. This team was formed in the northwest of the parish, comprising the townlands of Waterdale, Clochan, Mullacuttra and Liscananaun in the Lackagh parish and it went under the name Ban Mor Padraic Pearses.

James Qualter, Loughgeorge made hurleys for them and if they needed others, Mike Skerrit from Claregalway was another hurley maker. People who had cut their own sticks and did the initial shaping could get their "caman" finished off nicely in Skerrits. Ban Mor Padraic Pearses made an immediate impact on the hurling scene by getting to the West Board Final where they drew with Liam Mellowes, but were beaten in the replay. They accepted an invitation after this, to rejoin Claregalway to form a senior hurling team.

During this period Thomas O Connor N.T. Claregalway played a noble part in ensuring the survival of hurling in Claregalway. He was also an officer in the West Board and on the County Board. Billy Morris and John McDonagh were also officers at this time.

Paddy Ruane served as County Board treasurer for 15 years.

Paddy Fahy (Cregboy) won an All-Ireland Junior Hurling medal with Galway in 1939.
"Butty" Duggan was in goal for Galway Minors in 1938, 1939 and 1940.

P.J. Hughes and Mattie Healy were County Players at this time.

In 1944 Carnmore registered their own Junior Hurling club. It only took them two years to become the Junior Hurling Champions when they defeated Clarinbridge in the '46 final. At this time, Claregalway players began transferring up to play for Carnmore. In the Senior Hurling Final the Army team (an Chead Cath Gaelach) defeated Carnmore 4-13 to 4-3. They again defeated Carnmore in the county semi-final in 1948.

The team which played in the 1947 final: was Patrick Beatty, Mike McDonagh, Jim Commins, Matt Grealish (Patcheen), Patrick Fahy, Peter Grealish (Seamus Pheadair), Martin Grealish (Ml), Mairtin Bodkin, Michael Commins, Tommy

Sports, Recreation and Pastimes

Hanley, Paddy Grealish (Patcheen), Peter Grealish (Ml), Martin Grealish (Seamus Pheadair), Paddy Ruane and Thomas Hanley. Subs: Martin Commins, Willie Killilea, Mick Lardner, Paddy Hanley, M. Grealish and J. Murphy

In 1952 in the West Board Junior Final at Clarinbridge, Claregalway played Carnmore in what was to be their biggest and last clash. The teams lined out as follows:

Claregalway:	*Carnmore:*
Michael (Butt) Duggan	Tom Leonard
George Fahy	Mike McDonagh
Jimmy O Dea	Paddy Murphy
Mick Glynn	Tom Hanley (John)
John Holland	Murty Grealish
Brian Fahy (Capt)	John Hynes
Pat Feeney	Jackie Hanley
Watty Duggan	Mattie Coneely
Tom Flaherty	Mairtin Kelly
Eamon Grealish	Martin Murphy
Paddy Raftery	Eddie Hanley
Mattie Duggan (Dan)	Peter Grealish (Ml)
Mike Monaghan	Mattie Hanley
Richie Fahy	Jack Murphy
Mattie Boyle	Thomas Hanley
Subs.	
John Glennon	M. Leonard

"The match came fully up to expectations as neighbours, Claregalway and Carnmore, fought a skilful desperate battle for honours with the former narrowly gaining the day. A draw would have been a fairer reflection of the game in which the lead changed hands several times and level pegging was frequent - a game, too, in which the more skilful and speedier Carnmore side went down to the determination of Claregalway. Claregalway 7-6 Carnmore 6-4." Connacht Tribune 30 Aug 1952

Claregalway went on to win the County that year beating Eyrecourt in the final. Alas the team grew old together and many subsequently retired. This led to a decline in the Claregalway club and not having entered a team one year, Carnmore was the only team allowed to enter the following year by the County Board. The Carnmore Club grew and with the club developing its own pitch the scene was set for further glories.

The most talked about hurler of this era was Martin Murphy. He first came to prominence as a college hurler with St. Mary's, Galway. From then on he

- 169 -

County Champions, Intermediate 1961 - Carnmore
Back Row (L to R): P. Fox (coach), M. Kenny, M. Collins, J. Conroy, P. Kenny, P. Hynes, J. Girvan, R. Kenny, C. Grealish, M. Walsh and M. Commins (manager). Front Row (L to R): M. Hanley, J. Greaney, J. Hanley, J. Murphy, E. Hanley, M. Fox, T. Leonard, M. Beatty and M. Hanley

enhanced his reputation with Carnmore and with Galway. He ended his hurling career in New York. He was only one of many that emigration took away from us and it is recurring theme in the history of the club.

("I have heard him described again and again as the best hurler who ever played in Gaelic Park, New York." Jimmy Conroy, Carnmore, Whitegate and Galway.)

In 1955 Carnmore beat Leitrim in the County Junior Final. Carnmore 5-10, Leitrim 1-2.

Carnmore: T. Leonard, M. McDonagh, J. Hynes, P. Kelly, J. Hanley, M. Murphy, M. Kelly, M. Fox, M. Conneely, P. Grealish, E. Hanley, G. Ruane, M. Hanley, P. Conneely and J. Conroy. Sub: J. Conroy.

The hurling careers of Jimmy Conroy and Mattie Fox were only just beginning at this stage and both were outstanding for their club and for Galway for many more years.

Their next biggest success came in 1961 when they became Intermediate Champions.

Carnmore 4-5, Loughrea 4-1.

Carnmore: J. Hanley, M. Kenny, M. Collins, C. Grealish, P. Hynes, T. Leonard, J. Conroy, J Conroy, P. Kenny, M. Walsh, M. Beatty, E. Hanley, M Hanley and M Leonard.

In 1958 the Carnmore Club took possession of their own ground, which over the years they have continued to develop into a lovely compact ground with a wonderful playing surface. From about 1955 to 1960 they organised a very

Sports, Recreation and Pastimes

successful seven-a-side tournament, which was hotly contested by all the local clubs. The prizes were sets of medals and suit lengths of clothes.

In the early seventies, they were again a force to be reckoned with at Senior Club level. During this time for a period of eight consecutive years the team which beat Carnmore went on to become County champions. This was the era of the knockout championship with no chance of a slip up. They were in two finals at this time:

1971 Carnmore 1-12 Tommy Larkins 5-2
1975 Carnmore 1-11 Ardrahan 4-5

This revival in Carnmore coincided with an upturn in the fortunes of the Galway team. Paddy Walsh, Michael Greaney, Padraig Fahy, Johnny Long, Jimmy Hughes, and Sean Murphy all lined out regularly with Galway. Jimmy Duggan won an All-Ireland under 21 medal in 1972. This was a significant victory for Galway in that it was their first national title for many years. In 1975 Galway achieved what many thought would never happen by winning the National League and reaching the McCarthy Cup final. Along the way Sean Murphy and Padraig Fahy gave outstanding performances while James Grealish played in earlier rounds of the league and came on in the All-Ireland final despite suffering a serious injury that year.

In 1981 a separate Juvenile Club was formed to cater for the growing demand of young people wanting to play the game and for the great number of competitions for the same.

Early success came in 1981 when they took a National Feile na Gael title beating Mervue in the final. That team was:

	Alan Kenny	
Noel Greaney	Danny Connell	Padraic Higgins
Declan Collins	Pat Killilea	Eamon Cormican
Michael Killilea		Eamon Cormican
Michael Fahy	Thomas Grealish	Thomas Lohan
Liam Fahy	Declan Heneghan	Noel Grealish

Subs: Donal Duggan, Steve Ruane, Sean Newell, Murty Killilea, Michael Grealish, and Tony Spellman. Their mentors were John Connell, Brian Fox, Roddy Kenny and Johnny Greaney.

In 1984 they beat Annaghdown in the Minor B final (4-10 to 4- 9) The team was:

	Tony Spellman	
Declan Flaherty	Danny Connell	Eamon Cormican
Declan Collins	Michael Collins	Sean Newell
P.J. O Hagan		Patrick Killilea
Liam Carr	Danny Grealish	Thomas Grealish
Paul Concannon	Noel Fox	Michael Killilea

Subs: Thomas Lohan, Roddy Grealish, Tom Newell, Stephen Ruane, Michael Fahy, Liam Fahy, Michael John Murphy, Tom Lenihan, Eamon Fox. Manager: Tom Lenihan. Coach: Padraig Fahy. Selectors: Paddy Joe Spellman, Seamus Concannon, John Fox, Michael Hanley and Jimmy Noone.

The Carnmore intermediate team. County champions 1988
Back Row (L to R): Tom Lenihan (Mgr), Danny O'Connell, Eamonn McDonagh, John Fox, Thomas Grealish, Michael Killilea, Liam Fahy, Tom Lenihan (junior), Declan Collins, Alan Kenny, Patrick Killilea, Rory Kenny, Michael Hanley, Padraig Fahy (coach) and Jimmy Duggan. *Front Row (L to R):* Johnny Greaney (selector), Ray Grealish, Tom Fox, Fergus Madden, Malachy Hanley (captain), Tony Spellman, Jimmy Noone, Murty Killilea, Gerry Fox, Sean Newell, Brendan Commins and Jack Hession (selector)

In 1987 they beat Rahoon in the County under 21B final while in the following year they regained senior status by defeating Craughwell in the Intermediate final. That team was:

	Tony Spellman	
Fergus Madden	John Fox	Murty Killilea
Declan Collins	Jimmy Noone	Sean Newell
	Malachy Hanley	Jerry Fox
Patrick Killilea	Liam Fahy	Thomas Grealish
Alan Kenny	Tom Lenihan	Michael Killilea

Subs: Brendan Commins, Danny Connell, Eamon McDonagh, Rory Kenny, Michael Hanley, Jimmy Duggan, Raymond Grealish and Tom Fox. Selectors: Tom Lenihan (manager), Padraig Fahy, Johnny Greaney and Jack Hession.

1990 Minor B hurling final. Carnmore 2-8, Beagh 1-4

Sports, Recreation and Pastimes

	K Walsh	
M Walsh	Brian Connell	Joe O'Connell
Declan Madden	Ronan Walsh	Declan O'Brien.
Paraic O'Connell		John O Hagan
Shane Walsh	Peter Fahy	Kevin Moran
Derek Long	Mickey Grealish	Geoffrey Keating

Junior B Hurling Final. Carnmore 2-8 Killimordaly 1-6

Team: Brendan Commins, Jimmy Duggan, Tom Fox, Michael Hanley (Capt), Malachy Hanley, Danny Connell, Eamonn Cormican, Declan O Brien, Noel Grealish, Shane Walsh, Sean Murphy, Mairtin Connell, Gerry Fox, Tom Lenihan and Paraic Connell. Subs: Mickey Grealish, Declan Madden, P.J. O Hagan, Jimmy Hughes, Derek Long, R. Donovan, J. O Hagan and Kevin Moran. Selectors: Johnny Duggan (Mgr.) Thomas Noone, Johnny Greaney and Michael Casserly.

This match was notable for the fact that Sean Murphy, after many years of outstanding service for Carnmore, won his first County medal.

The Carnmore Junior B champions 1992
Back Row (L to R): Johnny Duggan (Mgr), Jimmy Hughes, Derek Long, Richard Donovan, John O'Hagan, Kevin Moran, Tom Lenihan, Eamonn Cormican, Noel Grealish, Tom Fox, Martin Connell, Padraig Connell, Gerry Fox, Thomas Noone (selector) and Johnny Greaney (selector). *Front Row (L to R):* PJ O'Hagan, Declan O'Brien, Sean Murphy, Shane Walsh, Malachy Hanley, Michael Hanley (captain), Brendan Commins, Mickey Grealish, Jimmy Duggan, Declan Madden and Michael Casserly (selector). *Sitting at front (L to R):* Trevor Casserly, Thomas Noone, Barry McCarten, George Hanley and Padraig Hanley.

Sports, Recreation and Pastimes

The early nineties saw the emergence of another very strong senior team. This team could lay claim to be the best ever sent out by the club as they were beaten on three occasions in County Finals by teams who subsequently went on to win All-Ireland Club titles. In 1992 they were beaten by a Joe Cooney led Sarsfields after a replay. They lost again to Sarsfields in 1993 who went on to become the first club to retain the All-Ireland club championship. They were back again in 1996 only to lose to Athenry.

The players involved in those finals were: Kenneth, Declan and Ronnie Walsh, Sean Newell, Jimmy Noone, Enda Flaherty, Declan Collins, Murty, Patrick and Michael Killilea, Rory and Alan Kenny, Ronan and Shane Walsh, Ray and Thomas Grealish, Peter, Damien and their cousin Liam Fahy, Brendan Commins, Alan Thompson, John Fox, Danny Grealish, Noel and Mickey Grealish, Danny, Mairtin and Padraig Connell, Malachy Hanley, Declan O Brien, John Keogh, Declan Madden and T.J. Hynes. Johnny Greaney was Team Manager. Padraig Fahy was Coach. Selectors were: Malachy Hanley, Martin Higgins and Paddy Walsh.

Murty Killilea and Ronan Walsh have won All-Ireland under 21 medals while Murty played in the 1993 All-Ireland Senior Final. Shane and Declan Walsh have won Minor, Vocational Schools and County Vocational, All-Ireland medals. Sean Newell and Derek Long have won All-Ireland County Vocational medals.

Over the years the club has been well served by many dedicated and outstanding clubmen. Among them Paddy Joe Spellman, J.J. Coneely, Johnny Greaney, Johnny Duggan, Tom Lenihan, Martin Leonard, Danny Potter, Johnny Kerrigan while Martina Casserly became the club's first female officer.

Tom Lenihan has also served as a referee, as Co Selector Under 21, Vice-Chairman, Assistant Treasurer and Treasurer of the Hurling Board.

Micheal Leonard's book on the GAA in Claregalway and Carnmore called *'Gaiscigh an Achreidh"* is a wonderful book and anyone who would like to know more about the parish should try and get to read it. Copies can still be bought from Johnny Greaney, Carnmore and Tom Lenihan, Lakeview.

The Claregalway Football Club

Interest in the Claregalway hurling team waned after the defeat by Fr. Tom Burke's hurling team in the West Board Junior Hurling Championships final in 1959. Also some of their best players emigrated; Séan and Mattie Glynn, Mullacuttra and Tom Lenihan, Lakeview went to the USA and Joe McTigue, Knockdoe, Mattie Keane, Mullacuttra and Martin Joe Flaherty, Mullacuttra went to England. Interest in football was very high with Galway winning three All Irelands in a row in the early sixties. A group of lads started to play football in Pat Ryan's field in Waterdale. These young lads were from Liscananaun,

- 174 -

Sports, Recreation and Pastimes

Mullacuttra and Waterdale. The leaders of that group of lads at the time were Peter Greally, Gortadooey, Paddy Gleannaun, Mullacuttra and Paddy Walsh and Martin Nally, Waterdale.

Then in early 1963 they decided to enter a football team in the West Board. They were called the Waterdale Football team. They didn't have a club at the time. All the decisions were made in Ryan's field.

The first football match played by the Waterdale Football team was a league game against a team by the name of St. Patricks in Ballyconneely, Connemara. We were told that they were very excited about playing this game; it was like an All Ireland final to them. We were told they went to first Mass in Claregalway that morning and then headed off for Ballyconneely. They hadn't a clue where Ballyconneely was. They didn't know if it was 50 miles or 500 miles away. They had only two cars and one of them a Hilman Minx had eleven people in it that morning, but they got there. The field was surrounded by two big drains of water and the sea was only a few hundred yards away. There were no changing rooms. The lads had to tog out in between furze bushes.

They had only fifteen players that day; namely: Joe Hanly, Claregalway, Paddy Walsh, Waterdale, Johnny Walsh, Liscananaun, Martin Nally, Waterdale, Johnny Gleannaun, Bawnmore, Padraig Concannon, Gortadooey, Séan Carr, Bawnmore, Peter Fox, Mullacuttra, Dinnie O'Brian, Waterdale, Willie Collins, Waterdale, Michael Walsh, Waterdale, Tom Walsh, Waterdale, Peter Greally, Gortadooey, Billie Greally, Gortadooey and Paddy Gleannaun, Mullacuttra.

After that game when they didn't do so well, players started to appear from outside the parish. Some players came from the Army in Renmore, others from the neighbouring parish Annaghdown, 'illegal of course'. It's said a player from Annaghdown was suspended for a year by his club for playing with the Waterdale Football team.

That Waterdale team lasted for about three or four years. Then about 1966/67 they got together with the rest of the parish and a club was formed under the name of the Claregalway Football club. The colours of the jerseys were as they are today, 'green and gold'. A continuation of the colours that the Claregalway Hurling Club had going back as far as the eighteen hundreds.

The officers of that first football club were:
Chairman: Tom Flaherty, Cahergowan,
Secretary: Peter Greally, Gortadooey,
Treasurer: Johnny Duggan, Cregboy.

They fielded a junior team that first year. They trained and played most of their football in Hession's field, beside Hession's shop in Claregalway. They found it hard at the beginning to get players to train, presumably because of the tradition of hurling within the parish, but with players like Seamus Concannon,

Gortadooey, Jack Hession, Peake, Malachy Qualter, Rooaunmore, Jimmy Hughes, Claregalway, Padraig Fahy, Ballincreg, Séan Murphy, Ballymurphy, Tommie and Fergus Madden, Killeen, Castlegar they kept it going. The arrival of Patsy O'Hagan in the early seventies from County Down, winner of two All Ireland medals in the sixties, was a great boost to the club. Patsy played out his final years with Claregalway and then helped with training and coaching the Claregalway footballers. Around that time also we had Jackie Morris who played football with Tuam Stars come and play with the local club. Later we had Gerry Hester, RIP from Roscommon, Wally French from Wexford, PJ McGovern from Cavan and Mick Higgins from Clonbur.

The first success for the club came in 1975 when they won the West Board league final. Around that time also a Juvenile committee was set up within the club to cater for the under age players and with men like Pat Heanaghan, Sean Flanagan, Tommie Moran, Paddy Gleannaun and Gerry Hester in charge, a lot of good players came to the fore. We had Val Hanly, Claregalway and Martin Cummins, Rooaunmore who went on to play minor football with Galway in those years.

Then the club had a long wait from that 1975 league win until 1986 when they won the North Board Junior football 'B' championship and the county final as well. In 1991 the efforts of the juvenile committee bore fruit when the club won the minor football championship and league under the guidance of Seamus Concannon, Montiagh. In 1993 the club won the North Board minor league, the North Board junior 'A' championship and the county football junior 'A' championship final. In 1996 they won the West Board junior football 'B' championship.

Then in 1997 they won the West Board minor league and the West Board U21 'B' championship. In 1998, thirty one years or so since the foundation of the club, they won Comartás Péil Soísir ná Gealtachtá, the West Board junior 'A' championship and the county junior 'A' championship. Three caps in one year and now they play intermediate football within the county for 1999. So as we move into the twenty-first century, things look good for Claregalway football.

Newspaper report on the 1998 Junior 'A' West Board Championship Final:

Claregalway   *1-8*
Micheal Breathnachs 0-8

Claregalway captured the West Board Junior 'A' Football Championship at Killanin on Sunday after a well merited but hard-earned victory over a gallant Micheal Breathnachs team.

It was a tense, tough, physical affair with both teams giving it everything for the

Sports, Recreation and Pastimes

hour before a large appreciative crowd. To add spice to the occasion, Micheal Breathnachs had only been beaten once this season in competitive football and that was by Claregalway in the Comórtas Paile na Gaeltachta final so revenge was very much in their minds.

It was Claregalway, however, who got the perfect start with a great goal by Derek Murray after a long ball over the top from midfielder Anthony Monaghan after three minutes. The victors went further ahead with a pointed free from Monaghan before Na Breathnaigh opened their account with a great point from corner forward Padraig O'Griofa.

Claregalway began to dominate proceedings with Padraig O'Conaill and Monaghan exerting their influence at midfield. They were ably assisted by star wing-back Rory Kenny and half-forward Niall McGovern. During this period they went further ahead with points from Monaghan on 14 minutes and a beauty from Kenny on 18 minutes. This left the score at 1-3 to 0-1.

However the Inverin side began a mini revival led by O'Griofa who added four unanswered points, three from frees, as the game reached the half-time interval. Full-back Colm O'Fatharta and midfielder Donncha O'Conghaile were very much to the fore as Breathnachs tried to get a grip on the game. Referee Mick Byrne brought the first half to a close with a minimum of margins between the sides: 1-3 to 0-5.

Whatever Micheal Breathnachs were told at half time seemed to do the trick as they came out with all guns blazing. Midfielder Donal O'Curraoin and wing forward Daithi Beaglach began to cause a lot of problems for the Claregalway defence with their direct running style.

Points from O'Griofa, Beaglach and corner forward Stiofain O'Mainnin soon followed and Breathnachs eased into a two point lead. Claregalway introduced Padraig Walsh and Paul Concannon in order to stem the flow of the game against them. They proved inspired moves as Walsh's physical presence and Concannon's experience began to settle the Claregalway side. Rory Kenny, Noel Grealish and Richard Donovan began to form a formidable line of defence which Breathnachs were finding increasingly hard to penetrate.

But they did get a golden opportunity in the 47th minute when Claregalway's goalkeeper Nigel Donovan mis-judged the hop of the ball which allowed Seosaimh O'Fatharta to fist it over his head. However the ball rolled agonisingly wide of the empty net. This proved a major turning point as the last ten minutes of the game belonged to Claregalway. Monaghan added two frees to fine efforts from Adrian Moran and O'Conaill to put Claregalway two points in front.

The Claregalway forwards were guilty of some terrible shooting in the final minutes of the game but Monaghan again steadied the ship with a fine point from play with the last kick of the game. Claregalway's heroes on the day were

Monaghan, O'Conaill, Walsh and the man of the match Rory Kenny. Best of Breathnachs were O'Griofa, the O'Fatharta brothers and Donncha O'Conghaile.

The Claregalway team were: N. Donovan, K. Watson, N. Grealish, G. Madden, M. Grealish, R. Donovan, R. Kenny, P. O'Conaill, A. Monaghan, A. Moran, P. Connell, N. McGovern, D. Murray, E. Davitt, K. McNamara and P. Walsh for K. Watson.

Newspaper report on the 1998 Junior County Final

Claregalway	2-13
Kilconly	2-4

A fit and determined Claregalway made club history when they stormed to victory in the final of the County Junior 'A' Football Championship at Menlough on Saturday and by doing so they have secured a place in next year's Intermediate competition, a fitting reward for a deserved win.

They proved far superior in most positions for a Kilconly side, which must be disappointed at this performance. They never produced the sort of football that brought them through the North Board in triumph and they didn't have the physical power of the new champions who adapted themselves to the heavy underfoot conditions much better than the losers.

All is not lost for Kilconly however and they are still in contention for promotion from the League. They are in the Divisional final of that competition and will be hoping to overcome Glynsk in a replay after the teams drew when they first met. It will be a big test for them after this morale sapping defeat but it does give them the opportunity to bounce back quickly.

Claregalway will naturally be delighted at this breakthrough. It is the fruition of some sterling foundation work at schoolboy and underage level in recent years and as a thriving hinterland of Galway City its rapidly expanding population will give the club the optimism that further progress can be made and on this evidence it would be well founded.

They swung into top form from the start and had six points on the board before they conceded one to the opposition. As expected their towering young midfielder Anthony Monaghan was again their central figure. Defying the slippery conditions his fielding, running and laying off were out of the top drawer and he was the main instigator of most Claregalway attacks.

He gave them an early advantage when he pointed a free from the hands and that lead was quickly doubled when Adrian Moran landed one from a free on the right wing while the same player then engineered a point from play to make it 0-3 to 0-0 in five minutes.

Monaghan then kicked an inspirational 50 metre free and Derek Murray stretched the difference to five points with a lovely effort from a difficult angle.

Sports, Recreation and Pastimes

The latter then let Kilconly off the hook though when he sent a penalty wide after Richard Donovan was taken down.

The losers made a number of switches including bringing Justin Dermody out to midfield and moving Pat Lally into the full forward line as they tried to stem the tide and they almost got their first score when a long range free by Brian Moran went inches the wrong side of the post. They were 0-6 to 0-0 behind thanks to a Niall McGovern point when Michael Morris raised their first white flag but then came disaster to them when Enda O'Connell drove to the net from close range.

A great point from play by Anthony Monaghan turned the screw further but when Shane Brady crossed from the right corner Brian Moran flicked to the roof of the net as Sean Higgins also ran in to make sure. That gave Kilconly some hope as they went in at half-time 1-7 to 1-1 behind but their hopes of a fightback were severely dented on the resumption when the rampant Monaghan converted three frees in the first five minutes.

Corner-forward Enda O'Connell, son of former Killererin stalwart Mick, then blasted a second goal to make the game safe for Claregalway at 2-10 to 1-1 but Kilconly battled away bravely and two points in a minute by Brian Moran – one a free, were followed by a magnificent Sean Higgins goal after Declan Collins had spotted him free. Richard O'Donovan, Anthony Monaghan and Niall McGovern pushed the score up to 2-13 for the winners while Brian Moran had a last gasp penalty saved by Nigel Donovan but then landed a point at the final whistle.

Top scorer Anthony Monaghan led the way for the winners and he got most assistance from goalie Nigel Donovan, Padraig Walsh, Adrian Moran, Niall McGovern, Richard Donovan and Enda O'Connell while 'keeper Niall Hannon, Martin Connolly, Declan and Kieran Collins, Sean Higgins, sub Stephen Curley and Brian Moran all tried non-stop for Kilconly.

The Claregalway team were: N. Donovan, K. Watson, S. Walsh, G. Madden, M. Grealish, P. Walsh, R. Kenny, A. Monaghan, P. O'Connell, A. Moran, R. Donovan, N. McGovern, E. O'Connell, E. Devitt and D. Murray. Sub: P. Concannon for Devitt.

The 1999 officers are:

President:	Tom Lenihan
Chairman:	Gerry Starken
Vice Chairman:	Kevin McNamara
Secretary:	Gerry Higgins
Asst Secretary:	Mary O'Connell
Treasurer:	Tom Newell
Asst Treasurer	Richard Donovan
PRO	Sean Flanagan

Handball

There was always a great handball tradition in the parish. The 'ballalley' beside the bridge was a very popular meeting place. In the days when the only other outdoor sport played in the parish was hurling, handball games were played there every Sunday and nearly every evening in summer. Some players were William Kemple from Lakeview, Commins and Casserly from Kiniska, Commins from Carnmore, Duggan from Montiagh and many others. A 'ballalley' was also built across from the national school in Carnmore in 1922 and it was a popular centre for years. The alley there had to be demolished in 1972 as it was in a dangerous condition. The County Council knocked down the old 'ballalley' in Claregalway in 1954 as it lay in the path of the proposed new road, and a new one was built in 1955. Handball continued to be popular and a club was reformed in 1974 and the game was very popular with large numbers playing.

At that time, some young players competed in the Community Games and had some success also in the County championships. In 1979, the team competed in the community games and went on to win in Connacht and played in the All-Ireland Final in Butlins. They lost the final there to Kilkenny but all received silver medals. The team was Tommy Duggan, Martin Commins, Kieran Moylan, Michael O'Hagan and Kevin Hestor. They were trained by Seamus O'Connell.

The building of the Leisure Centre in Lakeview in 1980 with its indoor facilities saw a decline in the interest of handball as an outdoor activity in the parish. However some people continue to keep the sport alive.

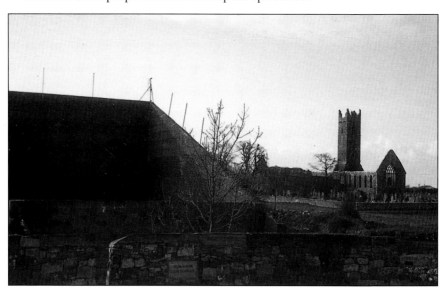

Claregalway handball alley with the Friary in the background

Chapter 14: The Famine

The period between 1845 and 1847 is generally referred to as 'the famine'. How it affected the parish of Claregalway can be seen from the census figures between 1841 and 1851.

The principal food of the ordinary people was the potato. When this crop became diseased the results were tragic. At that time early marriages were the norm and usually implied large families. The custom was that the already small farm was sub divided to provide the newly weds with their own division. After a number of such partitions the units became completely uneconomic. In order to survive it became necessary to rent small parcels solely for the growing of potatoes. These conacre lettings from the local landlord usually meant that he profited the most. Landless farm workers were known to accept a small conacre plot in lieu of wages. At that time it was customary for most households to keep a pig. This animal was fed on scraps. However as even this food became scarce the number of pigs dropped off.

Naturally the parish of Claregalway did not fare any better that the rest of the country. In the Barony of Clare some 18 families comprising 299 people were lost in a 10-year period. During the same period, in the Barony of Dunkellin part of the parish, only 198 families out of a total of 422 survived. In the 10 year period between 1841 and 1851 we find that the number of families fell from 671 to 529 or from a population of 4,042 to 2,763. Therefore the parish lost almost one third of its parishioners in that period.

The Famine

How the Townlands fared:

Townland	1841			1851			Change
	Male	Female	Total	Male	Female	Total	
Cahergowan	319	285	604	246	226	472	*-132*
Caherlea	24	29	53	23	21	44	*-9*
Carnmore East	1	2	3	12	12	24	*21*
Carnmore West	292	295	587	170	178	348	*-239*
Claregalway	84	75	159	66	67	133	*-26*
Cloughaun	26	25	51	10	11	21	*-30*
Cloon	91	96	187	53	61	114	*-73*
Cloonacauneen	19	15	34	22	19	41	*7*
Cregboy	163	151	314	90	86	176	*-138*
Curraghmore	3	2	5	4	4	8	*3*
Gortadooey	60	53	113	55	53	108	*-5*
Gortatleva	54	53	107	44	45	89	*-18*
Gortcloonmore	54	43	97	37	27	64	*-33*
Kiltrogue	81	88	169	44	32	76	*-93*
Kiniska	104	77	181	81	74	155	*-26*
Knockdoemore	59	58	117	31	30	61	*-56*
Loughgeorge	34	26	60	21	15	36	*-24*
Lakeview	52	55	107	26	35	61	*-46*
Lecarrowmore	50	37	87	7	9	16	*-71*
Lissarulla	56	45	101	50	51	101	*0*
Lydacan	54	69	123	49	73	122	*-1*
Montiagh North	4	5	9	3	2	5	*-4*
Montiagh South	149	140	289	110	128	238	*-51*
Mullaghruttery	59	49	108	21	34	35	*-73*
Peake	53	51	104	9	13	22	*-82*
Pollaghrevagh	39	35	74	16	13	29	*-45*
Rockwood	3	3	6	2	2	4	*-2*
Rooaunmore	28	26	54	22	13	55	*1*
Waterdale	70	69	139	47	58	105	*-34*
Totals:	**2,085**	**1,957**	**4,042**	**1,371**	**1,392**	**2,763**	***-1279***

The Famine

When people were finally reduced to absolute poverty a 'solution' was formulated which consisted of the construction of workhouses. There was one such structure to each poor law district and it was capable of housing 1,000 persons. However in order to be accepted it was a condition that you would surrender your cabin and plot of land. Unfortunately this meant that when the famine ended very many people were left by the roadside. In most instances the surrendered cabins were demolished when their occupants entered the workhouses. This was an easy task, as the vast majority of these structures comprised a one-room mud walled cabin. Between 1841 and 1851 some 173 houses disappeared from the locality. The workhouses in the general area were situated at Ballinasloe, Clifden, Gort, and Loughrea. People from Claregalway were accommodated either in Galway or Tuam.

The Famine

The table below sets out the position regarding houses between 1841 and 1851.

Townland	1841	1851
Cahergowan	96	89
Caherlea	7	6
Carnmore East	1	5
Carnmore West	108	63
Claregalway	19	19
Cloughaun	8	4
Cloon	27	23
Cloonacauneen	5	5
Cregboy	55	31
Curraghmore	1	2
Gortadooey	18	15
Gortatleva	16	15
Gortcloonmore	16	13
Kiltrogue	31	12
Kiniska	29	33
Knockdoemore	20	11
Loughgeorge	8	3
Lakeview	18	12
Lecarrowmore	14	3
Lissarulla	16	15
Lydacan	18	18
Montiagh North	1	1
Montiagh South	47	43
Mullaghruttery	17	8
Peake	21	5
Pollaghrevagh	10	4
Rockwood	1	1
Rooaunmore	9	7
Waterdale	24	22
Totals:	661	488

The Famine

People from Montiagh said that the famine did not affect them as badly as in other parts of the parish, due to the nature of the soil. They were then sowing in boggy land and the blight did not seem to be as harmful there.

The British Government arranged to have 'relief works' undertaken in order to provide employment for labourers. With this in view a Lt. CS Miller was sent to the Claregalway area to examine possible schemes and to have further monies made available for road works, should he consider it to be necessary. In 1848 very few people seem to have been employed but when the drainage of the Corrib began it was expected that more people would be employed.

Claims for monies for schemes were lodged but in fact were rarely approved or if sanctioned were for sums far less than had been applied for. An application from the Barony of Clare for approximately £17,000 only merited approval for about £6,000. However this appears to be very generous as another sanction of £105 was given in response to a further request for £17,000. The Barony of Dunkellin got very poor responses to requests for £27,000 and £42,000 as they only received £311 and £100 respectively.

In reply to a request for more details on Claregalway, the receiving officer, James Morris reported the following:

Estimated area in statute acres	*11,514*
Net annual value to P.L.V.	*£4,423-10-0*
Population in 1841	*3,873*
Highest number of persons given	
Food in one day	*2,966*
Number of persons on relief list	*1,942*

The figure of 2,966 people in one day equates to most of the parish and would appear to be a once off only. In 1848 in one week only, 450 'paupers' were relieved at a cost of £15-3-5 _. In a report sent to Britain it was stated that from a third to a half of the potatoes were useless. The people were now only planting potatoes and the survival of the population was now dependent on a good yield. The turnips had generally failed and the small holders could not be persuaded to grow them as they expected that the potato disease would disappear. The wheat and oats were giving a very poor return, specially the wheat. Barley too was poor with the grain falling from the ear and some areas were affected by smut.

A goodly number of farmers had only themselves to blame in later years as they used blighted potatoes as seed thereby spreading the disease to the new crop.

Chapter 15: Townlands and Placenames

Introduction

Claregalway Parish, as we know it today, covers a total area of over 12,000 statute acres. Historically, Ireland was divided into counties, which were subdivided into Baronies. Baronies were formed in the 16th century, and used for administrative purposes up until the late 19th century. The majority of Claregalway (7,080 acres approx.) lies in the Barony of Dunkellin and the remainder is contained within the Barony of Clare.

Claregalway itself is divided into 30 official townlands, used for present day administration. Townlands vary in size and most do not contain a town, indeed some lack inhabitants. Natural features such as the Clare River or manmade structures such as the N17 (Galway to Tuam) main road sometimes define their boundaries. The official townland names may not always be used, as locals may still use the older Irish townlands and placenames. As is in the case all over Ireland, our local placenames are derived from various sources. Most are very old and have been passed down through the centuries by word of mouth or manuscript. These factors and the anglicised versions of Gaelic names have led to some placenames being lost or bearing little or no resemblance to the present features. Names such as Curraghmore (large boggy place) or Gortatleva (field of the hill) have changed only in spelling over the years.

In the following listings we have described Claregalway using the official townlands, along with some facts and local features. We have attempted to include as many local names as possible and have had to pick the most common spellings for some names. Included under each townland is the total area1 and its value2 under the Griffiths Poor Law Valuation of 1855; also included are the family names that appear in the same Valuation.

[1] **Area is given in acres, roods and perches where 1 acre = 4 roods = 160 perches**

[2] **Value is given in old pounds, shillings and pence; £1 = 20s = 240d**

The following is a list of the Claregalway townlands:

Carnmore
Carnmore East
Carnmore West

Townlands and Placenames

Caherlea
Cahergowan / Summerfield
Claregalway
Cloon
Cloonacauneen
Cloughaun
Cregboy
Curraghmore
Gortadooey
Gortatleva
Gortcloonmore
Kiltrogue
Kiniska
Knockdoemore
Lakeview
Lissarulla
Loughgeorge
Lecarrowmore
Lydacan
Montiagh South
Montiagh North
Mullaghruttery
Peake
Pollaghrevagh
Rockwood
Rooaunmore
Waterdale

Carnmore/Cairn Mór

(Great heap of stones)

Area: 180 acres 3 roods 24 perches
Poor Law Valuation: £19 10^s 6^d
Landlord: Valentine Blake
Population 1851: 12 people in 3 houses
Family Names: Kenny and Rabbitt
Placenames: Gortaleasa

Carnmore is at the extreme eastern side of the Parish adjoining Athenry along the Monivea Road where Johnny Greaney now lives. The land is mainly good.

The boundary between the Barony of Dunkellin and the Barony of Clare went through the east end of Carnmore (about where Greaney Glass is now). Farmers

- 187 -

Townlands and Placenames

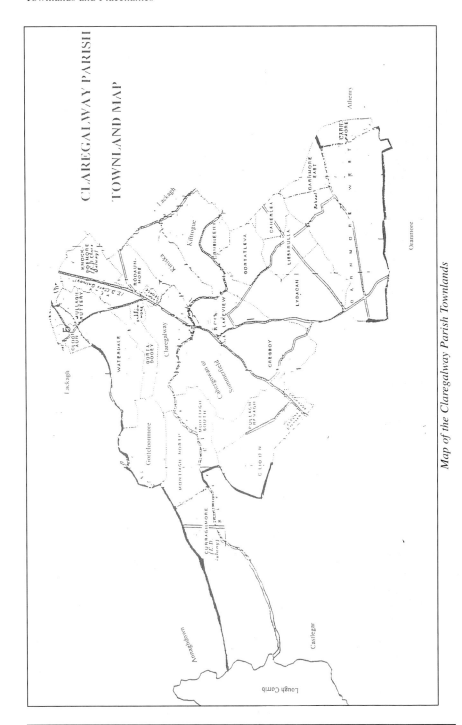

Map of the Claregalway Parish Townlands

who had their land in the Clare Barony were counted as being in Carnmore West, those whose land straddled the boundary and had some in each Barony were counted as being in Carnmore East while those who had all their land in the Barony of Dunkellin were counted as being in just Carnmore.

Aerial view of the Claregalway crossroads about 1970. The old church can barely be seen in the bottom right hand corner. Shows Hession's shop and Hughes' old house and shop.

Carnmore East/Cairn Mór

(Great heap of stones)

Area: 221 acres 3 roods 25 perches
Poor Law Valuation 1855: £7 18s 0d
Landlord: Valentine Blake
Population 1851: 24 people in 5 houses
Family Names: Fox, Hynes, Rooney and Veitch.
Placenames: Sean Bhaile Beag and Lochán Buí.

Carnmore East is on the extreme eastern side of the Claregalway Parish adjoining Lackagh and the Athenry parishes. The land here is of mixed quality. There is a turlough in the area and the remains of a small lisheen. Some stone tools were discovered in this area a few years ago.

Townlands and Placenames

There were traces of an old village in Foxes land near Hynes house and on the night of the big wind in 1839 the storm played havoc with the houses and a few years later the famine put an end to what houses remained.

Carnmore West/Cairn Mór

(Great heap of stones)
Area: 2041 acres 3 roods 29 perches
Poor Law Valuation 1855: £359 12^s 6^d
Landlord: Valentine Blake
Population 1851: 348 people in 63 houses
Family Names: Beatty, Behan, Burke, Butler, Carr, Cavanagh, Collins, Costello, Egan, Fahy, Finnegan, Ford, Fox, Grealish, Hanley, Higgins, Holland, Holmes, Hynes, Kelly, Kenny, Lardner, Linskey, Mahon, Morris, Quinn, Rabbitt, Rooney, Ruane, Rushe, Small and Walsh.
Placenames: Bearna an tSalann, Boithrín Tobar Núa, Caher, Clais Bhrein, Cloch Maol, Cnocán Dorethy, Cuinne Geal, Gortaleasa, Páirc Garbh and Páirc na Rasaí.

Carnmore West is the largest townland in the parish, stretching from the airport to Greaney Glass and lies between Glenascaul and Lydacan. In this townland is the airport, school, community centre and GAA pitch. The land is of good quality. There is a souterrain in the area and a number of ringforts.

There is also a *lisheen* or children's burial ground within the townland. This *lisheen* is in Eddie Hanley's field and was used as a burial ground for adults as well as children until about 1950. The *lisheen* is sited within a ringfort. There was also a Mass rock in this field but it was moved many years ago. While Mass was being said in secret, during Penal times, there used to be a man on guard to look out for the authorities. This field is one of the highest points in the parish from which there is a marvellous view. According to the old people if you had good eyesight you could see seven counties from that point – presumably on a clear day.

The remains of *Cloch Maol* castle can still be seen. There are burials around this castle where according to local tradition *"Seán agus trifichead Seáin"* are buried. There is also a monument of stones similar in form to a fort nearby.

Caherlea/Cathair Líath

(The grey fort)
Area: 147 acres 3 roods 36 perches
Poor Law Valuation 1855: £39 0^s 0^d
Landlord: H. Lynch
Population 1851: 44 people in 6 houses

Townlands and Placenames

Family Names: Collins, Duggan, Fox, Kerrigan and Melody.
Placenames:

Caherlea is one of the smaller townlands and it adjoins Lisheenavalla (which is in the Lackagh parish). Land is mainly good there and suitable for all kinds of farming. Taking the Irish translation of Cathair Líath to be a grey stone fort would indicate that there was some ruins or fortress in the area at one time but no visible evidence has been found.

Cahergowan/Cathair Ghabhain or Summerfield/ Páirc an tSamhraidh

(**Fort of the blacksmith/calves**)
Area: 841 acres 0 roods 25 perches
Poor Law Valuation 1855: £384 13^s 0^d
Landlord: Lord Clanmorris
Population 1851: 472 in 89 houses
Family Names: Boyle, Burke, Clanmorris, Cody, Cogwell, Conor, Corcuit, Cullinan, Donoghue, Duffy, Duggan, Egan, Fahy, Flaherty, Flesk, Ford, Fox, Gobbobs, Hession, Holland, Hughes, Joyce, Kelly, Lenihan, Lynskey, Moloney, Moran, Murphy, Prendergast, Tully, Walsh and Wren.
Placenames: Clogher, Casuala, Carrow Keel, Páircín na Bpoll, Poll na gCapall, Tobar Padraic, Cnocán Droighnean, Cúinne na Sceach, Cnocán Lurghan and Garaide an Uisce. (Tobar Padraic refers to an actual tobar or spring well that is located behind Dunleavy's shop.)

Cahergowan is unusual in that it has two official names, Summerfield and Cahergowan. Both are used but Cahergowan would be used more frequently. This townland is large and has always been heavily populated. The river Clare separates it from the townland of Claregalway and it stretches along the N17 as far as Pollaghrevagh and on the western side it adjoins Montiagh South.

Clogher or Clochár is an old name that indicates a monastic settlement. The Taylor and Skinner road map of 1777 shows Summerville Blake Esq. as the occupant of the big house. At the back of the ball alley there is an old ruin of a church and this was used as a burial ground until recently. There are two pubs and three shops in Cahergowan. The land is mainly arable with some outcrop of rock and hazel and some low-lying land that is liable to flooding. There is also some bog but no turf is cut there now.

Near Hessions shop, an old mile stone stands which is engraved with the figure '5' indicating that this spot is 5 Irish miles from Eyre Square, Galway.

- 191 -

Claregalway/Baile an Chláir/Baile Chláir na Gaillimhe
(Town of the plain. In the past, Claregalway was also known as Clare-yn-Dowl.)

The Claregalway village pump

Area: 585 acres 0 roods 0 perches
Poor Law Valuation 1855: £228 0^s 0^d
Landlord: Lord Clanmorris
Population 1851: 133 people in 19 houses
Family Names: Allen, Byrne, Casserley, Duggan, Finnerty and Ryan.
Placenames: Cloonbiggen, Móinín Ribeach, Léana, Cúinne Cam, Bóithrín O'Kane and Bóithrín Lachach.

The Claregalway townland stretches from the Claregalway bridge to the Garda barracks and westward along the river as far as Gortcloonmore. The village of Claregalway itself does not lie within this townland. The parish name was taken from this townland possibly because the original church was located on the grounds of the 13th century Franciscan Friary, one of the main landmarks in the area. Claregalway's present-day graveyard surrounds the ruins of the friary. A short distance from the friary stands the remains of a 15th century castle, overlooking the Clare River. The Nine Arches Bridge also lies within the Claregalway townland. A new landmark is the SMA house opposite the friary.

Cloonbiggen is a better known name for part of Claregalway townland. A reference exists in an article about the friary in 1387 when six acres of land in Cloynbiggan were given to the friars.

There is also a small river, which rises from a spring near Loughgeorge, and it flows through Cloonbiggen into the Clare River. There are some spring wells in this area also. One is known as Tobar Dubh. The land is mainly good but some of it is low lying and liable to flooding in winter.

The origin of the name Claregalway is not clear. Variations used in the past include Baile An Chláir meaning Town of the Plank, (used for crossing the river) and Town of the Plain. Baile Chláir Na Gaillimhe is a direct translation of Claregalway and has been in use for the last 80 years.

Cloon /Cluain

(Meadow)

Area: 440 acres 3 roods 7 perches
Poor Law Valuation: £100 4^s 0^p
Landlord: James Ffrench
Population 1851: 187 people in 27 houses
Family Names: Concannon, Connor, Davock, Earner, Fahy, Feeney, Flesk, Garvey, Higgins, Kelly, Mannion, Moran, Reilly and Wall
Place Names:

Cloon is situated 2 miles from Claregalway village on the western side of the N17. It lies between the townlands of Cloonacauneen and Pollaghrevagh. Cloon and Pollaghrevagh are separated by a by-road, with Cloon lying to the left as you go into the area, although most people living along the boundary would actually use Cloon as their address.

The land within Cloon is classed as 233 acres being bog-land and the remaining 207 acres is fertile land suitable for all types of farming.

Cloonacauneen /Cluain an Chainin

(Meadow of the dust specks)

Area: 29 acres 0 roods 16 perches
Poor Law Valuation: £13 5^s 0^d
Landlord: Robert Faire
Population 1851: 41 people in 5 houses
Family Names: No record.
Place Names: 'Holmes Hill'

There is another townland of the same name in the Castlegar parish and both join at the top of Holmes' Hill. There are no houses there now. The land is of mixed quality. It lies next to the Cloon townland and the N17.

Cloughaun /Clochan

(River/Stepping Stone)

Area: 11 acres 1 roods 39 perches
Poor Law Valuation 1855: £9 10^s 0^d
Landlord: James S. Lambert
Population 1851: 21 people in 4 houses
Family Names: Golding, Nolana and Rabbitt.
Placenames:

Cloughaun townland is the smallest townland in the parish. In reality the townland is divided between the parishes of Claregalway and Lackagh. The roads to Liscananaun and Baunmore from Baunmore Cross divide the townland and parishes. The land here is of mixed quality. There are no traces of any historical monument in the townland in the present day.

Thatching in progress at Skerret's old house in Claregalway

Cregboy/Creag Bui/Creig Bui
(Yellow Rock)

Area: 676 acres 0 roods 8 perches
Poor Law Valuation: £222 6^s 0^d
Landlord: James Galbraith
Population 1851: 176 people in 31 houses
Family names in 1855: Boyle, Burke, Casserly, Tully, Hession, Corenit, Maloney, McDonagh, Morris, Murphy Quinn, Samways, Daly, Heany, Moran, Long, Giles, Connolly, Wade, Kearns and Kelly.
Placenames: Baile Fanach, Gort na Guaillini

Baile Fanach (Bally Faunagh) is an old name for Cregboy and there is evidence of it being used in 1847. It was used by the teachers of Claregalway School up until 1960. There are several definitions in the dictionary for 'fanach' such as aimless, wandering and futile. Gort na Guaillini is the old name of the part of Cregboy that joins Lydacan, where the Fahys and Shaughnessy family presently live. It is defined as 'fields with triangles'.

The land is of mixed quality. Some very good and dry, suitable for all kinds of farming and some with rocky out-crops with hazel.

Townlands and Placenames

Cregboy is situated off the N17 and extends from the Claregalway/Oranmore road as far as the Kiltulla road.

The first 'milestone' in the Parish was standing near Ruane's house, near the Kiltulla road, but was removed from there by the County Council. It was re-erected in 1998 at a different location nearby. This stone is inscribed with the figure '4'.

Curraghmore/Currach Mór

(Large swampy field)

Area: 792 acres 3 roods 11 perches
Poor Law Valuation 1855: £30 0^s 0^d
Landlord: Lord Clanmorris
Population in 1851: 8 people in 2 houses
Family Names: Burke and Feeney.
Placenames: Curraghline.

Curraghmore is a large townland lying at the most westerly part of the parish and running as far as the shores of Lough Corrib. At present it has no human inhabitants. The Galway to Headford road known as the Curraghline runs through Curraghmore. It was built during the mid 19th century, prior to which boats ferried people across the Cregg river and the Clare River too.

The Feeney family was the last family to live there. They left around 1960. The Clare River runs alongside Curraghmore and as the land is low lying it is prone to flooding in winter or indeed any time of severe rainfall.

Most of Curraghmore is peat bog. Although a lot of turf is harvested there every summer, a lot of the area is virgin bogland known as *Gaelige* as *Eanach*. The remainder of the land is good pastureland in summer.

Gortadooey /Gort a Dubha / Gort an Dúaigh

(Black field)

Area: 229 acres 2 roods 26 perches
Poor Law Valuation 1855: £42 0^s 0^d
Landlord: James S. Lambert
Population 1851: 108 people in 15 houses.
Family Names: Collins, Concannon, Cassidy, Duggan, Grealy, Glynn, Fahy, Henegan, Lambert, Lenehan and Moloney.
Placenames: Ceann na Gairde, Crochan na Creithe, Tolan Ruid and Cappagh Eoghan.

Gortadooey lies between Waterdale and Claregalway off the Mullaghruttery road. Gortadooey got its name from the land in the area because when it was dug it was blackish in colour. Land there is mainly of good quality although some is

- 195 -

liable to flooding.

There was supposed to be a well in the area that had a dark dye which, when mixed with other material substances made a type of ink. It is said the friars in Claregalway used it for writing. James Greally was the herdsman for the landlord and his descendants lived in the same house until about 1980.

Greally's old herds house in Gortadooey

Gortatleva / Gort an tSleibhe
(Field of the Mountain)
Area: 336 acres 2 roods 27 perches
Poor Law Valuation: £106 13^s 0^d
Landlord: Andrew H. Lynch
Population 1851: 89 people in 15 houses
Family Names: Bodkin, Cavanagh, McDonagh, Qualter, Walsh, Williams, Hughes, O'Brien, Carr and Murphy.
Placenames: Garraigh Raven

There was a pub in this townland in the past, across the road from Walshs. Most of the land is of good quality and is suitable for all types of farming, but also has some low-lying land, which is liable to flooding. Gortatleva is situated next to Lydacan.

Townlands and Placenames

Gortcloonmore /Gort Clúain Mor

(The big meadow)

<u>Area</u>: 517 acres 2 roods 39 perches
<u>Poor Law Valuation 1855</u>: £50 10^s 0^d
<u>Landlord</u>: James S Lambert
<u>Population 1851</u>: 64 people in 13 houses
<u>Family Names</u>: Duggan, Feeney, Greally, Noon and Qualter.
<u>Placenames</u>: An Loch bheag

Gortcloonmore adjoins the Waterdale River on the north side and Montiagh North at the other end. Gortcloonmore is mainly low lying but has a mixture of land ranging from good grazing pastures to bog. Turf is cut there and in the past it supplied many households in the parish with winter fuel. It has a small population today, with one family home inhabited, another not in everyday use and the Autistic Society/Western Health Board have a house and farm there as well. During the early 20th century, when the Waterdale Estate was divided, some Gortcloonmore families moved to land they got in the division.

Kiltrogue /Cill Tróg

(Trog's church)

<u>Area</u>: 98 acres 0 roods 0 perches
<u>Poor Law Valuation 1855</u>: £49 14^s 0^d
<u>Landlord</u>: Lord Bishop of Cashel
<u>Population in 1851</u>: 76 people in 12 houses
Family Names: Currane, Duffy, Egan, Greaney, Kelly, Kenny, Kyne, Moylan, O'Dea and Ryan.
<u>Placenames</u>: Tonn an Cnoic

Similar to Cloughaun, the Kiltrogue townland is also a strange division. The townland is split into land that is in the Claregalway parish and the remainder is in Lackagh. Of the land in Claregalway, the area is in two parts, both of which are fully surrounded by the Lackagh part of Kiltrogue.

The land is good and suitable for all kinds of farming. Kiltrogue got its name from St. Trog who had a church there, only the bare remains of which survive to this day. A lisheen is also close by. Kiltrogue Castle, which is still in good order, lies in Lackagh parish.

- 197 -

Townlands and Placenames

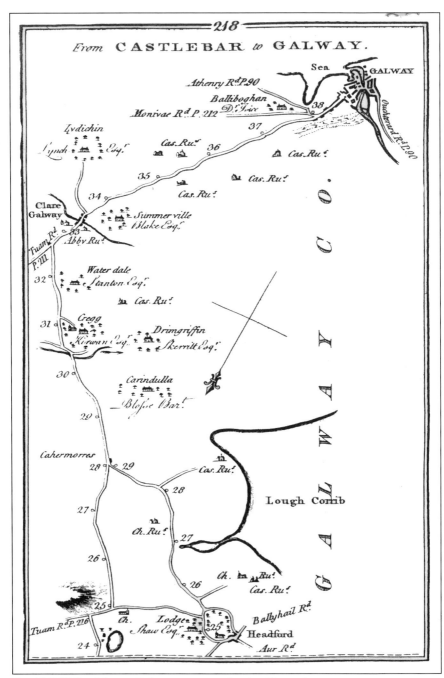

An old 1783 Castlebar to Galway route map showing Claregalway

Townlands and Placenames

Kiniska /Cinn Uisce
(Water's head / River mouth)

<u>Area</u>: 505 acres 0 roods 22 perches
<u>Poor Law Valuation 1855</u>: £192 5^s 0^d
<u>Landlord</u>: Lord Clanmorris
<u>Population 1851</u>: 155 people in 33 houses
<u>Family Names</u>: Burke, Casserley, Commins, Connell, Kelly, Long, Nalty and Shaughnessy.
<u>Placenames</u>: Bun an Uisce, Caraun (Carán), Pollanrumpa and Tón an Cnoic.

Kiniska adjoins the Clare River and Kiltrogue. The quality of land is mainly good with some low-lying land beside Kiniska River. Kiniska River rises, as the name would suggest at Bun an Uisce and joins the Clare River about one mile away. There is a children's burial ground not far from Bun an Uisce and the last children were buried at the turn of the century. There is a souterrain or cave near the village.

Lord Clanmorris retained 18 acres for his own use for hunting. It was described as a fox cover in the Griffiths Valuation of 1855; that area may have been the wood that was on Pat Duggan's land until about 1953 when it was cut down. The herdsman at that time was Patrick Nalty.

Knockdoemore/Cnoc Tuadh Mór
(Hill of the big axe)

<u>Area</u>: 269 acres 1 roods 30 perches
<u>Poor Law Valuation 1855</u>: £86 11^s 0^p
<u>Landlord</u>: William Burke
<u>Population 1851</u>: 61 people in 11 houses
<u>Family Names</u>: Bane, Browne, Comer, Connell, Lardner and Pearse.
<u>Placenames</u>: Tinkers Lane and Baile Úi Chonaill.
<u>Historical sites</u>: Enclosure and Ringfort.

Knockdoemore is situated to the east of the N17. The land is mainly very good with some rocky outcrops. Knockdoemore is at the base of where the famous *Battle of Knockdoe* was fought in 1504.

Tinkers Lane runs through Knockdoemore from the N17 to the Roscommon road. Baile Úi Chonaill has been associated a lot with the O'Connell families. Thomas Browne was the herdsman for the landlord in 1855.

Lakeview / Radharc na Locha

<u>Area</u>: 352 acres 3 roods 18 perches
<u>Poor Law Valuation 1855</u>: £157 7^s 0^d

Landlord: James Galbraith
Population in 1851: 61 people in 12 houses
Family Names: Hession, Galway, Commons, Duggan, Cordial, Morris, Lynch, Small, Murphy and Giles.
Placenames: Droim Na Gaoithe, Turloch Bréige and Bóithrín De Burca.

Lakeview is the name of the townland where the present church, school and leisure centre lie. The old post office, which was owned by the Cahill family until 1927 was also in this townland. This was situated across the road from Dunleavey's bar, not far from the Nine Arches Bridge. Local knowledge tells us of a church situated in the same area in the past but very little is known about it.

Most of the land is of good quality with some low lying land near the river which floods in very wet weather when the Clare River floods the surrounding land, hence the name "Turloch Breige" (False Lake). "Droim Na Gaoithe" is the name on the Ordnance Survey maps. Radharc Na Locha is a direct translation of Lakeview.

Lissarulla / Lios a Rúla

(Ploughed fort)

Area: 305 acres 3 roods 20 perches
Poor Law Valuation 1855: £118 7^s 0^d
Landlord: Andrew H Lynch
Population 1851: 101 people in 15 houses
Family Names: Murphy, Hanley, Qualter, Finnerty, Culkeen and Cunneer.
Placenames: Ballymurphy and Ballinacreg.

Lissarulla lies between Lydacan and Caherlea. Lissarulla is the official name on the Ordnance Survey maps covering Ballymurphy and Ballinacreg but is not used by locals as often as the unofficial ones.

Ballymurphy or *Baile Uí Mhurchú* got its name from all the Murphys who lived there. It is also the more commonly used name by locals to this day. Ballinacreg or *Baile Na Creige* is not an official townland either but it is on the Ordnance Survey maps as a recognised village name.

There is a ruin of an old castle near Ballymurphy and also the ruins of an old settlement cluster.

Loughgeorge / Leacht Seoirse

(George's stone)

Area: 31 acres 3 roods 38 perches
Poor Law Valuation 1855: £20 15^s 0^d
Landlord: Directors of Alliance Insurance company

Townlands and Placenames

Population 1851: 36 people in 3 houses
Family Names: O'Brien and Scully.
Placenames: Cimín.

Loughgeorge is located along the N17 (the Galway to Tuam road)

All the land is good and while the local Garda Barracks is not in Loughgeorge itself, the Garda District is known as Loughgeorge. There is a well-known pub and restaurant named Kynes Central Tavern. The Galway GAA football board has purchased a field in Loughgeorge to be used for training county teams.

Loughgeorge or Leacht Seoirse means George's Stone and it is believed that a man named George fell from his horse, was killed and is buried under a large stone in the area. The Cimín is the name of the field across the road from Kynes Restaurant. It was reputed to have been used as a cattle pound in the past.

The third milestone is standing in this townland and is inscribed with the figure '6'.

Lecarrowmore / Leath Ceathru Mór

(Big half quarter)

Area: 47 acres 1 roods 20 perches
Poor Law Valuation 1855: £17 10^s 0^d
Landlord: Lord Dunsandle
Population 1851: 16 people in 3 houses
Family Names: O'Brien, Cassidy and Kirrane.
Placenames:

Lecarrowmore is on the left after you pass the Garda Barracks on the Mullacuttra road. Land is mainly good.

Up to the last century, a ceathru represented a unit of measure of about 16 acres and was commonly used in describing the size of farmlands.

Lydacan / Lideachán/ Laighdeacán

(Small triangular fields)

Area: 852 acres 2 roods 26 perches
Poor Law Valuation 1855: £280 7^s 0^d
Landlord: Andrew H Lynch
Population 1851: 122 people in 18 houses
Family Names: Collins, Fahy, McDonald, Malony, Cullinan, Walsh, Gardinder, Glynn, Flesk, Flynn, Dillon, Kemple, Sheridan, O'Dea and Qualter.
Placenames: An Fheilm, Cathair na Finneoige, Cnoc na Leacht, Cnocán Aoibeann, Geata na Geann, Gort na gCuailíní, Páirc an Asail, Rock Road and Tónruadh.

Townlands and Placenames

Historical Sites: Ringfort, Lisheen, Castle and Souterrain

This townland is unique within the parish in that it was a parish at one stage with a church. Lydacan lies between Lakeview and Gortatleva and extends as far as the River Clare.

One feature of the area was the landlord's house. The house was burned in 1922 and the occupants, the Greated family, moved away and bought a farm in Co. Wexford. Their land in Lydacan was divided among the local farmers at the time. Also beside the Lydacan Castle was a constabulary hut. The land is mostly fertile with some acres of rocky outcrops and has hazel growing there.

Cnoc Na Leacht is the Irish name for Lydacan Hill. It got its name from an old custom of building small heaps of stones inside the wall while a corpse was been taken to the church.

Cnocan Aoibeann is the name of the fields owned by John Fahy and is situated at the back of the commercial truck garage.

Geata Na Geann was the name of the gate that was at the back entrance to Greated's Castle. This gate was in turn given to Canon Moran to be used at the entrance to the old Claregalway Church and were to be seen there until 1974 when the church and walls were knocked.

Tonrnadh 'Tonroe' is that part of Lydacan between Carnmore and Lydacan. The area gets its name from the red ferns to be seen locally.

Cathair Na Finneoige is the Irish name for the old fort beside the rockroad at Lydacan.

Páirc an Asail: Name of the field beside Lydacan castle where the Greateds kept a few asses.

Montiagh South / Mointeach Theas

(House of turf)

Area: 331 acres 2 roods 23 perches
Poor Law Valuation 1855: £84 5ˢ 0ᵈ
Landlord: Lord Clanmorris
Population 1851: 238 people in 43 houses
Family Names: Burke, Collins, Duggan, Glynn, Heavey, Lenihan, Moran, Noone, Thorpey, Keany and Wall.
Placenames: Leana, An Barlan, Garrai Bán, Garrai Beag, Gort Clúain mBuilan, Oilean na mBad, Oilean Fada, Bearna bHuí, an Cheibh, Garrai na Móna and Boithrín na Blathaí.

The townland of Montiagh is located along the Clare River between Cahergowan, Cloon and Pollaghrevagh and at the extreme westside it adjoins Sylaun in the parish of Castlegar. As in the parish of Claregalway, Irish was the

Townlands and Placenames

An aerial view of Claregalway village taken in 1996 from the Montiagh direction. More houses have been built since then.

spoken language but it survived more so in Montiagh than in other parts of the parish.

There was a hedge school here as well in the past. Tomásín was the name of the teacher and his reward for the teaching of the pupils was vegetables and groceries.

There was also a *lisheen* there; no child has been buried there since the 1930s.

As the river is so close to the village, boats were very important in the past for the transporting of turf, hay and other products. They were also used for shooting and fishing. The type of boat that was used was a flat bottom boat, which was suitable for travelling over flooded land.

There are none of those boats in use now, only the standard lake boats. Fishing was a very important part of the lifestyle in Montiagh in the past. Salmon were very plentiful then and the catch would be transported to hotels in Galway City, hidden in cartloads of turf.

The land is mainly low lying except where the village is situated, and in winter is liable to flooding from the nearby Clare River. Most of the land is good pasture. There is also some bog, and turf is still cut there up to the present time.

Bringing the turf home. Taken around the 1930s, this photo shows turf being transported on the Clare River at Montiagh. Shown are: Sally Concannon (née Moran), her son John Concannon, Catherine Duggan (née Giles) and her husband Valentine Duggan. In the boat is Sean Ó'Noone.

Townlands and Placenames

Montiagh North / Mointeach Thaudh

(House of turf)

Area: 454 acres 2 roods 17 perches
Poor Law Valuation 1855: £48 0^s 0^d
Landlord: Lord Clanmorris
Population 1851: 5 people in 1 house
Family Names: Duggan
Placenames:

The Clare River separates Montiagh North from Montiagh South. The land is low lying and floods in the winter but it is good pastureland in summer. There is also a bog there and part of the cut away bog (200 acres) was acquired by the Forestry in 1960 and planted. It is now a large wood. Turf is still cut in the remaining bog. Montiagh North adjoins Curraghmore to the west and Gortcloonmore to the North. There hasn't been anybody living there for the past hundred years.

Mullaghruttery / Mullacuttra / Mullach Otraigh / Mullach Chrotaire

(Hill of the red cat)

Area: 180 acres 0 roods 16 perches
Poor Law Valuation 1855: £74 11^s 0^d
Landlord: James S. Lambert
Population 1851: 55 people in 8 houses.
Family Names: Connell, Glynn, Golding, Herwood, Hogan, Keane, Hughes, Lambert and Lyons.
Placenames:

It is told in a story from Irish folklore that the name Mullacuttra originated from Mullach a 'Chait Rua' which was a Great Red Cat that guarded a treasure buried in the area in olden times.

Land is arable, suitable for grazing and tillage. Mullaghruttery is on the right as you go to Corrandulla. It adjoins Peake. A feature of the area is the striking stone walls dividing the fields.

Peake / Péic

(High point)

Area: 220 acres 2 roods 0 perches
Poor Law Valuation 1855: £85 0^s 0^d
Landlord: William Burke
Population 1851: 22 people in 5 houses

Townlands and Placenames

Family Names: Browne, Carthy, Forde and Griffin.
Placenames:

The townland is situated on the left as you go to Tuam after passing Loughgeorge. Land is arable and suitable for grazing and tillage. There are very nice stone walls dividing the fields here.

Pollaghrevagh / Pollach Ríabach
(Rough hollow)

Area: 417 acres 3 roods 28 perches
Poor Law Valuation 1855: £92 3ˢ 0ᵈ
Landlord: James Ffrench
Population 1851: 29 people in 4 houses
Family Names: Ffrench, Hardiman, O'Brien, Nohilly, Nolan, Wall, Moran, Kineen and Quinn.
Placenames:

Pollaghrevagh lies between Cahergowan and Cloon off the N17. Most of the land is fertile, and there is also some woodland and bog. Locals seldom use the name Pollaghrevagh.

Old number '4' milestone at Pollaghrevagh on the Galway road, indicating four Irish miles to Galway

Rockwood / Leach na Coille
(Rock in the wood)

Area: 41 acres 0 roods 34 perches
Poor Law Valuation 1851: £45 0ˢ 0ᵈ
Landlord: John Galway
Family Names 1855: Galway
Placenames: Holmes hill
Population 1851: 4 people in 1 house

Rockwood is situated on the left as one travels into Galway from Claregalway. It begins at Kiltulla Road and ends at the top of Holmes hill. The only house in this area at the time was the

- 206 -

landlord's house. This is the last remaining landlord's house in the parish to this day. In recent times the house went into disrepair for some years until the Divilly family bought it and restored it to its former glory.

Rooaunmore / Ruadh án Mór
(Large area of red ferns)
<u>Area</u>: 220 acres 2 roods 0 perches
<u>Poor Law Valuation 1855</u>: £72 11s 0d
<u>Landlord</u>: Lessor
<u>Population in 1851</u>: 35 people in 7 houses
<u>Family Names</u>: Hughes, Gaynor, Mooney, O'Brien, Smith, McGrath and Clancy.
<u>Placenames</u>:

Rooaunmore is situated on the Roscommon road adjoining Kiniska, Loughgeorge and Knockdoemore. In the past there were very few houses in the area as the landlord retained all the land because of its good quality. Due to the size of the fields, horse races were held there in the early part of this century.

Here in Rooaunmore is the only remaining forge to be found in the parish. It has been in the Smith family since the last century. Presently Michael Smith is the owner and he continues with this trade to this day.

Waterdale / Eochaill
(Yew wood)

Arched water gully in Waterdale

Area: 679 acres 3 roods 0 perches
Poor Law Valuation 1855: £225 12^s 0^d
Landlords: Lambert owned 610 acres 1 roods 34 perches. Blake owned 69 acres 1 roods 0 perches.
Population in 1851: 105 people in 22 houses
Family Names: Blake, Carley, Cullinan, Duggan, Glenane, Keeney, Moran, Walsh and Golding.
Placenames: Leana Clocha, Baile Na Móna, Páirc na Ceartan and Waterdale River.

The old name Eochaill meant yew wood and bears no resemblance to the English name Waterdale that was given to the area by the Anglo Normans who owned the land. There is another name for part of Waterdale known as Leana Clocha; the Keany family live in that area now. In the past many families lived in Leana Clocha but when the land was divided among the tenants, some built their new houses in Waterdale.

Waterdale townland was once one whole estate owned by Lady Lambert. She lived in Waterdale house. There was a church beside the house. The land was divided in 1908 when Lady Lambert left. There are very good examples of an old ring fort and also a *lisheen* - a fairies field. Over half the land is of good quality with the remainder bog or low-lying land liable to flooding.

The fourth milestone in the parish is situated near the entrance to Waterdale village. This stone is inscribed with the figure '7'.

Keaney's thatched house in Leana na Clocha in Waterdale, reputed to be the oldest inhabited thatch house in Connacht

Chapter 16: The Church and Parish Priests

Early History

As we approach the dawn of the second millennium, the parish of Claregalway has one church, a parish priest, and one curate, catering for an ever-growing population. However, should the population explosion that is now taking place, due to the influx of an increasing number of suburbanites, be sustained, we might again be blessed with two churches, as we had in the eighteenth century, prior to the establishment of the parish boundary as we now know it. The parish church of Claregalway was situated in Lakeview, adjacent to the present church, while the parish of "Lydecane," which is currently spelt "Lydacan" had its church in Cregboy.

When the history of this millennium was being recorded in the so-called "Dark Ages," the parish of Claregalway did not exist in its present form. Records show that in 1484, the then Archbishop of Tuam gave the parish of St. Nicholas in Galway, which had been attached to his diocese since 1324, the status of "exempt jurisdiction". Why he decided to give this parish a type of independence is unsure, but what is known is that he subsequently annexed the Parish of St. James at Balenclear (now Baile an Chlair). Eventually these latter territories and others were assimilated, until a district was arrived at which corresponds basically to the present diocese of Galway. When Pope Innocent VIII ratified the Archbishop's decision, it freed Galway and Claregalway, both originally part of the Annaghdown diocese, from the Tuam Archdiocese. In earlier centuries Tuam had been at loggerheads with Annaghdown, which had long striven for its own identity.

Before this independence was bestowed upon Claregalway, information on priests in the parish is scarce. Among the names recorded in the late fourteenth or early fifteenth century are:

David Valensis	
James Cachyr	1418
Cormac O'Callanayn	1419
Urmanus O'Madagayn	1419
Brandon Ymulcroyan	1429
Philip Macmaylayn	1430
Donald O'Mulcroyan	1430
John O'Douna	1480

Risteardus de Burgo 1492
Gilleduff O'Brouder 1648

It is recorded that Cormac O'Callanayn required a papal dispensation to qualify for ordination, as he was *"the son of an unmarried man and an unmarried mother."* He became the Canon of Annaghdown and then he was transferred to what was called the 'Vicarage' of Claregalway. An unverified story says that a son of his was later Parish Priest of Claregalway.

Matthew Lynch Fitz-Dominick

In the Register of Priests, who had to register in 1704 in accordance with the Act requiring them to do so, there is the following details for Matthew Lynch Fitz-Dominick: Place of abode: Town of Galway. Age: 85. Parish: 'that part of the parish of Clare-Galway which lies in the East Liberties of Galway. Ordained: 29-3-1659 at Avilla in the kingdom of Spain by Don Martinus de Bonilla, Bishop of Avilla.

Mr. Nicholas Lynch

An extract from the 'Wardenship of Galway' contains a letter dated 12th September 1732, Louvain from Richard Hennessy to Rev. Patrick Bermingham, Warden in which the following words occur: *'Mr. Nich. Lynch is now sure of his parish of Claregalway. I lodged the money for the new bull in Sr. Francis' hands yesterday. You need not give yourself any more trouble about this affair.'*

In 1735 he was a candidate for the post of vicar in the college in Galway, as another document dated October 29 in the same year is summarised as follows: *'Protest by Father Nicholas Lynch, candidate for the post of vicar in Galway College in the room of Father Walter Bodkin deceased, against the election of Father Andrew Lynch Fitz-Thomas.'*

Fr. Walter Burke

The following letter was written on 9th April 1753 by John Kirwan to Rev. Augustine Kirwan about Fr. Burkes's successor: *'Uncle Kirwan wrote to you in his last letter that the parish of Claregalway was vacant by the death of Fr. Walter Burke and that he spoke to Fr. Antho. Blake about it for you who made answer he was mindful of you. In a few days after he called a chapter (meeting) and asked the vicars one by one according to seniority if they would accept it. They all refused till it came to Fr. Dominick Browne who accepted of it, which was contrary to our expectation.'*

The letter tells us the procedures followed in those days for the selecting of ministers.

The Church and Parish Priests

Fr. Dominick Browne

There is a manuscript in the National Library which contains the following extract dated 8th June 1765: *'Death, in Galway the Rev. Mr. Dominick Browne, a worthy Roman Catholic clergyman, parish priest of Minlough and Claregalway.'*

Rev. Thomas Kirwan

In the same manuscript as mentioned above, there is an extract dated 18th August 1767: *'Death at Galway, the Rev. Mr. Thomas Kirwan, a titular Vicar of that town and parish priest of the parish of Claregalway.'*

Fr. Andrew Kenny 1770-1805

Fr. Kenny left Ireland in 1750 for the University of Alcala where he studied in the College of St. George the Martyr and was ordained priest in the year 1756 by Augustinius Gonzales Piscador, D.D. Bishop of Tricomoriensis.

Fr.Andrew Kenny made a detailed return, dated 15th November 1800, that gives an invaluable picture of the workings of the parish at this period. The return was in reply to certain queries sent to parish priests by the Archbishop of Tuam, Rev. Edward Dillon at the request of the Government. He states that he was in charge of the parish for thirty years at that date. The return describes the parish income and also discusses regulations for marriage that were followed in Claregalway.

The following is a summary:

The number of houses in the parish at that time was 400, and the population was 2,150. To support the priest, as well as an assistant priest, the head of each household paid eight pence twice a year, at Christmas and Easter while the woman of the house was expected to contribute one penny. Young male wage earners paid two pence and young women who were working were expected to pay one penny. The total of these dues, along with some contributions from the better off, came to £35 for the whole parish. These twice-yearly contributions were made, or expected, when the people of each village congregated at a local house with their priest who heard confessions, distributed Holy Communion, instructed the adults and children in their faith, and settled disputes between neighbours. A different house was chosen for the next community meeting.

The parish priest's income from dues was augmented by payments made at christenings, marriages and deaths. An average of 150 christenings per year brought in about £11-10-0. Funeral offerings to the priest varied, with the more affluent paying half a guinea, while donations from the less well off varied from between half-a-crown and 6s 6d. A contribution was not expected from those of very poor means. The annual income from this source came to about £6. The annual income from wedding offerings yielded an average of £11-15-0, a not inconsiderable amount, which helped greatly towards the upkeep of the parish. At each wedding, the bridegroom placed half-a-crown on the collection plate at the end of the ceremony, while guests contributed anything from 6d to a shilling each. The priest collected anything from between five to thirty shillings for a marriage.

Fr. Kenny estimated his yearly income at approximately £66, of which a third, amounting to £22 was paid to his curate. This left him with the sum of £44, of which he spent £20 on grazing and fodder for his horse.

Fr. Kenny died in July 1822 at the age of 90, having being a priest for 66 years.

A tomb inside the Franciscan Friary

Fr. Tadhg Ó'Murchú (Thady Murphy) - 1805

Fr Murphy was P.P. at the time of the French landing at Killala and when the parish church was situated opposite the village parish-pump. There is a church document that references a parish of *'Ledicane'* with Thady Murphy as the parish priest. Was there, at least for a period a separate parish of Lydacan? If there was a parish in Lydacan then there must have been a parish church. There were reports that there was a church on the top of Lydacan Hill.

Fr. Ó'Murchú is buried in the Friary. His flagstone in the north transept has the following inscription:

"Lord have mercy on the Soul of the Rev. Thady
Murphy PP of Claregalway who departed this

The Church and Parish Priests

Life the 12th day of August 1805 aged 63 years.
This monument was erected by his brother
Geoffrey Murphy in memory of him. Requiscat in
Pace. Amen. "

The inscription is surmounted by a chalice and host with a biretta on either side.

Fr. Malachy Mannin 1816-1830

Fr. Mannin, fondly known as *'an sagart mór'*. An old document relating to the Wardenship of Galway states: *'10ᵗʰ September 1809, Claregalway. Petition of Honor Higgins, widow, to the warden complaining of Rev. Malachy Mannin, who possessed himself of ground she ought to have.'* The tradition about him in the parish was that he had a strong personality, although the above extract does not show him in a favourable light.

The following is an interesting story about him. The landlord of Cahergowan had made a seizure of cattle in the village for non-payment of rent and amongst the animals seized was a poor widow's cow. Fr. Mannin intervened but the bailiffs referred him to the landlord. The priest was getting his own milk supply from this cow but that is not suggested as the reason for his action. He set out for a place called 'Béal Áth na Lúb' in Co. Mayo on horseback. He received no satisfaction and thereupon he scraped the threshold of the house with the sole of his boot and departed. He had not gone very long when fire broke out and a messenger was sent after him to ask him to return and extinguish the fire but he refused. This occurred twice and the fire could not be extinguished – as soon as it was extinguished in one spot it broke out in another, until after twelve months the house was destroyed. The value of this story no doubt is that it gives evidence of a tradition that this priest was a fearless champion of the oppressed.

A sundial made of slate, which belonged to him, is preserved in the National Museum, Dublin. It bears the following inscription:

'Constructed by R. Molloy for the
Revᵈ. M.M. P.P. C.G. 22 August 1828'

In this inscription, M.M. are his initials and C.G. is for Claregalway.

In 1828, Fr. Thomas E. Gill was appointed administrator, to help the ageing parish priest, but whether he ever took up duty or not is uncertain. A Fr. B. Adams served in the parish but is not credited with the title of parish priest. His tenancy was perhaps a stopgap measure before the arrival of Fr. P. O'Kane.

Fr. P. O'Kane - 1838

He is said to have been suspended or at least removed from the parish for addiction to drink. He was a native of Kiniska. After his retirement he lived in a

The Church and Parish Priests

house down the (then) bóithrín leading to the new gate into the graveyard around the Friary. He is buried in the Friary.

In 1838 a direct exchange took place between the parishes of Spiddal and Claregalway, with Fr. O'Kane moving to the coast and the ill-fated Fr. Hosty transferring to this parish.

Fr. Thomas Hosty 1838-1848

Fr. Hosty's arrival coincided with construction of the new church, which was to replace the penal-day, thatched roof chapel, which was also situated in Lakeview, a short distance away. It was completed in 1838 but on the 6th January 1839, the 'Night of the Big Wind' also known as 'Oiche na gaoithe moire', the roof was blown off and the church was almost destroyed.

The priest and the people were shattered. They had given their money, time and voluntary labour over the years and now with many of their own homes destroyed they could not do or give any more. After reflecting on the matter for a time, Fr. Hosty concluded that the only solution was for him to go to America and appeal to the people there to help them in their plight. So he set off and travelled a good deal there, specially to cities where there were large numbers of Irish and, according to the story, collected a lot of money.

When his task was almost complete he began to prepare to return home. Things then were not the same as they are now and banks could not transact money between one country and another – it had to be carried by person. So Fr. Hosty arranged to have a friend from the parish who was already in America to travel home with him. The evening before they were due to sail home he withdrew the money he had collected from the bank and was to meet his friend at the quayside early next morning.

At that time according to the story a bell would be rung three times before a ship sailed. The first a while before the sailing, the second ringing a short time before but when the bell rang for the third time if a person was not already on board then he should get on immediately. His friend was already at the quayside before the first bell and the priest had not arrived. When he had not come by the second bell he was getting very worried. But when the third bell rang he still had not arrived. As he had an idea of the name of the place where he was staying for the night, a hotel not far from the port, he went and told his story to the police. They found the priest shot dead in a cellar underneath the hotel together with a couple of skeletons but there was no money.

It is related that when he failed to return, his sister, who had lived with him, was affected mentally and that she burned the parochial books. A successor was not appointed pending his expected return. Fr. Michael Kavanagh was appointed interim C.C. until the appointment of Fr. James Commins in 1848.

The Church and Parish Priests

Fr. James Cummins 1850-1862

Fr. Commins, who was noted for his support of agrarian reform, served until 1862, when he was transferred to Castlegar as P.P. He died in 1880.

Fr. Thomas Walsh 1865-1876

His successor, Fr. Thomas Walsh came from Rossmuc, where he had been parish priest for 25 years. He was said to have been a great preacher and to have tried to become a 'missioner', probably a Redemptorist, but for health reasons could not achieve it.

Fr. Walsh is remembered as an advocate of tenant rights in the Land War and may have been one of the priests involved in the Nolan and Trench Election Petition court case that was tried by the notorious Judge Keogh in 1872.

A Captain John Nolan had been elected to Parliament by a large majority. The local bishops and clergy had strongly supported him, chiefly because the family of his opponent, a Captain Trench, was active in Proselytism. Capt. Trench appealed and the petition was heard in Galway in April and May 1872. Judge Keogh found that Capt. Nolan had been elected by the undue influence and intimidation exercised on the voters by the Archbishop of Tuam (McHale), the bishops of Clonfert (Duggan) and Galway (McEvilly) and twenty nine named priests, such intimidation being in some cases exercised in the very churches, and awarded the seat to Capt. Trench.

Among the priests named was Fr. Thomas Walsh. Evidence was given by a parishioner, Edward Morris, who was active in the Trench interest, that Fr. Walsh, in the chapel on January 21st 1872, wished the people to vote for Capt. Nolan – those who had votes – and that he wished that those who voted for Capt. Trench 'would be Trenched'. He also called a man, called Martin Cullenan, 'a millers dog'. Cullenan was a bailiff of Lord Clanmorris and also a supporter of Trench. Lord Clanmorris was landlord of some of the parishioners and the allusion was to the fact that Cullenan acted as an agent for the purchase of corn for some miller in Galway.

Counsel for the other side in cross examination suggested that the phrase 'would be Trenched' was said as a joke, and the witness admitted that the people laughed, but nevertheless the result was as stated and those against whom the decision was given – in addition to the fact that Capt. Nolan was unseated, were liable to criminal prosecution.

The first to be placed on trial was the bishop of Clonfert, Dr. Patrick Duggan, in February 1873, in the first year of his episcopate. It created a major sensation. It was the first time in these islands that a Catholic bishop had stood in the dock since the trial of Oliver Plunkett in 1681. He was found not guilty and in the event, the prosecution against the others was abandoned.

- 215 -

Fr. Walsh was obviously not afraid of controversy. He served for twelve years, during which period he had the assistance of the following curates: Fr. James Craddock (1870-1873), Fr. Patrick Lally (1873-1874) and Fr. Malachy Hanley (1874-1878). Fr. Walsh died on the 16th March 1876 and was buried under the church - on the site of the present structure.

Fr. Martin Commins 1876-1909

Fr. Martin Commins (Mairtin O "Mullags") succeeded Fr. Walsh and served until his death on the 14th April 1909. Fr. Commins entered Maynooth in 1862 and was ordained in 1869. After serving as a C.C. in Rahoon, Lisdoonvarna, and St. Nicholas South and West, he was appointed parish priest in Claregalway in March 1876.

He has been described as a strongly built man with a pleasant disposition. Is seems that he got on very well with the local gentry, though he didn't cultivate them *("bhí sé istigh leis na daoine móra ar fad")*. It appears that his good sense of humour endeared him to all of his parishioners, rich and poor alike. He broke with the old tradition of having first communion and confirmation on the same day and he refused to confirm anyone under the age of 12. Another change was enforced upon him when he discontinued the practice of saying Mass for All Soul's Day in the Friary, due to a decline in the numbers attending and instead moved back to the church.

His tenure in Claregalway gave him the opportunity to make many improvements in the parish. As well as renovating the church, he was responsible for the construction of the parochial house and affecting improvements to the Friary cemetery. Two Connell brothers from Kiniska built the surrounding wall in 1890. A different set of brothers, Fitzpatrick's from Bohermore, were employed by Fr. Commins to build Carnmore School in 1885. He was much in favour of education and as such was very strict on school attendance. He spared no effort to get parents to send their

Cardinal Conway stopped at the old church while en route to the opening of the Galway cathedral

The Church and Parish Priests

children to school regularly.

In Fr. Martin's time the parish had a parish clerk who was known as Micheáilín Cléireach. He served Mass for the parish priest and at the times of the 'stations', he brought the priest's bag to the house in which the 'stations' were to be held the previous evening and helped with the preparations, the erecting of the altar etc. and usually stayed the night. He was an excellent seanachai and people from the neighbouring houses used to gather in to listen to him. Raftery's well known poem 'Seanchas na Sgeiche' was first obtained by Dr. Douglas Hyde from a manuscript of Micheáilíns, either written by him or taken down from him by someone else.

He and the parish priest of Lackagh, the Rev. James Heany did the stations in common. They did them in Lackagh parish and in Claregalway parish on alternate weeks. Fr. Martin came in a sidecar and Fr. James, as he was known, came on horseback. He is remembered as a dignified and somewhat aloof figure. On his arrival, the man in whose house the stations were being held, had to rub down and exercise his horse. He heard confessions and had his breakfast with Fr. Martin.

"An t-Athair Máirtín", as he was known in the parish, was much interested in land and farmed very extensively. It was this interest in farming that eventually brought him trouble and a measure of unpopularity. His main "crime", as it was thought of at the time, was his acquisition of a large tract of land in Crusheeny and he had a lot of stock on it. It was widely believed that he had bought the land, which was to have been divided amongst the parishioners, chiefly those from Montiagh, who felt very aggrieved. To his credit he employed many men and fed them well, limiting his profits. Eventually he was obliged to give up his farm, which was divided by the Congested Districts Board.

Due to Fr. Commins's failing health, Rev. J.T. O'Kelly was appointed to assist him. Fr. Commins was taken to a hospital in Dublin, where he died on 14th April 1909, having served the people of Claregalway for 33 years.

He was buried outside the walls of the Friary and a handsome Celtic cross marks his grave. The inscription reads:

> *'Pray for the soul of the Rev.*
> *Martin Commins P.P.*
> *Claregalway from 1876 to 14th*
> *April 1909.'*

Fr. Redmond McHugh 1909-1912

Fr. McHugh's tenure of Claregalway was brief but it made a lasting impact in many ways. He was a native of Baile Bán, Headford and came to the parish from Rosmuc, where he had been P.P. for some years.

He was a keen advocate of the Temperance movement and lost no opportunity in urging the men to take and keep the pledge. To further this cause and to provide a counter attraction to the public house, he founded a parish band composed of members of the Claregalway Temperance Society.

Fr McHugh provided seating in the body of the chapel and put in a new high altar and made other improvements. The old altar of wood was transferred to the abbey.

He liked to pay informal visits and discuss their affairs with them, prices, crops etc. He was skilled and interested in such matters and his advice, practical and shrewd was always received with appreciation. He opposed customs that savoured of superstition e.g. the custom of three women sitting on the coffin at funerals. There was also a custom of nailing an ass's shoe on the door of an outhouse or stable, probably for luck.

He was transferred to the parish of Castlegar in 1912.

The parochial house

Fr. Matthew Griffin 1912-1915

Fr. Matthew Griffin, whose tenure of the parish was equally brief, succeeded Fr. McHugh. He was remembered as a gentle, kindly man. He was fond of horses and always kept a pair.

The most momentous event that occurred during his time was the outbreak of the 1914-18 war. He was remembered as exhorting the young men to join the British army in the defence of Catholic Belgium and saying that if England were defeated, Ireland's condition would become like what it had been during the Penal Days.

He was a native of Moycullen parish. He was transferred to the neighbouring parish of Oranmore in 1915, much to his regret as he had become much attached to the parish and was well liked by the people.

Canon Patrick J. Moran 1915-1946

The next parish priest was Canon Padraic S. ("Pa") O'Morain, a native of Castlebar who was ordained on 17th of June 1900, at the age of 25. He spent time in Achonry, Kilfenora, Castlegar, Lettermore and Liscannor (twice, earlier as a C.C. and from 1914-15 as administrator) prior to his appointment to Claregalway in 1915.

In physique he was tall and lithe and active to a very unusual degree. He came to the parish in the prime of his life probably when he was not much more than forty. It is remembered that for many years afterwards he would never trouble to open a gate no matter how high. He simply placed one hand on it and vaulted over it.

A devotee of the Irish language, Canon Moran made extensive use of Irish in the liturgy, including direct translation of the epistle and gospel from Latin. He organised a "feis" every year and was also a member of Coiste Gnotha of the Gaelic League. His large collection of books, all annotated in Irish, is now housed in St. Mary's College library in Galway.

He translated into Irish and published St. Alphonsus Liquori's 'Visit to the Blessed Sacrament' (1934). It had an introduction by the Most Rev. Dr. Magean, Bishop of Down and Connor. Credited by none less than the President of Ireland, Sean T O'Ceallaigh as *"one of the best Irish scholars in the country"*, it is said that it was largely due to his efforts that Irish is still living and in use amongst the older people in Claregalway. He promoted devotion to St. James (to whom the Claregalway church was dedicated) and he also preferred the name Bridget to Delia.

The habit of celebrating Mass in the friary, as was stated earlier, had ceased under Fr. Commins, but his two successors Fr. McHugh and Fr. Griffin, reintroduced the practice. Canon Moran had two words to describe the Franciscan abode: "Norman" and "alien", sufficient reasons for him to bring the

Canon Patrick Moran, parish priest of Claregalway

The Church and Parish Priests

2nd of November Mass back to the church again. At a later stage, when some itinerants took shelter in the covered portion of the friary, he had that part of the roof removed.

He also had an interest in education and was responsible for the building of the new school in Claregalway and also the renovations to the Carnmore School. He visited the school in Claregalway regularly, Carnmore and Bawnmore less frequently. He used to quiz the pupils on the Gospel and such, often in Irish. Pupils whom he examined at the time admitted that Canon Moran terrified them. He was very strict with children at first confession. On one such occasion he expressed satisfaction with only two pupils from among the first communicants. He was held in awe by the older people too, many of whom openly feared him. Householders were very terrified when their turn for the "stations" came round. Initially he would satisfy himself as to the sturdiness of the table-cum-altar, after which he invariably lifted the cloth to check for dirt. If he found it necessary to clean the table and use his own cloth it meant embarrassment for the family. By all accounts he appeared to have been a domineering man, although it seems that anybody who stood up to him fared well.

Another aspect of his character was his well-known love of dogs. The following anecdote is worth relating. The Canon met a man in Montiagh, out with his dog and because his own dogs were named in Irish and understood Irish, he said *"Dia dhuit, a Sheain, bhfuil Bearla ag an madra?"* to which the man replied. *"Nil a Athair, ach tuigeann se as."*

He was also a lover of horses and he was a member of the council of the Connemara Breeders Association. He sponsored a cup for the County Ploughing Championships and attended annually to present the trophy. His interest in matters agricultural was also evident in that he was a member of the Agricultural Production Consultative Council, and from 1931 on he was Chairman of the Galway County Committee of Agriculture. This committee printed an obituary for Canon Moran stating that he *"had a major part in the successful development of agriculture"* and also that *"he gave his constant help and wise direction"*. *Because of the way he worked for all farmers, especially the small farmers, his death meant "a grievous loss to the farming community...and more especially to the smaller landholders".* The committee also stated that his life served three main causes, the Holy Church and agriculture being two, and along with these, his country.

Evidence shows that he was involved in the 1916 events, not directly, but he did supply two revolvers to the forces gathering at Moyode. He was also rumoured to have been a member of Sinn Fein. His close friend Eamon De Valera later confessed that he was shocked to learn of the extent of Canon Moran's involvement in the republican movement.

The Black and Tans' frequent raids on his house obliged him to sleep away from

The Church and Parish Priests

home, often staying as a guest of Mrs Greated in Lydacan Castle. Later when the castle was burnt down during the agrarian troubles, Canon Moran rebuked the people, and put a curse on the land saying that it wouldn't yield crops. Taking all this into account, one piece of information that doesn't add up is that Canon Moran removed a fellow republican, and later a renowned poet, Mairtin O'Cadhain from his post as headmaster in Carnmore school. Mr O'Cadhain had been drilling the pupils in out of the way fields in Carnmore, using their 'camáns', but it appears that the single incident that precipitated the demise of the once strong friendship actually occurred inside the school building. The headmaster had a photograph of James Connolly displayed in the school and when Canon Moran saw it, he told him to take it down as he was, in the Canon's word a "communist". Mr. O'Cadhain refused and from that confrontation, things went rapidly downhill.

The Canon who had been unwell for some eighteen months prior to his death, as a result of an accident when he was knocked down by a lorry while returning from the funeral of a parishioner, became "eccentric" to say the least. On one occasion while travelling from Galway he is reported to have been so abusive to a passenger that the conductor was obliged to stop the bus.

Another close friend, with whom relations became strained, was the then Bishop of Galway, Dr Michael Browne. At a Mass in Claregalway, possibly the Confirmation Mass, Canon Moran vaulted the altar rails, an action that so displeased the bishop that he ordered him into the sacristy and reprimanded him. The coolness between the two clergymen seems to have persisted to the very end. When the Canon was on his deathbed, the Bishop visited him with a view to reconciling their differences. It is said however, that the Canon stubborn to the last, foiled the bishop's good intentions by pretending he was already dead.

He died on 8th July 1946. Whatever differences existed between himself and Bishop Browne were not in evidence when the Bishop paid him a tribute at his funeral. Amongst the compliments he bestowed on his erstwhile "adversary" were that *"he did not spare himself any privation or hardship attending to the people"* and *"Canon Moran gave the example of a blameless life, of unshaken fidelity to the highest ideals of the Catholic priest."* He also commented on the Canon's strong feelings and positive convictions on many subjects, which, he said may have caused offence to some people, but that on that day everyone should forgive. (This message must not have made much of an impression on Mairtin O'Cadhain, who is reputed to have danced on the Canon's grave).

On a final note, the esteem in which Canon Moran was held was evidenced by the presence at his funeral of an t-Uachtaran Sean T O'Ceallaigh and an Taoiseach Eamon De Valera.

Amongst the clergy present that day were some of the priests who were to serve in the parish after the Canon, and also his two living predecessors.

The Church and Parish Priests

Very Rev. R. Canon McHugh, P.P. Clarenbridge.
Very Rev. M. Canon Griffin, P.P. Oranmore.
Very Rev. P. O' Dea, P.P. Kilbeacanty.
Rev. M. D. Forde, Adm. Oughterard.
Rev. G. Callanan, C.C. College House, Galway.

Whether Canon Moran will be remembered as a champion for the Church, the Irish language or as a ferocious man who ruled with an iron hand and struck fear and resentment into many is debatable, but what is undeniable is that he will be remembered and for some long time to come.

Canon Patrick O'Dea 1946-1957

Canon Patrick O'Dea, parish priest of Claregalway

Canon Patrick O'Dea succeeded Canon Moran. He was appointed parish priest on 8th August 1946 and served until his death on the 20th April 1957. A native of Kilfenora, Co. Clare, he was ordained in St. Patrick's College Maynooth on 21st June 1914. Prior to his appointment in Claregalway, he served as curate in Rahoon, Oughterard, Lettermore, and Gort. He also served as Administrator in Moycullen and Rosmuc where he was to serve as parish priest at a later date. He was parish priest of Kilbeacanty prior to his appointment in Claregalway.

Unlike his predecessor Canon Moran, Canon O'Dea was a quiet unassuming man. At first the parishioners were very wary of him. This was understandable, as Canon Moran in his long reign had left an indelible mark on them. Gradually however the people became less apprehensive and Canon O'Dea quickly gained the respect, and admiration of his parishioners. When his health started to fail in June 1956 he was admitted to St. Bride's nursing home. His remains were interred in the church grounds on 22nd April 1957. In the intervening period between his illness and death, Fr. Paddy Carroll was appointed as Administrator. While in Claregalway Fr. Carroll started a branch of the legion of Mary and also of the Pioneer Total Abstinence Association.

Fr. M. D. Forde 1957-1969

Fr. Forde was born in Milltown on 17th August 1906. He was educated in Kilgeverin N.S., where his mother taught, and later in St. Mary's College and Maynooth. After his ordination in 1930, he served in the parish of Saint Nicholas S.W. for two months. He also served in Lettermore, Ennistymon, and Oughterard, (where he was noted for his love of drama and is remembered for his moving portrayal of Christ in the Holy Week ceremonies in the Pro-

Cathedral). He later served in Gort and Rahoon (where he was also chaplain to the Central Hospital, now University College Hospital). He returned to St. Nicholas's as Administrator and P.P. until his transfer to the parish of Claregalway as successor to Canon O'Dea.

Fr. Forde is remembered as a quiet retiring man who carried out extensive repairs to the church and had further plans for renovations which had to be shelved due to his deteriorating health. It is said that when ill, he never complained and bore his suffering very well. A man of great compassion, he had, during his years as a hospital chaplain, been a source of great consolation to the seriously and terminally ill. Fr. Forde served until his death in 1969.

Canon Gerard F. Callanan 1968-1996

Canon Gerard Callanan, parish priest of Claregalway

Canon Gerald F. Callanan (then Fr. Callanan), who had been assisting the then ailing Fr. Forde for a year prior to his death, was appointed Parish Priest in 1968, a post he held until his retirement on 11th October 1996. Canon Callanan was born on 16th February 1920 in Ennistymon, Co Clare. He attended Maynooth and was ordained in the Pro-Cathedral Galway in June 1944.

Canon Callanan was a man of boundless energy who quickly undertook the daunting challenge of replacing the church which had served the people of Claregalway for 135 years with a modern edifice, in keeping with the changes in the liturgy arising from the second Vatican Council. (See photographs). Dr. Michael Browne, Bishop of Galway, consecrated it on the 15th of August 1975. The commemorative plaque reads as follows:

> Haec Ecclesia Dedicata Est
> 15a Augusti 1975
> In Honorem
> B.V. Mariae Coelum Assumptae
> Et S. Jacobi
> A Michaelo Browne
> Episcopo Galv. et Duac
> Gerardo Callanan Parocho

The first major event in the new church was the First Communion celebrations, which had been postponed until September of that year. The last funeral in the old church was of John Concannon from Montiagh and the first funeral in the

The Church and Parish Priests

new church was of James Keane from Mullacuttra.

Canon Callanan next set about improving the educational facilities in the parish as both schools were in need of renovation. His initial plan was to accommodate all the children of the parish in one large school located in Claregalway. The old building in Carnmore had fallen into disrepair and the thinking of the time was that it would make educational and economic sense to amalgamate the two schools. This generated some heated debate in the Carnmore school area and after further discussion it was agreed to build a new school in Carnmore as well as extending and refurbishing the Claregalway School.

Canon Callanan conducted his duties without the help of a curate for the greater part of his tenure. In 1989 Fr. Raymond Browne, a priest of the Elphin Diocese, who was working in the Galway Regional Marriage Tribunal, assisted at the weekends. Due to the sharp increase in the population of the parish, Fr. Sean Kilcoyne was appointed curate on January 5'h 1991, the first such permanent appointment to the parish this century. The Canon initiated the construction of a new house, adjacent to the Parish Priest's house, on the site of the building once occupied by Tomas O'Connor, a former Principal of Claregalway N.S. Fr. Kilcoyne served in the parish until 29th September 1995.

Canon Callanan celebrated the golden jubilee of his ordination in the summer of 1994. Many tributes were paid to him for his outstanding work for the people of the parish over a period of twenty-five years and presentations were made as a token of the esteem in which he was held. On the request of the bishop he agreed to carry on until a replacement could be found, a difficult task due to the shortage of priests in the diocese as a result of the decline in the number of vocations over a number of years. He used his time "constructively" as once again he set about another construction project; a retirement home for himself at the rear of the parochial house.

The church and its surrounds were a credit to Canon Callanan, who manicured the lawns with meticulous care. He retired on October 11th 1996 and looked forward to many contented hours fishing on his beloved Clare River. He died on 15th January 1999.

Canon Noel Mullin.

Canon Noel Mullin was born in Shrule on 2nd January 1938. He was ordained in Maynooth on June 23rd 1963. He served as curate in Rossaveal from July 1963 until July 1964 when he was transferred to Gort where he served until July 1965. His next position was Dean to St. Mary's College where he served until his appointment as chaplain to Merlin Park hospital on July 12th 1968. On September 1st 1972 he became chaplain in the Galway Regional Technical College, and the Holy Family School, Renmore. On the 9th October 1981 he was transferred to

- 224 -

The Church and Parish Priests

The present church

Galway Cathedral as C.C. and became the Diocesan Secretary on July 10th 1987. Approaching the end of Canon Callanan's tenure, Fr. Mullin assisted in some of the parochial duties and was appointed Parish Priest upon Canon Callanan's retirement. On the same day, Fr. Thomas Marrinan was appointed to serve as curate.

Fr. Mullin's arrival coincided with preparations for a historic event in the history of the parish, namely the first ever ordination in Claregalway church. David Cribbin from Cahergowan and a member of the Society of St. Columban was to be ordained in the Parish on the 4th January 1997. Fr. Mullin immediately became involved with the various parish groups involved in co-ordinating this event.

It was apparent even at this early stage in his ministry that he was willing to tap into the enormous reservoir of good will in the parish. Since his arrival, Fr Mullin has called to visit practically every house in the Parish. On September 26th 1997 Fr. Mullin was elevated to Canon of Cathedral Chapter. A fitting tribute to a dedicated and much loved Minister of the Church. On the same day Fr. Marrinan was appointed as chaplain to University College Hospital Galway. Once again the parish was deprived of the services of a full time curate. However, Fr. Ian O'Neill who was ordained on 8th June 1997 was appointed Diocesan Secretary with a brief to assist Canon Mullin, primarily at weekends. Such is the decline in vocations, that in the not too distant future, historians may well look back to the days when each parish enjoyed the blessings of a full-time parish priest. Or then again, we might experience a substantial increase in vocations. The rule on celibacy might be revoked, or even a more radical change might allow women to be ordained. Maybe then the aspirations expressed in the opening sentences of this chapter might materialise. Things on this earth happen in cycles. God has decreed it that way, and God's Will will prevail come what may.

The old church in the late 1960s

Church Building (1839 – 1974)

The previous church building, which was demolished in 1974, was similar to the majority of churches that were built in the 19th century. Cruciform in shape, it was somewhat smaller than the current day structure. A large stained glass window adorned the gable end at the front of the church. It had three doors, one on each transept, and one at the rear. There were three galleries, named locally as the Carnmore gallery, the Claregalway gallery, and the grand gallery. Mass times on Sundays and holy days were at 8.30a.m., referred to locally as first Mass, and at 11a.m. or second Mass. The vast majority of worshippers went to first Mass.

There were many local customs, as there undoubtedly were in all rural communities. The women occupied seats on the left, the men on the right. Men, except for members of the choir who used the Claregalway gallery on occasion, occupied both galleries over the transepts. It is said that a woman never set foot in the Carnmore gallery. Women, almost entirely elderly, occupied the seats on both transepts. They usually had their own favourite seat. Both sexes used the grand gallery. Those customs were adhered to with few exceptions. Maybe the occasional traveller might inadvertently stray into "foreign" territory, and that "separatist" custom was tailor made for the "show off" who craved special attention, and would break ranks just to be noticed.

The old church in the 1920s

Confessions were held on Saturday afternoon. One day for the girls, one for the boys, one for the women and one for the men. At Sunday Mass this order was repeated for communicants, the girls to receive 1st etc. If there were 5 Sundays in the month, members of the Sodality would be first to receive Holy Communion. Many parishioners were saddened by the demise of the old church, but the "comforts" of the new church compensated somewhat. Undoubtedly, the same sentiments will be expressed sometime in the future.

Pre-Reformation Church Building

This is situated close to the handball alley, directly south of the Friary. There is a path or driveway leading to it from the riverbank. Almost nothing is known about this building. It is assumed that it was built around the same time as the friary and was destroyed during the time of the Suppression of the Monasteries in the 16th century. However according to local folklore the building was a hospital or infirmary that was associated with the Friary. People with infectious diseases were normally kept apart from the rest of the congregation. Parts of the walls are still standing. It was used as a burial ground.

The Church and Parish Priests

Inside the old Claregalway graveyard, beside the handball alley

Graveyards

The parish has one graveyard currently in use, which is situated adjacent to the Claregalway Friary. However, other burial grounds (small graveyards and lisheens) are scattered throughout the parish. The most notable being: Montiagh, Waterdale, Lydacan, Carnmore, Kiltrogue, Kiniska and Clogher. Undoubtedly there are others, like the previous mentioned ones, which have fallen into disrepair, no one having been buried in them for the greater part of the century. The last account we have of a burial taking place in one of those small graveyards was in Montiagh in 1933. It was a young child, whose father was originally from the village, but was residing in Bohermore, Galway. He was a man by the name of Duggan, and he brought his deceased child out to his native village for burial.

One of the reasons for so many little graveyards scattered throughout the parish was more than likely due to the many deaths that occurred during the famine years. Many were buried in beds of straw matted together, because there were no coffins, and this procedure was referred to locally as *"Mata Taoi"*.

There is a *lisheen* in Eddie Hanley's field in Carnmore West that is sited within a ringfort. There were people being buried there up to the mid 1950s. Mícheál Ó'Heidhin, Carnmore, tells us:

"I myself was at a funeral there of an infant about 1946 but there were a few more buried there afterwards. I remember four or five funerals there when I was going to school (most I believe from Mountain West, Oranmore). There are two

The Church and Parish Priests

The lisheen in Eddie Hanley's field in Carnmore

headstones there – one of them has two names: James Grealish and Michael Cooley on the one stone with a date of 1890. The other one has the name Mary Donoghue aged 53, buried 1898."

Those burial places are often referred to as children's graveyards, because it was mostly unbaptised children that were buried in them. The Montiagh burial ground might be an exception because there was a monastery nearby some centuries ago. That was before any road existed between the village and Galway. The priests at that time used a short cut to Galway that was later called "The Priest's Way" (Clochán an tSagairt).

The oldest recorded date on a headstone in the friary is 1648. The engravings on many of the old headstones near the friary are unusual in that many denote the particular trade or occupation that the person had. For instance an anvil, hammer or pincers while another shows a plough. There were many other engravings.

The new graveyard that was added on to the friary about 1900 was under the Galway County Health District and the earliest record of caretakers is 1936. The following is a list of caretakers:

Mr. Patrick Lenihan	from 1936 to 1939
Miss Sabina Lenihan	from 1939 to 1945
Mr. Patrick Monaghan	from 1946 to 1947
Re. P. O'Dea PP	from 1947 to 1948
Mr. James Hession	from 1948 to 1988
Mr. Seamus O'Connell	from 1988 to present time

Receipt for two grave spaces in Claregalway cemetery in 1950 for a price of 15 shillings (75 pence)

Chapter 17: Snippets

Marriage: February 15th 1896, Varden and Hession. Patrick, son of Peter Varden, Anbally, Cummer, to Kate Annie, daughter of Thomas Hession, Merchant, Claregalway.

Confirmation (Tuam Herald Sat. July 24th 1854) Six hundred plus were confirmed by His Grace, the Archbishop of Tuam in Claregalway on Tuesday. His Grace attended at the request of right Rev. Dr. O' Donnell who was ill and unable to officiate. Large crowds attended. His Grace reflected high credit upon the zealous labours of the truly worthy and amiable P.P the Rev. James Cummins.

Mailcar Robbery (The Connacht Tribune Sat. Oct. 27th 1923) The horse-drawn mailcar from Galway to Tuam was held up at two o' clock on Monday morning by two men at Cregboy. It is stated that the large sums of money going to the banks were amongst the registered letters seized. One of the men presented a rifle and the second had a revolver and caught the horse by the head and brought him in a by-road for about thirty or forty yards. The driver was then pulled off the car and told to go back the road. One of the raiders jumped up on the car and emptied the contents of the ten mailbags on the road. They told the driver to go and that he would find all the mails at the Claregalway post-office.

For Sale Two storey high slated licensed premises for sale by public auction on Thursday 15th May 1913 at Loughgeorge.

The Galway Vindicator, March 18th 1853 Galway Union - Electoral Returns.

The electoral returns of guardians for the Galway Union have been completed. Ten elections have been made:
Electoral Division of Galway:
West Ward - John Gunning, Joseph Grealy and James Martyn.
North Ward - John Redington, John Blakeney and John Harrison.
South Ward - A.R. Mullins, R.N. Somerville and W.G. Murray.
Claregalway - Michael Burke.

Liscananaun - William Clancy.

Unusual Incident at Claregalway Upon hearing a scream, passengers on the Galway - Claregalway bus were horrified to see an elderly woman, Mrs Margaret Kearney of Rooaunmore, Loughgeorge fell through the emergency door on to the road below. The incident occurred near Castlegar on Saturday evening. The woman who was conscious was found to be suffering from severe injuries and shock and was taken to Galway Central Hospital.

Transport For many years, the common mode of transport for people in Claregalway and elsewhere were the bicycle, trap and cart. It was not until the

Snippets

1930's and 1940's when a public service was introduced. The first bus in the area was known as the "Charrabang". It was owned by the Flanagans and it was a single wheeled bus. Later they named it the "Magnet".

The first Government run service were the Great Southern Railways. After that came another state service which was the Irish Omnibus Company.

The first person to own a tractor in Claregalway was a man named Kirwan. He had a model T-Ford. The first car of the Parish was owned by Foxes of Rockwood. Soon after both Jimmy Leonard and Walter Walsh owned one too. (1930's -40's)

(Not many people went to Galway or Dublin for a day out but those who went to Dublin travelled by steam train. The only traffic that passed from Tuam to Galway were the traders on their way to market. - John Casserley)

Claregalway Farmers Summoned for Obstruction. Co. Council Discussion. (The Connacht Tribune Saturday July 6th 1929) Farmers from Claregalway crowded the public gallery at the meeting of the Galway County Council on Saturday when Mr. Kyne voiced their grievance in regard to the slippery condition of the Claregalway - Galway road. Mr. Kyne explained that owing to the tarring of the road, horses could not draw loads over it and when one side was sanded, the traffic kept to that side, with the result that the civic guards summoned the drivers of the horse carts for obstruction. The district justice adjourned the case pending that meeting of the county council. It was stated that unless the traffic was spread over the whole road there would be a serious accident. After much debate the County Surveyor mentioned that if he got instructions to sand the Claregalway road he would do so but it was only a temporary measure - an order accordingly was given.

An old wooden child rocking cot – belonging to the Wall family

Snippets

Carnmore Airstrip Representatives from the Galway Chamber Of Commerce and Industry and the County Development Team met the Minister for Transport Jim Mitchell to lobby for the development of the Carnmore Airstrip. A statement from the Chamber of Commerce and Industry said that negotiations with the Dept. of Transport had started for the development of the airfield.

War 1939-1945 (Concannon Interview) During the war there was a local security and defence force in Claregalway. Some of the women involved were: Nurse Keane, Mrs. McHugh, Mrs. Glynn, Mrs. Flaherty, Mary Coady, Mrs. Cullinan, Rita Hession, Mrs. Monaghan, Julia Glynn and Nora Glynn. The women did not fight; they were the nurses and were there as a back up. The Government supplied the uniforms. The L.D.F. became the present F.C.A.

Ring Forts There is an underground tunnel going from Mullacuttra to Knockdoe and Waterdale. Reportedly, a pot of gold was hidden there and there was a cat guarding it in Mullacuttra. There is also an old fort in Mick Glynn's field in Knockdoe.

Houses:

Turf Houses

There was a turf house in the Montiagh area but it did not last very long.

Stone Houses

The very old houses were made of stone and all of them were thatched. All the stones came to this village from Angliham near Castlegar, down the Clare River across the Curragh Line. Stones were taken over the river for about two miles by boat to build the houses.

Household: During the war only a half a gallon of paraffin was given for a month. There was no light, not even candles to be had.

Electricity came in 1953-55 to Cahergowan up to Mullacuttra, bypassing Loughgeorge and into Annaghdown.

Water came in the 1970's. Before that, water was brought up from drains, springs, wells or rivers.

Newsletters - Summer 1977 to Autumn 1981

Summer 1977

1. Community Games, 1973, first year's participation.
2. Gun Club - formed October 1965.
   Objectives:
   a) Improving shooting facilities by restocking and controlled shooting.
   b) Controlling vermin.
   c) Add to range of leisure activities.
3. I.C.A. Claregalway Guild formed 26th Jan. 1976.

- 233 -

Snippets

Michael 'the Hiker' O'Connell, a well known character around Claregalway

No.2 Christmas 1977

1. Community Games.
Norann Flaherty qualified for the U-16 final and won the All - Ireland 1500M final in her age group.
2. Current Parish Clubs:
a) Community Council - Chairman, Seamus O' Connell; Secretary, Mary Reilly.
b) Football Club - Chairman, Patsy O' Hagan; Sec., Tom Lenihan.
c) School Management - Chairman, Rev. Fr. Callanan; Sec. Kathleen Dunleavy.
d) Hurling Club - Chairman, Martin Higgins; Sec. P.J. Spelman.
e) Handball - Chairman, Johnny Moran; Sec. Michael Casserly.
f) I.C.A. - Chairwoman, Agnes Lenihan; Sec. Marie Dempsey.
g) I.F.A. - Chairman, George Glynn; Sec. Martin Cormican.
h) Community Games - Chairman, Patsy O' Hagan; Sec. Sean Mannion.
i) Gun Club - Chairman, Seoirse Morris; Sec. David McSweeney.
j) Pioneer Club - Chairman, Sean Walsh; Sec. Mattie Keane.

Snippets

No.3 May 1978.

1. Census Results
1768 parishioners:

Under 5	190
5 – 13	335
13 – 21	237
21 – 66	830
66+	176

(1/3 under 13)

2. Carnmore Ladies Club Founded

Two goals:
a) To provide both social and cultural outlets for females of the area.
b) To organise activities and to encourage a healthy outlook for the youth of the district.

No.4 July 1978.

1. 30th June 1978, Johnny Glynn retired. Here since 1962.
2. 10th June 1978, Trinity of Ordinations:

Fr. Des Forde, Fr. Martin Glynn, Fr. Martin O' Connell, all ordained on the same day.

Fr. Glynn, Lydacan attended Claregalway and St. Mary's, studied in St. Patrick's College, Thurles. Going to Patterson, New Jersey, U.S.A.

Fr. O' Connell, Kiniska, attended Claregalway, studied in Kiltegan, Co. Wicklow, going to Nigeria.

Fr. Forde attended school in Galway, studied in St. Patrick's College, Thurles, going to Galway Diocese.

No.6 Christmas 1978.

Camogie, St. Ita's - Claregalway/Carnmore:
Officers: Marguerite Flaherty, Moira Cullinan, Rita Hanley, Kay O' Hagan and Christina Grealish.

No.9 Autumn 1979.

1. Moira Cullinan off to Kenya for two years with Concern.
2. For the third successive year, hurlers lost the All - Ireland final in Mosney, this time to Toomevara, Tipperary.

No.11 Autumn 1980.

1. Fund raising scheme: Mayor of Claregalway,
Mrs. Maudie Moran, Mr. Patrick Cormican, Mr. Michael Hession, Mr. Dave Lohan and Mr. Joe Hanley.
2. Hurlers got bronze medals in Mosney, lost to Limerick in the Semi-Final.

Snippets

No.12 Christmas 1980.

1. Maudie Moran, first mayor, 29th November 1980. Money raised £9,582. Great jubilation especially by the women when the result was announced. She wondered if her husband would ever get used to calling her "your worship!"

No.13 Spring 1981

1. A parent's association for the Claregalway School was set up.

Chairman: Gearoid Hartigan; Secretary: Mrs. Maura Lohan; Treasurer: Martin Fleming and PRO: Mrs Pauline Doyle.

On the 24th April 1981, Charles J. Haughey, Taoiseach will open centre. Blessing by his Lordship, Dr. Eamon Casey.

Chapter 18: Parish Organisations and Clubs

Claregalway Amenity Group

The Claregalway Amenity Group was formed in December 1995 arising from local meetings that expressed serious concern about the overall development of Claregalway. The purpose of the group's existence is to improve the physical appearance of Claregalway.

Within three years of its establishment, the following works were carried out:
- Provision of 30 plus townland names in Claregalway and surrounding areas.
- Restoration of three pumps in Claregalway and surrounding areas.
- Provision of bottle and clothes banks in Dunleavey's car park.
- Implementation of FÁS scheme in November 1996.
- Landscaped the area adjacent to Claregalway National School.
- Erection of Famine Stone in the above-mentioned area.
- Planted trees on the main road.
- Cleaned up park near Rockwood and installed new benches.
- Re-erected milestones at Hessions Shop and across from Rockwood Park.

The biggest and most ambitious project to date is the restoration of the Nine Arches Bridge at Claregalway. This was done in conjunction with Galway County Council and FÁS. This was a very worthwhile project and restored a feature which had been absent for over forty years, thereby putting it back into its natural habitat.

Claregalway Agriculture Show

The first agriculture show to be held in the parish of Claregalway took place on Sunday, 18th August 1991. A group of people got together and formed a committee and set about putting a great show together. There were 160 classes at the show in the various sections. The different categories were: ponies, cattle, sheep, dogs, farm produce, home baking, flowers, crafts, photography and art. The first show was also seen as a day out for all the family and with that theme in mind, the committee introduced a large children's section and several novelty events and side shows. One of the most enjoyable of these events was the Donkey Derby. The venue for the first show was the Claregalway Leisure Centre and the adjoining GAA grounds in Lakeview, Claregalway. The first executive committee was: Chairman: Raymond Halpin. Secretary: Bernadette Moran, Treasurer: Declan Shaughnessy, Vice Chairman: Joseph Naughton. Recording

Secretary: Lorna Walsh.

The show increased in popularity and size over the following years and in 1994 moved to a new venue. This venue was Duffys Claregalway Equestrian Centre in Rockwood, Claregalway. By this time the number of classes had increased to 226 and exhibitors were travelling to it from all over Ireland to display their fine exhibits.

Today the show still attracts entries from all over Ireland, including Northern Ireland, as well as a great deal of local entries. It is a great opportunity for local competitors to compete with some of the finest exhibits throughout the country. Over the years the committee have tried to introduce something new to the programme of events each year, and their latest event – the obstacle course for dogs – has proved very successful. The show is affiliated to the Irish Shows Association and the Irish Pony Society.

Carnmore Community Centre

The first meeting was held on Carnmore National School on 2nd October 1984. There were 120 people present. The meeting agreed that a community centre be built. The committee elected was: Chairperson: Willie Greaney, Secretary: Catherine Quinlan, Treasurer: Kathleen Caulfield. Also about 30 people were elected as committee members and to sub-committees.

Planning permission was sought and permission was granted on 30th January 1985. The centre was built between 1985 and 1988 at an approximate cost of £160,000. Frank Fahey TD, Department of Sport approved a grant of £30,000. The site was acquired from local GAA grounds. Funds were raised through the local community and also a once off members' draw that was supported by surrounding parishes. The committee also got an interest free loan from Meitheal to repay the final part of the debt.

The GAA trustees signed over the site to the community on 1st October 1984. Micheál Ó hEidhin, Jack Murphy, John McDonagh and Patrick Ruane.

The trustees of the centre are: Jack Beatty, Martin Greaney, Willie Greaney, J.J. Connealy, Martin Leonard, Billy Grealish and Johnny Greaney.

Carnmore Ladies Club

The Carnmore Ladies Club is a community-based group first formed in November 1978.

The original group met under the auspices of the Hurling Club in the old clubhouse. Its original aim was an outlet for the at home mothers to meet and participate and lend support to local events.

During their twenty-one years of existence they have certainly succeeded very well in doing just that. Their activities over that time included: an annual sports day, arts and crafts, cooking, dress making, upholstery, painting, Irish, set dancing, guest speakers on various topics etc and of course they have helped out with hurling, drama and community centre events.

The highlights of each year were and still are:

- A sponsored walk each May in aid of some chosen charity.
- A senior citizens Christmas party held at the community centre.
- A Santa party for local children, catering for between 100 and 150 and of course their annual outing to various locations around the country.

The group meet each week and many of its founder members are still active in the club. They meet at the community centre at 8.30 on Monday nights and a céad míle fáilte is extended to old and new members.

Claregalway Community Centre

First committee of the Claregalway Leisure Centre at the official opening, 1980

The building of the Claregalway Community Centre first came to light in the minutes of a meeting of the Claregalway Football Club in early 1976. It seems that the Football Club set up a committee to see if they could purchase land for a playing pitch. That committee was Patsy O'Hagan, Gerry Hestor, Fergus Madden and Tom Lenihan. This committee purchased the present ground where the centre is now built. The Football Club paid £30,000 for the land, which was purchased from Martin O'Boyle. The Claregalway Football Club, in conjunction with the local community council of that time, set out to raise funds for the

Parish Organisations and Clubs

building of the community centre. Almost £200,000 was raised through various fund raising events and a substantial grant was received from the Government of the time. The centre was opened in May 1980 by the then Taoiseach, Charles J. Haughey.

The Centre caters for basketball, indoor soccer, badminton, volleyball, drama, scouts, indoor hurling, aerobics and Olympic handball. There are four meeting rooms, two dressing rooms with showers, a kitchen and a full-length stage with curtains. The community is indebted to all the committees who gave of their time to run the Centre since 1980. The 1999 committee is composed of:

Chairman:	Tony Clarke
Secretary:	Mary Reidy
Treasurer:	Hubert Newell
PRO:	Mary Casserly
Members:	Maura Hart, Mary Flood and Gerry Moran.

Pioneer Total Abstinence Association - Claregalway

It was in 1838 that Fr. Matthew founded the Temperance movement in Ireland. Followed by Fr. Cullan S.J. from 1889 to 1898. By 1903, 30,000 had taken the pledge. By 1957, under the stewardship of Fr. Sean McCarron, the Pioneer membership had risen to 500,000. The Association continued to grow for almost twenty years. Its members formed one of the largest and most significant 'subcultures' in Irish life, coming from all walks of life.

It was at this time that the Pioneer Total Abstinence Association of the Sacred Heart was set up in Claregalway on 14th January 1957.

The following thirteen names were passed by the Central Council as the first members of the new Pioneer Centre attached to the church of Our Lady and St. James, Claregalway.

Maura Gillespie N.T., Claregalway
Josephine O'Connell, Knockdoe
Thomas Grealy, Montiagh
Brigid Grealy, Gortadooey
Bridie Concannon, Cregboy
Brigid Flaherty, Cahergowan
Bridget Duggan, Cregboy
Bridgie Flaherty, Mullacuttra
Maureen Duggan, Cregboy
Maureen Kemphe, Lakeview
Patrick Caulfield, Kiltrogue
Michael Leonard, Lydacan
John Buckley, Loughgeorge

Like it was in the whole country, respect for the Association grew and the young people of Claregalway were eager to join the movement. It was fashionable to wear the Pin. In the seventies and eighties, Sean Walsh and John O'Hanlon gave much of their time to the youth of Claregalway involved in the movement. In a changing world, the crusade against the abuse of alcohol provides us with an opportunity to reflect. The relevance of the past can apply to modern Ireland.

The alarming rise in teenage and underage drinking is attracting growing concern among all sections of society. There have been calls for well-prepared alcohol awareness programmes for schools and additional state support for alcoholic rehabilitation centres. Will we allow the movement to die forever in Claregalway?

May the Holy Spirit help us to get life into perspective. May He give special help to our young people to accept the challenge of Temperance and use the precious gift of youth in a balanced and healthy way. Their future concerns us all.

The Claregalway Festival of Drama

'What time is it? Almost half ten; nearly time to open.' And it was with these words that the first annual Claregalway Drama Festival did open, although it was at a slightly earlier time – half past eight, on Sunday the 21st March 1982 – that the Demesne Players from Montbellew took to the stage with their production of John B. Keane's *Many Young Man of Twenty*.

The clock must be put back some months from this night, however, to when a committee was formed in answer to a request from the National Theatre Festival Directorate of the Amateur Drama League. The request was simple - would the community be interested in hosting a drama festival in its then fledgling Leisure Centre? Those doubty souls who accepted this challenge did so with relish, finding scarcely a problem with the fact that the centre did not even have a stage on which to perform! In response to this most immediate problem, the Leisure Centre Committee was cajoled into bringing forward longer-term plans, money was borrowed and the stage was built and fitted out. The infancy of this new development was evident, mostly in the primitive backstage area. There was no proper dressing rooms, showers or toilets – *'go around to the facilities at the front of the hall or else take to the fields!'* – but it nevertheless served its function admirably. The drama groups came and eight nights of first-class live theatre were enjoyed by good crowds in relative comfort. The founding committee was:

Mary Moran (senior), Maudie Moran, Agnes Lenihan, Ann Flaherty, Liz Hession, Francis Moran, Peter Duggan, Tommy Moran, Philip Cribbin, Michael Fleming, Gearóid Hartigan, Michael Hession, Tom Lenihan, Winnie Heneghan and Margaret Hester.

Parish Organisations and Clubs

The first committee of the Claregalway Drama Festival committee, 1983
Back Row (L to R): Francis Moran, Peter Duggan, Michael Fleming, Tom Lenihan, Michael Hession, Tom Moran, Philip Cribbin and Gearóid Hartigan *Front Row (L to R):* Liz Hession, Ann Flaherty, Mary Moran, Linda Henderson (adjudicator), Maudie Moran, Winnie Heneghan and Agnes Lenihan

Over the following years, improvements were gradually made to the facilities. Then came the Festival's greatest challenge to date, and a sure reflection of its strength. It had been receiving very favourable comments from participants and others involved on many different levels, both inside and outside the drama circuit, and this culminated in the committee being asked to host the 1989 All-Ireland Drama Festival Final of the Confined section of the competition. Those involved 'grasped the nettle', as it were, eagerly, and further major improvements were made to the Centre. The single largest improvement was the installation of three-phase power, allowing for the addition of a new electrical heating system and increased stage lighting capability. In addition, however, there were significant improvements made to the backstage dressing rooms, including the construction of toilets and showers. The Finals were highly successful and even resulted in the creation of the Claregalway Perpetual trophy, which is now presented annually at the All-Ireland Confined Finals. It recognises the commitment of the Claregalway Drama Festival committee in fostering a sense of spirit and enterprise in community development and has spread the name of a little village on the Clare river to areas of the country where it would otherwise be unheard of.

At its inception and in the first Festival programme, the original Drama Festival Committee set out three aims. The first of these was to *'offer the people of the*

Parish Organisations and Clubs

area an opportunity to enjoy the best in live theatre'. To the date of this publication, the Festival has seen the performance of some 216 productions and 130 plays, and has offered the best in live theatre to a vast number of people from outside the area of Claregalway, as well as inside it.

The second aim was to *'stimulate those in the parish with experience and/or an interest in acting to form a local drama group'*, and with the birth of Compántas Lir and its subsequent successes, this objective could well and truly be said to have been attained, with the added bonus of having provided an outlet for much dramatic talent in the area.

The third aim set out by the committee was *'to make the best possible use of the new Leisure Centre'*. By its staging of continuous successful Festivals and its addition of some £60,000 of additional facilities, the Drama Festival has enabled the Centre to broaden the scope of its activities and can be proud that it has indeed contributed in no small way to the realisation of much of the potential of this important community resource.

Much credit is due to the committee members, some of whom are there since the beginning of the Festival, who have given selflessly of their time and energy down through the years. The 1999 committee is:

Hugh Farrell, Mary Kelly, John Brennan, Mary McCarthy, Helen Cahalan, Mary Cribbin, Mary Duggan, Mary Duffy, Mary Fleming, Gearóid Hartigan, Michael Hession, Agnes Lenihan, Tom Lenihan, Gerry Loughnane, Seamus McNulty, Francis Moran, Mary Moran (senior) and Ann Murphy.

Others who do not feature on the founding or current committee lists but who have had a loyal association with the Festival throughout the years either as former committee members or helpers are Simon Kavanagh, John Mannion (Lydacan), Niall Devitt, Jimmy Moran, Moira Cullinan, Emily Hartigan, Peadar Conboy, Delo Collier, John Mannion (Lakeview and Galway), Gerry Moran, Kevin Duffy, Carmel Kenny, Liam Glynn, Tony Doyle, Jackie Kenny, Michael Spelman, Evelyn Kenny, Jan Graham, Mairéad Geraghty, Anne Giles, Johnny Geraghty and Róisín Kane.

The Drama Festival has, by now, become somewhat of an institution in the area and long may it continue to benefit, excite but most importantly, entertain the people of Claregalway each March.

Amateur Drama Group

Local interest in amateur drama spans a sixty-year period. The first known reference to a drama group in the area is the Lackagh Drama Group which was founded by Mairtin O Dugain, Timire Gaeilge, who produced "An tUacht" which won the Feile Dramaiochta in Taibhdhearc na Gaillimhe in 1937 and was third in the All Ireland Drama finals in the Mansion House, Dublin. The members of

Parish Organisations and Clubs

the group included James Hession (father of Michael who has maintained the family tradition with Compantas Lir), Maureen Hanlon, (Corbally), Mai Glynn (Lackagh), Julie Shaughnessy (Lackagh) and Mattie Murtagh (Carraun Cross)

During the forties there was an upsurge of interest in Claregalway. One of the successful productions during this period was "The Courting of Mary Doyle" which was staged in Keaveney's Hall, Cummer on November 10th 1940. An indication of the group's popularity can be gleaned from the fact that eight buses ferried patrons to the performance! Other noted productions during the war years included, "Mrs Mulligan's Millions" and "Troubled Bachelors". Among those who were involved at that time were: Tommy Newell, Seamus Glynn, John Casserly (Cregboy), Brigid Tarpey, Micheal Hanley, Martin Hughes, Garda McGrath, Nora Farragher, Mary Moran (who is still very involved in the Claregalway Drama Festival), Der Morris, James Hession, Larry Fox and Katie Duggan.

After a lapse of some years there was a revival of interest from the mid fifties with the re-formation of a drama group. The most prominent members included: Johnny Casserley (Cahergowan), Peter Newell, Liam O'Connell, Maire Gillespie, Mary Newell, Bridgie Duggan, Padraig Grealish (Tonroe), Mattie Boyle, Kitty Boyle, Maura Keaney, Tommy Moran (Lakeview), Tom Hughes, Rita Hession, Maggie Skerrit, John Casserley (Cregboy), Johnny Gillespie, Garda Seamus Glynn, and Garda Guheen (father of Carmel Kenny, one of the founding members of the current group). During this period the Claregalway members performed in halls around the county such as Cummer, Athenry, Roscahill, Camus and An Taibhdhearc. The group's successful productions included "Old Acquaintance", "The Damsel from Dublin", "Down in Mulligan's Farm" and "Mary Ellen at the Bottom of Galway Bay".

1963 saw another revival of interest in drama in Claregalway with the production of Jude Flynn's "Sunset in the Valley" which was performed at various venues throughout Galway. The members of the time included Maudie Moran, Brigid Duggan, Tommy Moran, Johnny Casserley, Padraig Grealish, Mattie Boyle, Tom Hughes and Seamus O'Connell.

The success of the Drama Festivals of 1982 and 1983 provided the inspiration that was needed to revive a local drama group. Liz Hession the first chairperson along with Carmel Kenny acquired the services of Sile Meehan who directed the Claregalway/Carnmore drama group's first production 'Ten Little Indians' by Agatha Christie. This ran for three nights in November 1983.

The cast and crew on that memorable occasion were Michael Spellman, Pat McCarton, Evelyn Kenny, Maureen Lenihan, Ray Kavanagh, Philip Cribbin, Carmel Kenny, Jackie Kenny, Michael Hession and Michael Fleming. Officers and stage crew included Liz Hession (chairperson), Mary Fleming (secretary), Evelyn Kenny (treasurer), Agnes Lenihan, Gearóid Hartigan and Tony Doyle

- 244 -

Parish Organisations and Clubs

(lighting), Michael O'Toole (music), Michael Healy, Galway (stage manager), Aiden Duggan and Gerry Dempsey (set construction), Mary Fleming and Mary Duggan (Carnmore, make up), Mary Duggan, Carnmore and Agnes Lenihan (props), Mary Moran, Maura Kavanagh and Mary Cribbin. In November 1983, Sile Meehan also produced 'Drama at Inish' by Lennox Robinson.

Philip Cribbin became the group's first local producer and he took the group on the first of his productions venture into festival competition with a one-act play 'Careful Rapture', which competed in the Kiltulla One-Act Drama Festival in Spring 1985.

This was followed by entering the three-act festival circuit in 1986 with 'The Country Boy' by John Murphy. In 1987, the group staged 'Anyone Could Rob a Bank' and this qualified for the All-Ireland Finals in Cavan. In 1988, he produced 'The Sorcerer's Tale' which qualified for the finals in Charleville. The following autumn, 'Halloween', the one act version of 'The Sorcerer's Tale', entered the one-act festival circuit and was placed second in the All-Ireland One-Act finals in Carlow.

The first production under the name Compantas Lir, the new name adopted by the group, was 'Them' by Tom Coffey in 1989. That autumn John Mannion, Lydacan, made his debut as director with Leonard Morley's 'Hell in High water' which again reached the All-Ireland One-Act finals in Carrick-on-Shannon.

The 1990 play was 'The Communication Cord' by Brian Friel and it reached the finals in Gorey. In November 1990, the group held its first ever Supper Theatre in the newly opened Carnmore Community Centre. The first one-act play in this event was 'On the Outside' by Tom Murphy and produced by Mary McCarthy. The three-act play of 1991 marked John Mannion's first three-act play as producer with M.J. Molloy's 'The Wood in the Whispering'. This production came third in the All-Ireland finals in Cavan with Philip Cribbin winning the first of his two All-Ireland acting awards. Frankie Moran won Best Lighting. The same year, Mike Graham produced 'The Marriage Plan' by Brian Friel for Midwest Radio's 'Festival of Radio Plays.

In 1992, Ann Greaney produced 'Aristocrats' by Brian Friel, which opened that year's All-Ireland finals in Claremorris. President Mary Robinson attended on the night.

In 1993 Ann Greaney produced 'Gaslight' by Patrick Hamilton.

The 1994 production was 'Mungos Mansion' by Walter Macken, produced by Michael Hession and it reached the All-Ireland Finals in Enniscorthy. 1994 also saw group member, Carnmore man Paddy Greaney, make his debut as a writer with his own play 'Nuts and Bolts', which had its world premiere at that year's Supper Theatre.

The 1995 production was 'Harvey' by Mary Chase and was produced by Michael

- 245 -

Hession. In 1996 and 1997, John Mannion produced 'Moll' and 'Sive' by John B. Keane respectively. The 1999 production was 'Poor Beast in the Rain' by Billy Roche, produced by Michael Hession. This play reached the All-Ireland finals in Derry.

Since the first Supper Theatre in 1990, plays and producers include:
'The Marriage Plan' by Mike Graham,
'The Yank Outsider' and 'A Fishy Business' by Vincent Moran,
'A Galway Girl' and 'Nuts and Bolts' by Philip Cribbin,
'The Proposal and 'A Pound on Demand' by Paddy Greaney,
'Three Knaves of Normandy' by John Noone,
'Cassidy's Chair', 'The Knave of Diamonds' and 'The Way of a Woman' by Brid Conneely,
'Cuckoo' by Malachy Noone,
'The Workhouse Ward' by Seamus McNulty.

Paddy Greaney's second play 'Mr. Nobody' had its world premiere at the Supper Theatre of 1998.

Over the years, many people have given their commitment, time and dedication to drama in Claregalway. All are indebted to them.

Irish Countrywomen's Association (ICA) in the 1950's

A branch of the ICA was founded in Claregalway on 25th January 1950. Mrs. Sheila Gillespie was elected President, Mrs. Tomas O'Connor Vice President, Brigid Mullin NT Secretary and Mary Ryan Treasurer. Forty members joined on that first night and each paid a subscription of 2s 6d.

Committee members were: Mrs. Cullinan NT, Rita Hession, Mrs. Lenihan, Mrs. Fallon, Sally Cormican, Kathleen Heneghan, Brigid Flaherty and Nora Fahy.

In the years that followed, membership increased and the ICA became a happy focal point for the women and girls of Claregalway, both from a work and social aspect. Fortnightly work meetings were held in Brigid Mullin's room in the Claregalway school. A bright turf fire burned in the hearth. Paraffin oil was supplied by Rita Hession for the lamp which threw light on the proceedings from the red brick mantlepiece.

Craftwork was a very important part of the activities of the guild. There was spinning and knitting, embroidery, lace making, firescreen making, sugán stools and weaving. Talents were shared and ideas passed around. Miss O'Gorman gave rushwork classes. There were cookery nights given by Miss Garvey. First Aid lessons were given by Nurse Marie McDonagh and certificates were awarded at the end of the course. Encouraged by Mrs. Cahill, Teachta to An Ghrianán who visited the guild in 1958, many members attended the college and brought back new and wonderful ideas.

Parish Organisations and Clubs

To raise funds, ceilis and dances were held in Hanly's hall at which many a romance began and blossomed. Hanly's was also the venue for the big ESB switch-on dance in 1952. The guild's play was performed there on 23rd March 1958. It was called *'Sugar for Jam'*.

Special meetings were held once a month to which members of other guilds were invited to give demonstrations. Pieces were often read from the 'Farmers Gazette' and meetings usually ended with a singsong. Tea and cakes were served by hostesses elected for the night.

Once a year in November, husbands and sons were drafted in to prepare the school for the visit of the Blood Transfusion Unit.

Another highlight was the annual bus outing when all members headed for such faraway places as Kilkee, Lahinch or Lisdoonvarna.

Many of the ICA Women have now passed away. We remember Mrs. Tomas O'Connor, Mrs. Lenihan, Maggie Skerrit, Mrs. Harney, Sheila Gillespie, Brid Mullins, Mrs. Boyle, Mary Newell, Mrs. Cullinan and Mrs. Glynn. They gave of their time and talents to ensure that the Claregalway ICA flourished in the 1950's when television was yet unheard of and life was simple and satisfying.

Claregalway ICA group on tour in Dublin, 1950s

Parish Organisations and Clubs

Irish Countrywomen's Association (ICA)

In 1975 a guild of the ICA was re-established in Claregalway in response to a request from ladies of the parish to promote traditional skills and social activities. So getting together, a number of ladies became members of the organisation better known as the ICA and it became one of the largest guilds in the county. The guild went from strength to strength with members taking part in all kinds of activities such as craftwork, cookery, drama, set dancing and make and model competitions etc. Members learned all kinds of traditional and modern craftwork. The ladies took part in and won several competitions for these activities.

The Claregalway guild members were noted for their proficiency in craftwork and cookery. Some received Brannraí awards and Demonstrators Bars for these skills and some received teacher diplomas for craftwork.

Courses were held an An Ghrianán, ICA Headquarters, Termonfechin, Co. Louth, where members attended classes to perfect their skills at home industries. The guild hosted many ICA functions including federation meetings, exhibitions, competitions and the ICA drama festival. Various social events were held and occasionally visiting guilds were entertained and an enjoyable recreational outing was organised each year. The guild flourished for about fifteen years, then other activities began in the area and the ladies found it difficult to commit to everything. As a result the ICA suffered. Membership declined and it was eventually decided to close the guild. Many good and enjoyable times are remembered by all that had any association with the guild.

Water Schemes

Extension of the County Council water supply, 1991

Parish Organisations and Clubs

Next to electricity, the provision of piped water was a major improvement to private houses and farms in the parish. Until electricity was provided in 1954/55, people depended on rivers, wells, hand-pumps and concrete tanks to supply the needs of households and livestock. Many areas in the parish got together and organised group water schemes. In most cases, wells were bored and later on, the supply of water was extended from Galway City to cater for the Claregalway and Carnmore areas.

Parish News Letter - Nuacht Chláir

The Claregalway Community Council started the first newsletter in the parish in 1977. It covered the current affairs and sports and continued for a number of years. The next effort to get a newsletter for the parish was started by Bernie Moran and Bernie Conroy. They provided a regular Nuacht Chláir for many years. John Geraghty, Padraic and Josephine Noone next took up the newsletter and published a bilingual version for a number of years also.

In 1996, at a local meeting, Mary Casserly and Josette Farrell explored the possibility of re-introducing the newsletter. Brian Place, Head of Science in the Galway Mayo Institute of Technology was approached and it took off from there. Brian had the resources and experience and was willing to give time and energy to the project. The first edition of the present Nuacht Chláir was issued in August 1996 and all 600 copies went very quickly.

There is a huge personal commitment in creating and publishing a newsletter, a task that all those involved in, underestimated at the start. However, this commitment is outweighed by the many and varied contributors, without whom publication would not be possible. The reason for our existence is to provide a facility for Claregalway and surrounding areas in spreading their news.

It is interesting to note that with the proliferation of technology and particularly the Internet, that sales of local newspapers countrywide is actually increasing. This strongly suggests a continuing need for local information.

We are happy to provide this service and whilst the information continues to flow, we will continue to provide this service.

Parish Organisations and Clubs

20/10/1940

> Tionólaḋ cruinniuġaḋ de Cómairle
> Paráirte Baile Cláir na Gaillṁe ar
> an Domnać, an 20ᵃᵈ lá, Deireaḋ Fóṁair 19.
> Bí an Canónac P. S. Ó Móráin
> i gceannas.
> Bí na baltai ar faḋ i látair.
> Léiġeaḋ m-ḃítir ó Cómḟriúnaiḋe
> na Connḋae aġ cur ríor ar Dálġairṫ
> na gCómairlí aġur puinneaḋ ġo leor cainn
> ar ġać poinnte innte.
> Duḃairt Ó. Ó h-Aṫarnaiġe ġo raiḃ ruar le
> leaṫ-ċéaḋ clann ran ḃParáirte naċ féiḋy
> leo ríor ḃió do ċur iḋtairġe ceaḋ airṗṫa
> Bí i gcá móin, fatai, aḋḃar, 7rl. aca aġur
> iy féiḋy leo díol reaċṫaine nó corċiġṗe de
> ṫae, iṁicra 7rl. do ċeannaċ má éiriġeann.
> leo dul ġo Gaillṁ ar an gċéaḋaoin nó ar an
> Saṫarn le fatai, corpce 7rl. do díol aċt
> muna druġ leo dul ar an marġaḋ ḃeiḋ riaḋ
> i gcruaḋ-ċár.

An extract from the minute book of the old parish council

Claregalway Parish Council

The first meeting of the Parish Council was held on 4th August 1940. Present at this meeting were: the very Rev. P.S. Canon Moran, George Glynn, Walter Walsh, Martin Fox, Micheál Ó Cathain, Michael Murphy, Tom Hanley, William Coady John Concannon, Tomás Ó Connor, Dan Harney, Martin Hughes, Tim Feeney, Tom Collins and John Egan.

It was stated in a minute book of the council, that its main purpose was to help

Parish Organisations and Clubs

the people of the parish during the Second World War, as food was scarce. Local landowners were asked to let some of their land to small holders so that potatoes and wheat could be sown. Seaweed was harvested in Oranmore and Galway docks and used as fertiliser for potatoes, sugar beet and other root crops.

An effort was also made to improve roads and bóithríns leading into land, and grants for that purpose were sought. At that time there was the danger that Germany might land planes in Ireland and a branch of the Local Security Force was organised in the area and the Parish Council asked that every help and co-operation be given to them (see photo). The last date in the minute book was 21st April 1944.

Claregalway Ploughing Society

The first ploughing match was held on Malachy Kelly's land, Loughgeorge, Claregalway on February 20'h 1937. The competition, which was held under the auspices of the County Committee of Agriculture, was organised by Mr. D. Harney, founding member of the Department's overseer, assisted by John Monaghan and Thomas Hughes, Knockdoe.

Seven teams participated in a competition of two classes, the Chill Plough class and the Swing Plough class. Mr. Cotter the County Instructor in Agriculture judged the competition.

We have no records of a competition being held in 1938. The county plough-match was held on the same lands in 1939. A committee was formed for that event. The committee consisted of L. Fox, T. Newell, P. Moran, P. Ruane, J. Hession, W. Morris, P. Moran (Tom), M. Lenihan, D. Noone, P. Qualter, M. Hughes and J. Monaghan.

Anther plough-match took place on the same lands in 1948. For that event a new committee was formed: J. Hession Chairman, P. Giles Secretary and P. Cullinan Treasurer.

This was a great success with 50 teams of horses or more. There has been no county plough-match held since in Claregalway but there were parish matches held in different lands up to the middle 1970's. There was an annual Social held in the late 1960's and early 1970's, which were a great success under a new committee. S. Concannon Chairman, M. O'Reilly Secretary, and K. Dunleavy Treasurer.

Another big event took place in Claregalway Leisure Centre in 1983, in honour of Tom Reilly, who won 5 All-Ireland's in a row. At this event, twelve surviving members were presented with trophies from the Club by the late J.J. Moore.

Parish Organisations and Clubs

Community Council

A Community Council was formed in Claregalway in 1977 after elections were held in all areas of the Parish. A list of all the needs within the parish were drawn up and with the help of Galway County Council and C.I.E., many of the requests were seen to. Such requests included:

- The provision of a lollypop person to help children to cross the main road at the church.
- The transport to Claregalway National School for pupils
- The Claregalway Parents Association was started
- A parish newsletter was also started

Many other works were also completed including improving some bad bends on roads in the parish. The Community Council was active for four years after which it disbanded as new members were hard to come by. The last meeting was held in 1982.

Claregalway Senior Citizens Committee

A committee was formed in the early 1980's to organise a Christmas Party for our Senior Citizens. The party was held in the Leisure Centre in the beginning but in later years it was held in Kynes Central Tavern, Loughgeorge. The party was a success from the start and numbers attending are increasing every year. The event starts with a Mass followed later by a dinner and dance. It is a very enjoyable occasion for all and it gives a chance for people to see their friends socially. The committee has in recent years extended their events to include a day outing also. This has also proved to be a big success. Perhaps as the millennium approaches a more regular event may be considered.

Claregalway I.F.A.

The Claregalway branch of the Irish Farmers Association began life on the 6th December 1960. It was then known as the National Farmers Association. Some officers at that time were Larry Fox, Mattie Cormican, Billy Morris and George Glynn.

At that time, prices for farm produce were very low and the government would not even include the farm leaders in talks on how to improve matters for farmers in general. A famous farmers' protest took place in the early 1960's and farmers from all over Ireland assembled in Dublin. The then Minister for Agriculture was Mr. Charlie Haughey and he refused to meet the farmers. This was followed by a sit-down outside the gates of the Dáil that lasted for days. The Claregalway representative was Mattie Cormican.

Parish Organisations and Clubs

At the present time there are 60 members in the branch. The Association is very strong nation-wide and there are new issues being dealt with constantly to improve all types of conditions for the farming sector.

Claregalway Community Action Group

The Claregalway Community Action Group was formed in September 1994 following a public meeting of the residents, representatives of the business community and parents that was held in the Claregalway Community Centre. This meeting was called to address a number of major concerns in relation to the safety and the appearance of the village and a committee was elected to pursue these issues and concerns at that meeting. Because two major national roads meet in the village, the major concern was for the safety of the residents of the area and the 300+ children in the National School.

The Action Committee set about their task by meeting with the County Manager and the Local County Councillors. Securing funding for projects absorbed most of the committees' time in lobbying Councillors, TD's, the Department of the Environment and the National Roads Authority.

As a result of this work warning lights were erected at either side of the school. A surface water drainage system was installed to prevent flooding in the village. Footpaths were re-laid and extended. Traffic calming measures were put in place resulting in a major reduction in the speed of traffic through the village with motorists for the most part obeying the pedestrian lights.

The road through the village was due to be resurfaced but due to the imminent installation of a sewerage system and a new trunk water main it was put on hold. Both schemes will be completed by the end of 2000. The Action Group was to the forefront in securing funding for the work on the N17 between Claregalway and Oranmore at Lydacan; this work will be completed in 1999.

The Claregalway Amenity Group was formed in 1995 to improve the amenity aspect and appearance of the village. The Amenity Group continues to do Trojan work in this regard.

The Action Group made submissions to "The Galway Transportation and Planning Study" and they eagerly await the report, which will be published shortly. This report will influence the planning of Galway City and its hinterland well into the next century. The Group is in the process of making a submission to Galway County Council in relation to the proposed bypass of Claregalway and the new Dual Carriageway linking Claregalway to the city.

The draft Development plan for Claregalway is due to be published shortly. As we move into the new Millennium we are hopeful and confident that Galway County Council in consultation and co-operation with Claregalway Action Group and Claregalway Amenity Group will ensure that Claregalway and it

Parish Organisations and Clubs

environs is a safe and attractive place to live, a place that fosters good community life.

Claregalway & District Fishing Club

The Clare River originates close to Ballyhaunis, County Mayo and flows through Irishtown, Milltown, Tuam, Corofin, Turloughmore and Lackagh, passing through Claregalway village before eventually entering Lough Corrib at Curraghmore.

Its natural beauty is the centrepiece to all the local attractions of the village such as the Franciscan Friary, the De Burgo Castle and the Nine Arch Bridge. The river in the past had very good game fishing with salmon and trout and also coarse fishing with pike, perch, roach, eels and the odd bream but stocks have deteriorated drastically in the past number of years. The Clare River has fantastic potential and advantages to offer to the people of Claregalway and great interest should be taken to preserve and develop the river.

It was for this very reason that the Claregalway & District Fishing Club was founded in 1991 by a group of concerned locals with its first meeting held in the Summerfield lounge. Some of the objectives of the Club are as follows:

1. To protect the local landowners legal fishing rights.
2. To ensure all fishing club members are adequately insured and to take away the onus from the landowner.
3. To restock where possible with trout and salmon fry.
4. The possibility of creating pools in the river to hold salmon from going upstream.
5. To promote, encourage and teach young children to fish.
6. To have proper access and arrangement of steps for climbing wire fences and walls as to avoid interference with landowners property.
7. To keep riverbanks clean and free from litter.
8. To erect lifebuoys along riverbanks for safety.
9. To facilitate angling for tourists.
10. To have close liaisons with other local clubs in the parish particularly the Claregalway Gun Club which would have similar interests.

Appendix A: School Attendance Rolls

Examination Rolls for Claregalway Girl's School: 1895-97 and 1899

Infant Roll	Age
Annie Fahy	6
Sarah Grealy	6
Ellen Qualter	7
Bridget Qualter	5
Margaret Morris	6
Kate Collins	6
Mary Duggan M	6

1ST CLASS

Bridget Grealy	7
Julia Duggan	7
Bridget Duggan	7
Sarah Codyre	10
Mary Codyre	9
Winny Concannon	8
Honoria Concannon	7
Honoria Smyth	7
Bridget Codyre	7

2ND CLASS

Ellen Duggan D	11
Bridget Quinn	8
Mary Qualter	8
Bridget Reilly	10
Bridget Holland	7
Margaret Glynn	7
Mary Moloney	8
Mary Duggan	8
Bridget Kane P	12
Margaret Hanly	10
Kate Long	8
Ellen Duggan P	8

- 255 -

School Attendance Rolls

Margaret Hanley	7
Winney Lully	8
Margaret Duggan T	12

3RD CLASS

Mary Grealy	12
Honoria Walsh	12
Mary A Hughes	8
Sarah Grealy	9
Margaret Duggan J	10
Mary Qualter	9
Sabina Wall	9
Sabina Lully	9
Margaret O'Dea	11
Kate Duggan H	12
Bridget Murphy	9

4TH CLASS

Minnie Morris	9
Mary Moylan	12
Bridget O'Dea	9
Mary O Kean	12
Sabina Hession	12
Maria Cullinan	10
Margaret Quinn	10
Kate Ryan	10
Bridget O Kean	10

5TH CLASS 1st stage

Winny Raftery	12
Mary Fox	12
Mary Raftery	10
Mary Carter	11
Julia Moloney	12
Mary Ryan	12

5TH CLASS 2nd stage

Florence Hession	13
Kate Giles	13
Mary Grealy	13
Margaret Commins	12
Honor Grealy	12
Kate Grealy	10

School Attendance Rolls

6ᵀᴴ CLASS 1ˢᵗ stage
Sarah Giles	16
Bridget Egan	13
Celia Casey	12
Honoria Qualter	12
Delia Carter	15

6ᵀᴴ CLASS 2ⁿᵈ stage
Kate Mooney	15
Honoria Monaghan	15

The new pupils of 1896 were:
Ellie Giles	6
Annie Quinn	5
Mary Corcoran	5
Tessie Carter	6
Bridget Forde	7

In 1897 the infant's class had as new pupils:
Margaret Fahy	6
Mary Morris	6
Mary Long	7
Delia Grealy	7
Annie Ryan	7
Julia Grealy	8
Annie Cullinan	9

In 1899, a new teacher Margaret Brady was present. The new infants of that year were:
Rebecca Cullinan	5
Margaret Duggan	5
Mary Duggan	7
Honoria Grealy	6
Bridget Corcoran	6
Sabina Duggan	8
Mary Scully	7

And the first class, who obviously entered in 1898 were:
Nora Holland	7
Julia Moran	7
Mary Duggan	8
Bridget Duggan	8
Julia Hynes	8

School Attendance Rolls

School Principals and Staff

Principals (boys)

George Carter	1878 - 1915
Thomas O'Reilly	1915 - 1920
James P. Donnellan	1921 - 1922
Tomas O Concubhair	1922 - 1962
Sean Mac Fhloinn	1962 - 1978
Boys and Girls amalgamated in 1970	
Maire Bn. Ui Lochlainn	1978 – 1991
Pat Coen	

Principals (girls)

Bedelia Daly	1895 - 1898
Margaret Brady	1899 - ?
Margaret Flood	1905 - 1931
Eibhlin Bn. Mhic Suibhne (Ni Muirghis)	1931 - 1940
Eibhlin Bn. Ui Dhuibhghiolla	1941 - 1963
Maire Bn. Ui Lochlainn	1963 - 1970

Assistants (boys)

Mary J. Carter	1906 - 1912
Mary D. Curran	1912 - 1915
Mollie Cullinan	1915 - 1954
Eibhlin Bn. Ui Ghriallaigh	1954 - 1980

Assistants (girls)

Eibhlin Bn. Mhic Suibhne	1919 - 1931
Brid Nic An Iomaire	1932 - 1936
Polin Ni Lorcain	1936 - 1943
Brid Bn. Ui Aodha	1943 - 1984

Recent and current staff

Sean Breathnach	1977
Brid Ni Eanachain	1978 - 79
Lourda Bn. Ui Mhurchu	1979
Maire Ni Eigertaigh	1980 - 1985
Padraigin Bn. Ui Chartain	1980
Aine Bhreathnach	1982 - 1984
Bernard Cuirc	1984
Padraigin Ni Mhaolain	1984
Mairead Bhreathnach	1984
Nora Bn. Ui Lochlainn	1984 - 1988

School Attendance Rolls

Maire Bn. Mhic Eacha	1985 - 1999
Valerie Bn. Ui Dhuda	1987 - 1988
Seosaimhin Ni Dhugain	1990
Eilis Aine Ni Annain	1991

School Attendance Rolls

Claregalway National School - Girls

Year	Pupils Name	Address	Occupation
07-06-09	Clancy Anne	Cregboy	Farmer
07-06-09	Shaughnessy Maggie	Cregboy	Farmer
07-06-09	Long Nora	Kiniska	Orphan
07-06-09	Greally Mary	Gort	Farmer
06-09-09	Concannon Maggie	Montiagh	Farmer
20-09-09	Long Bridget	Kiniska	Farmer
04-10-09	Skevill Maggie	Claregalway	Carpenter
15-02-10	Hession Sara	Claregalway	Shopkeeper
15-02-10	Hession Delia	Claregalway	Shopkeeper
21-03-10	McDonagh Maggie	Lakeview	Farmer
04-04-10	Glynn Christina	Kiltulla	Farmer
11-04-10	Walsh Mary	Gortatleva	Farmer
13-04-10	Casey Mary	Claregalway	Farmer
02-05-10	Connell Ellen	Kiniska	Farmer
16-05-10	Donoghue Winnie	Kiniska	Farmer
23-05-10	Concannon Maggie	Montiagh	Farmer
02-06-10	Shaughnessy Kate	Cregboy	Farmer
18-04-10	Carr Delia	Cregboy	Farmer
15-06-10	Walsh Nora T	Lydacan	Farmer
06-10	Duggan Ellen	Montiagh	Farmer
03-07-11	Walsh Mary		Farmer
05-07-10	Conroy Winnie	Kiniska	Farmer
31-08-10	Hughes Maggie	Claregalway	Farmer
26-09-10	Donnelan Maggie	Cloughaun	Farmer
16-11-11	Walsh Sadie	Caherlea	Farmer
16-01-11	Walsh Mary E	Caherlea	Farmer
06-03-11	Clancy Delia	Cregboy	Farmer
16-03-11	Walsh Bridie	Lydacan	Farmer
16-03-11	Walsh Ellen	Lydacan	Farmer
24-04-11	Long Mary	Kiniska	Farmer
01-05-11	Hession Rita	Claregalway	Shopkeeper
02-05-11	Noone Mary	Summerfield	Farmer
01-05-11	Flaherty Anne	Lydacan	Farmer
07-05-11	Flaherty Winnie	Lydacan	Farmer
01-05-11	Kerrigan Winnie	Caherlea	Farmer
15-05-11	Walsh Maggie	Caherlea	Farmer
15-05-11	Loftus Winnie	Gort	Farmer
15-05-11	Duggan Julia	Montiagh	Farmer
22-05-11	Moran Delia	Cloon	Farmer
22-05-11	Flesk Delia	Cloon	Farmer

School Attendance Rolls

22-05-11	McCahill Bridget	Claregalway	Farmer
22-05-11	Ffrench Nellie	Loughgeorge	Shopkeeper
07-06-11	Kemple Mary	Lydacan	Farmer
29-05-11	Duggan Julia P	Montiagh	Farmer
17-07-11	Flaherty Sara	Lydacan	Farmer
30-07-11	Quinn Julia	Cregboy	Farmer
30-07-11	Greally Winnie	Gurth a doe	Farmer
30-07-11	Duggan Anne	Kiltrogue	Farmer
30-07-11	Lenihan Nora	Claregalway	Shopkeeper
30-07-11	Kemple Kate	Lisheenavalla	Farmer
30-07-11	McDonagh Nora	Lakeview	Farmer
30-07-11	Moran Nora	Lakeview	Farmer
30-07-11	Kemple Nora	Lisheenavalla	Farmer
30-07-11	Duggan Julia	Gort	Farmer
30-07-11	Murphy Kate	Ballymurphy	Farmer
08-11	Flaherty Kathleen	Carnmore	Farmer
06-09-11	Greally Mary	Gort	Farmer
01-03-10	McDonagh Maggie	Lakeview	Farmer
09-01-12	Walsh Mary	Carnmore	Farmer
04-03-12	Long Anne	Kiniska	Farmer
15-04-12	Donohue Ellen	Kiniska	Farmer
16-04-12	Connel Bridget	Kiniska	Farmer
23-04-12	Moran Nora	Cloon	Farmer
29-04-12	Moran Mary	Cloon	Herd
29-04-12	Moran Nora	Cloonbiggen	Farmer
29-04-12	Shaughnessey Brid	Cregboy	Farmer
29-04-12	Moran Margaret	Lakeview	Herd
29-05-12	Carr Mary	Cregboy	Farmer
16-01-12	Walsh Sadie	Caherlea	Farmer
05-06-12	Kemple Delia	Lydacan	Farmer
20-05-12	Ffrench Pauline	Loughgeorge	Shopkeeper
08-07-12	Duggan Bridget	Montiagh	Farmer
13-04-10	Casey Mary	Claregalway	Farmer
06-09-09	Skerritt Maggie	Claregalway	Carpenter
05-07-10	Conroy Winnie	Claregalway	Farmer
14-12-12	Connell Winnie	Gort	Herd
11-01-13	Loftus Winnie	Gort	Farmer
14-04-13	Walsh Mary	Ballinacurry	Farmer
08-06-12	Shaughnessy Kate	Cregboy	Farmer
05-05-13	Kerrigan Nora	Caherlea	Farmer
13-05-13	Lenihan Delia	Clogher	Farmer
14-05-13	Flaherty Mary	Summerfield	Farmer

School Attendance Rolls

19-05-13	Greally Bridget	Gort	Farmer
26-05-13	Greally Maria	Gort	Farmer
26-05-13	Greally Mary	Gort	Farmer
26-05-13	O'Brien Mary	Cregboy	Farmer
26-05-13	Flaherty Annie	Lydacan	Farmer
16-06-13	Forde Delia	Clogher	Farmer
30-06-13	Lenihan Sabina	Claregalway	Shopkeeper
07-07-13	Fahy Ellen	Cregboy	Farmer
22-07-13	Grealish Bridget	Lydacan	Farmer
22-07-13	Flaherty Ellen	Lydacan	Farmer
02-09-13	Duggan Delia	Cloon	Farmer
09-09-13	Duggan Ellen	Montiagh	Farmer
11-09-13	Kane Mary E	Cregboy	Farmer
16-09-13	Beattie Beta	Carnmore	Orphan
16-09-13	Fahy Mary	Carnmore	Farmer
16-09-13	Walsh Maggie	Caherlea	Farmer
16-09-13	Connell Ellen	Kiniska	Farmer
17-11-13	Flaherty Winnie	Lydacan	Farmer
13-03-19	Flaherty Brigid	Summerfield	Farmer
15-03-19	Kerrane Kathleen	Gurth a'dubha	Farmer
15-03-19	Flaherty Brigid	Lakeview	Farmer
14-03-19	Flesk Bridie	Cloon	Farmer
14-12-19	Cahill Margt.	Claregalway	Postman
01-02-19	Carr Brigid	Cregboy	Farmer
29-03-19	Moran Sarah	Cloonbiggen	Farmer
29-03-19	Duggan Annie	Cloon	Farmer
03-05-19	Forde Brigid	Cahergowan	Farmer
08-11-19	Bodkin Mary	Gortatleva	Farmer
06-12-19	Walsh Brigid	Ballinacregg	Farmer
08-11-19	Moran Brigid	Clogher	Farmer
08-11-19	Moran Brigid	Kiltrogue	Farmer
04-10-19	Duggan Mary	Montiagh	Farmer
08-11-19	Fahy Celia	Cregboy	Farmer
08-11-19	Loftus Mary	Gort	Farmer
04-10-19	Duggan Annie	Kiltrogue	Farmer
05-07-19	Greally Mary	Gort	Farmer
29-09-19	Shaughnessy Kate	Cregboy	Farmer
27-09-19	Flesk Brigid	Cloon	Farmer
05-07-19	Moran Brigid	Cloon	Farmer
27-09-19	Greally Brigid	Gort	Farmer
29-11-19	Kelly Margt.	Cloon	Farmer
29-11-19	Duggan Winnie (Tom)	Montiagh	Farmer

School Attendance Rolls

29-11-19	Sheirdan Brigid	Lydacan	Farmer
29-11-19	Flesk Mary	Cloon	Orphan
29-11-19	Donohue Mary	Claregalway	Farmer
29-11-19	Duggan Nora	Kiltrogue	Farmer
29-11-11	Raftery Brigid	Cahergowan	Farmer
29-11-19	Casserly Mary	Cregboy	Farmer
29-11-19	Nally Mary E.	Cloon	Farmer
29-11-19	Beattie Brigid	Lydacan	Farmer
29-11-19	Flesk Julia	Cloon	Farmer
29-11-19	Flesk Sabina	Cloon	Farmer
29-11-19	Duggan Ellen (J)	Montiagh	Farmer
29-11-19	Coen Winnie	Summerfield	Farmer
29-11-19	Morris May	Cregboy	Farmer
29-11-19	Duggan Julia	Kiltrogue	Farmer
29-11-19	Keane Mary	Lydacan	Farmer
06-12-19	Duggan Brigid	Kiltrogue	Farmer
06-12-19	Commins Brigid	Kiniska	Farmer
06-12-19	Flaherty Brigid	Cahergowan	Farmer
13-12-19	Duggan Ellen	Montiagh	Farmer
13-12-19	Moran Nora	Cloon	Farmer
13-12-19	Beattie Mary	Lydacan	Farmer
13-12-19	Casserly Brigid	Kiniska	Farmer
18-12-19	Duggan Winnie	Montiagh	Farmer
20-12-19	Glynn Christine	Kiltulla	Farmer
20-12-19	Cahill Brigid	Claregalway	Farmer
20-12-19	Duggan Brigid	Cloon	Farmer
29-12-19	Duggan Brigid	Montiagh	Farmer
18-10-20	Greally Mrgt.	Cloonbiggen	Farmer
13-10-20	Duggan Julia	Kiltrogue	Farmer
23-10-20	Duggan Nora	Kiltrogue	Farmer
24-10-20	Morris Mary	Cregboy	Farmer
04-12-20	Duggan Ellen	Montiagh	Farmer
04-12-20	Duggan Mary	Montiagh	Farmer
10-01-20	Morris May	Cregboy	Farmer
11-01-21	Commins Brigid	Kiniska	Farmer
11-01-21	Duggan Bina	Montiagh	Farmer
13-01-21	Duggan Winnie	Montiagh	Farmer
10-01-21	Lenihan Norah	Lakeview	Farmer
12-01-21	Greally Kathleen	Cloonbiggen	Farmer
22-01-21	Walsh Brigid	Ballinacregg	Farmer
22-01-21	Loftus Mary	Gort	Farmer
24-01-21	Duggan Brigid Tom	Kiltrogue	Farmer

School Attendance Rolls

24 01-21	Loftus Julia	Gort	Farmer
24-01-21	Duggan Mary	Kiltrogue	Farmer
24-01-21	Ffrench Nellie	Knocklawn	Farmer
24-01-21	Kelly Mary	Cloon	Farmer
01-02-21	Moran Brigid	Kiltrogue	Farmer
16-04-21	Bodkin Mary	Gortatleva	Farmer
13-04-21	Walsh Brigid	Ballinacregg	Farmer
02-05-21	Duggan Julia	Kiltrogue	Farmer
02-05-21	Duggan Nora	Kiltrogue	Farmer
13-06-21	Long Kathleen	Kiniska	Farmer
13-06-21	McGuiness Mary	Crusheen	Farmer
14-06-21	Carr Mary	Gortatleva	Farmer
16-06-21	Long Anne	Kiniska	Farmer
21-05-21	Walsh Margt.	Summerfield	Farmer
11-06-21	Conroy Winnie	Kiniska	Farmer
18-06-21	Flaherty Brighid	Summerfield	Farmer
02-07-21	Moran May	Cloon	Herd
22-10-21	Flaherty Katie	Lydacan	Farmer
02-21	Greally Kathleen	Cloonbiggen	Farmer
02-21	McGuiness Mary	Crusheen	Farmer
02-21	Bodkin Mary	Gortatleva	Farmer
17-12-21	Long Kathleen	Kiniska	Farmer
17-12-21	Duggan Mary	Montiagh	Farmer
24-12-21	Moran Nora	Cloon	Farmer
28-01-22	Moran Mary	Cloon	Herd
28-01-22	Duggan Brighid	Kiltrogue	Farmer
28-01-22	Duggan Winnifred	Kiltrogue	Farmer
28-01-22	Moran Brigid	Kiltrogue	Farmer
04-02-22	Duggan Julia	Kiltrogue	Farmer
04-02-22	Duggan Nora	Kiltrogue	Farmer
28-01-22	Carr Mary	Gortatleva	Farmer
11-02-22	Donnellan Maggie	Clogher	Farmer
11-02-22	Loftus Mary	Gort	Farmer
11-02-22	Forde Margt	Clogher	Farmer
17-02-21	Long Kathleen	Kiniska	Farmer
04-03-22	Casserly Brighid	Kiniska	Farmer
01-04-22	Duggan Brighid	Kiltrogue	Farmer
01-04-22	Duggan Winifred	Kiltrogue	Farmer
01-04-22	Moran May	Cloon	Herd
13-05-22	Duggan Brighid	Cloon	Farmer
31-03-22	Duggan Mary	Kiltrogue	Farmer
31-03-22	Fahy Evelyn	Cregboy	Farmer

School Attendance Rolls

31-03-22	Flaherty Nora	Cruskeen	Farmer
13-01-22	Duggan Mary	Kiltrogue	Farmer
17-01-25	Glynn Mary	Lydacan	Farmer
17-01-25	Bodkin Ellen	Gortatleva	Farmer
17-11-23	Casserly Mary	Kiniska	Farmer
17-11-23	Duggan Brighid	Montiagh	Farmer
15-11-24	Qualter Mary	Cloon	Farmer
10-01-21	Hanly Brighid	Colon	Farmer
10-01-21	McDonagh Nelie	Gortatleva	Farmer
10-01-21	Fahy Eveleen	Gortnagooleeny	Farmer
11-11-22	Duffy Norah	Loughgeorge	Tailor
25-11-22	Kerrane Kathleen	Gurth a'dhubha	Farmer
23-09-23	Fahy Mary	Carnmore	Farmer
25-11-22	Moran Sara	Cloon	Farmer
23-12-22	Greally Maria	Gortcloonmore	Farmer
23-12-22	Duggan Mary	Kiltrogue	Farmer
11-11-23	Moran Mary	Cloon	Farmer
23-12-22	Fahy Mary	Carnmore	Farmer
23-12-22	Commins Brighid	Kiniska	Farmer
23-12-23	Duggan Ellen	Montiagh	Farmer
23-12-23	Greally Nellie	Cloonbiggen	Farmer
13-12-22	Long Nora	Kiniska	Farmer
13-12-22	Casserly Brighid	Kiniska	Farmer
13-12-22	Duggan Julia	Kiltrogue	Farmer
13-12-22	Long Kathleen	Kiniska	Farmer
13-12-22	Duggan Anne	Kiltrogue	Farmer
13-12-22	Casserly Mary	Kiniska	Farmer
13-12-22	Carr Mary	Gortatleva	Farmer
10-02-22	Kerrigan Nora	Caherlea	Farmer
10-02-22	Allen Katie	Ballinacregg	Farmer
10-02-22	Ford Brighid	Cahergowan	Farmer
10-02-22	Stephens Mary	Gortatleva	Farmer
10-02-22	Flaherty Ellen	Lydacan	Farmer
13-01-22	Moran Sara	Cloon	Farmer
13-01-22	Duggan Brigid	Kiltrogue	Farmer
10-02-22	Moran Brighid	Kiltrogue	Farmer
10-02-22	Duggan Mary	Montiagh	Farmer
17-03-22	Duggan Mary	Kiltrogue	Farmer
17-03-22	Duggan Brighid	Kiltrogue	Farmer
17-03-22	Duggan Winnie	Kiltrogue	Farmer
27-01-23	Moran Sadie	Cloon	Farmer
03-23	Fox Teresa	Rockwood	Farmer

School Attendance Rolls

04-10-23	Fox Agnes	Rockwood	Farmer
04-10-23	Carr Mary	Cregboy	Farmer
28-06-23	Lenihan Sabina	Claregalway	Shopkeeper
28-06-23	Lenihan Brighid	Lakeview	Farmer
24-04-23	Casserly Margt	Kiniska	Farmer
31-03-23	Forde Winnie	Cahergowan	Farmer
31-03-23	Connell Brighid	Kiniska	Farmer
24-04-23	Duggan Sara	Montiagh	Farmer
14-05-23	Long Mary A	Kiniska	Farmer
21-05-23	Glynn Sara	Lydacan	Farmer
22-05-23	Quinn Brigid	Claregalway	Farmer
04-06-23	Casserly Katie	Kiniska	Farmer
04-06-23	Flaherty Eileen	Cahergowan	Farmer
22-12-23	Greally Sara	Cloonbiggen	Farmer
24-04-23	Casserly Mary	Kiniska	Farmer
05-05-23	Shaughnessy Brighid	Cregboy	Farmer
12-05-23	Donohue Ellen	Kiniska	Farmer
19-05-23	Carr Mary	Cregboy	Farmer
02-06-23	Moran Winnie	Cloonbiggen	Farmer

School Attendance Rolls

Claregalway National School - Boys

Year	Pupil's Name	Address	Occupation
14-05-19	Long, Joe	Kiniska	Farmer
14-05-19	Forde, Thomas	Peake	Farmer
14-05-19	Tommie Morris	Cregboy	Farmer
03-06-19	Commins James	Kiniska	Farmer
03-06-19	Lenihan Willie	Lakeview	Farmer
23-02-20	Stephens Joseph	Gortatleva	Farmer
26-02-20	Kelly Michael	Cloon	Farmer
26-02-20	Casserly Michael	Kiniska	Farmer
10-05-20	Casserly Padraic	Kiniska	Farmer
08-06-20	Kerrane Michael	Gorta'dubha	Farmer
09-06-20	Glynn John Joe	Cloon	Farmer
09-06-20	Feeney Francis	Gorta'dubha	Farmer
14-06-20	Duggan Malachy	Kiltrogue	Farmer
16-06-20	Moran Martin	Cloon	Farmer
16-06-20	Flaherty Michael	Cahergowan	Farmer
01-07-20	Sheridan John	Tonroe	Farmer
11-01-20	Noone Patrick	Lakeview	Farmer
25-01-20	Noone John	Lakeview	Farmer
07-03-21	Duggan Peter	Montiagh	Farmer
26-04-21	Forde William	Gorta'dubha	Farmer
02-05-21	Commons Patrick	Kiniska	Farmer
06-05-21	Hughes Michael	Claregalway	Farmer
06-05-21	Lenihan Patrick	Lakeview	Farmer
07-06-21	Duggan Michael	Montiagh	Farmer
07-06-21	Glynn Michael J	Lydacan	Farmer
08-06-21	Morris Patrick	Cregboy	Farmer
09-06-21	Morris John	Cregboy	Farmer
03-02-22	Moran Malachy	Clogher	Farmer
03-04-22	Ffrench Emmet	Rocklawn	Farmer
15-05-22	Kelly John	Cloon	Farmer
19-06-22	Quinn Michael	Cregboy	R.Q.

- 267 -

School Attendance Rolls

Carnmore National School - Boys

Name	Age	Residence	Entry date
1 Thomas Beattie	12	Carnmore	16-6-85
2 Roger Grealish	13	Lisheenavalla	"
3 Martin Hanley	11	Carnmore	"
4 Pat Holland	12	Lisheenavalla	"
5 Martin Fox Michael	13	Carnmore	"
6 Michael Murphy Ml.	7	Ballymurphy	"
7 Michael Murphy Pat	8	Ballymurphy	"
8 Martin Grealish	9	Carnmore	"
9 William Grealish	10	Lisheenavalla	"
10 Thomas Collins	10	Carnmore	"
11 Pat Hanley	9	Carnmore	"
12 Laurance Carr	9	Carnmore	"
13 John Carr Pat	10	Carnmore	"
14 John Carr John	11	Carnmore	"
15 Tom O'Brien	12	Carnmore	"
16 Richard Spratt	15	Cashla	"
17 Thomas Joyce	12	Cregmore	"
18 Pat Grealish Michael	12	Carnmore	"
19 Pat Donohue	11	Carnmore	"
20 Thomas Murphy	9	Ballymurphy	"
21 Michael Kenny Peter	12	Lydacan	"
22 Thomas Clarke	7	Carnmore	"
23 Pat Murphy	6	Ballymurphy	"
24 Tom Fox Tom	10	Carnmore	"
25 Pat Fox Tom	12	Carnmore	"
26 Martin Fox Tom	8	Carnmore	"
27 Pat Grealish James	9	Carnmore	"
28 Tom Fox Michael	8	Carnmore	"
29 Pat Carr John	11	Carnmore	"
30 John Moran	11	Carnmore	"
31 John Beatty	9	Carnmore	"
32 James Spratt	14	Cashla	"
33 James Collins	9	Carnmore	"
34 Martin Rooney	11	Carnmore	"
35 John Kenny Michl	7	Carnmore	"
36 John Kenny Pat	9	Carnmore	"
37 Michael Grealish J	7	Carnmore	"
38 John Grealish Mich l	7	Carnmore	"
39 Michael Moran	8	Carnmore	"
40 Thomas Spratt	9	Cashla	"

School Attendance Rolls

41 Peter Naughton	7	Lisheenavalla	"
42 Pat Fahy	11	Carnmore	"
43 Thomas Fahy	8	Carnmore	"
44 Michael Kenny Pat	6	Carnmore	"
45 Patrick Beattie	6	Carnmore	"
46 Tom Hanley	5	Carnmore	"
47 Pat Silke	6	Carnmore	"
48 Pat Fox Michael	6	Carnmore	19-12-85
49 Pat Hanly John	6	Carnmore	16-6-85
50 James Grealish Peter	6	Carnmore	"
51 Michael Carr John	5	Carnmore	"
52 James Grealish James	6	Carnmore	"
53 John Mullins	8	Lisheenavalla	18-6-85
54 Ned Clarke	5	Carnmore	"
55 Michael Mullin	15	Lisheenavalla	22-6-85
56 Michael Qualter	11	Lisheenavalla	22-6-85
57 John Kelly	14	Castlelambert	"
58 James Qualter	8	Carnmore	"
59 James Conway	9	Lisheenavalla	"
60 James White	8	Cregmore	"
61 Michael Collins	6	Lisheenavalla	"
62 Michael Higgins	6	Cregmore	"
63 Joseph Robert Spratt	4	Cashla	23-6-85
64 Pat Collins		Lisheenavalla	24-6-85
65 Martin Clarke	12	Carnmore	6-7-85
66 Pat Clarke	11	Carnmore	6-7-85
67 Thomas Mullin Michl	11	Cashla	"
68 Pat Carr Pat	5	Carnmore	"
69 Michael Collins Tom	5	Carnmore	"
70 John Killalay	6	Caherlay	"
71 Pat Killalay	4	Caherlay	"
72 John Caulfield	13	Cashla	7-7-85
73 Thomas Egan	15	Cashla	"
74 Pat Egan	13	Cashla	"
75 John Mullin	14	Cashla	8-7-85
76 Pat Carr John	16	Carnmore	"
77 Michael Carr John	13	Carnmore	"
78 Pat McGralton	16	Cashla	13-7-85
79 Michael Hanley John	11		"
80 William Collins John	4	Lisheenavalla	20-7-85
81 Peter Grealish James	4	Carnmore	"
82 Tom Conway	4	Lisheenavalla	21-7-85

School Attendance Rolls

83 Michael Killalay	10	Caherlay	"
84 Andrew Cunningham	12	Cashla	"
85 Willie Hynes Tom	11	Cashla	27-7-85
86 John Qualter	6	Lydacan	"
87 Ned Commins	6	Carnmore	"
88 James Commins	4	Carnmore	"
89 Pat Holland	6	Lisheenavalla	3-8-85
90 Tom Kelly John	4	Caherlay	11-8-85
91 John Cooney	10	Carnmore	17-8-85
92 Tom Cooney	9	Carnmore	"
93 Thomas Naughton	6	Lisheenavalla	"
94 James Murphy Pat	4	Ballymurphy	24-8-85
95 Andrew Forde	5	Lisheenavalla	7-9-85
96 Pat Jordan	9	Lydacan	"
97 Martin Jordan	7	Lydacan	"
98 Michael Hynes John	10	Carnmore	14-9-85
99 William Beattie	5	Carnmore	21-9-85
100 Michael Conway	11	Lisheenavalla	28-9-85
101 Thomas Hynes	8	Carnmore	23-11-85
102 John Briggs	7	Cashla	18- 1-86
103 James Harte	7	Cregmore	8- 2-86
104 Patrick Broderick	6	Cashla	19-7-86
105 Patrick Quilty	7	Cregmore	"
106 Patrick Kelly	7	Castlelambert	16-8-86
107 Thomas Ruane	6	Castlelambert	23-8-86
108 John Grealish Jr	3	Carnmore	4-10-86
109 Michael Hanley Pat	5	Carnmore	5-10-86
110 Michael Murphy Jn.	5	Ballymurphy	2-11-86
111 Thomas Murphy	7	Ballymurphy	6-12-86
112 Martin Duggan		Lisheenavalla	14-12-86
113 Matthew Ruane	8	Castlelambert	22-2-87
114 John Hanley	4	Carnmore	18-4-87
115 Pat Duggan		Lisheenavalla	2-5-87
116 Thomas Ruane		Castlelambert	16-5-87
117 William Higgins		Cregmore	"
118 John Holland		Lisheenavalla	23-5-87
119 John Kelly	5	Newtown	19-9-87
120 Pat Commins	5	Carnmore	20-9-87
121 Pat Conway	5	Lisheenavalla	10-10-87
121 Pat Kelly	11	Newtown	2-12-87
122 John Egan	12	Cashla	16-1-88
123 Michael Egan	7	Cashla	"

School Attendance Rolls

124 Pat Kelly	4	Caherlea	24-1-88
125 John Collins	5	Lisheenavalla	16-3-88
126 Pat Holmes	3	Carnmore	23-4-88
127 Roger Grealish	4	Carnmore	30-4-88
128 John Larner	4	Carnmore	"
129 Laurence Donohue	9	Carnmore	"
130 Edward Duggan	4	Lisheenavalla	15-5-88
131 Michael Roche	5	Carnmore	29-5-88
132 Pat Conway	4	Lisheenavalla	6-6-88
133 John Conway	8	Lisheenavalla	6-8-88
134 Thomas Ruane	5	Carnmore	20-8-88
135 Timothy Carr	5	Carnmore	13-5-89
136 John Kelly Jn.	3	Caherlea	14-5-89
137 John Grealsih	5	Carnmore	14-10-89
137 Denis Rabbit	10	Carnmore	"
138 John Hynes	9	Carnmore	"
139 Pat Higgins	4	Lisheenavalla	23-6-90

School Attendance Rolls

Carnmore National School - Girls

1 Margaret Fox	13	Carnmore	16-6-85
2 Nora O'Brien	14	Carnmore	"
3 Mary Fox	14	Carnmore	"
4 Winnie Grealish	12	Lisheenavalla	"
5 Annie Collins	12	Carnmore	"
6 Kate Murphy	12	Ballymurphy	"
7 Bridget Beattie	13	Carnmore	"
8 Bridget Fox Michl	11	Carnmore	"
9 Margaret Grealish Ml	14	Carnmore	"
10 Bridget Kenny	11	Carnmore	"
11 Bridget Fox Michl	11	Carnmore	"
12 Mary Hynes	12	Carnmore	"
13 Mary Mooney	12	Carnmore	"
14 Honoria Cooney	13	Carnmore	"
15 Bridget Fahy	13	Carnmore	"
16 Mary Higgins	14	Carnmore	"
17 Margaret Grealish J	12	Carnmore	"
18 Mary Ruane	7	Ballymurphy	"
19 Bridget Silke	12	Carnmore	"
20 Mary Jane Spratt	16	Cashla	"
21 Mary Anne Broderick	12	Cashla	"
22 Kate Kenny	10	Lydacan	"
23 Nora Joyce	8	Cregmore	"
24 Bridget Holland	9	Carnmore	"
25 Nony Higgins	8	Carnmore	"
26 Lissie Silke	9	Carnmore	"
27 Mary Grealish James	7	Carnmore	"
28 Mary Rabbit	10	Carnmore	"
29 Catherine Grealish	7	Carnmore	"
30 Julia Lally	12	Carnmore	"
31 Ellen Carr	9	Carnmore	"
32 Nora Hynes John	12	Carnmore	"
33 Nora Hanly	10	Carnmore	"
34 Julia Hanley	9	Carnmore	"
35 Margaret Grealish P.	9	Carnmore	"
36 Julia Kenny	8	Lydacan	"
37 Ellen Hynes	9	Carnmore	"
38 Kate Quirk	9	Carnmore	"
39 Susanna Spratt	8	Cashla	"
40 Margaret Quirk	17	Carnmore	"
41 Ellen Broderick	9	Cashla	"

School Attendance Rolls

42 Kate Kenny	4	Carnmore	"
43 Margaret Murphy Ml	6	Ballymurphy	10-7-86
44 Mary Forde	6	Lisheenavalla	"
45 Catherine Joyce	5	Cregmore	16-6-85
46 Anne Fox	4	Carnmore	
47 Julia Quirk		Carnmore	
48 Sarah Mgt. Spratt	6	Cashla	
49 Julia Grealish	3	Carnmore	
50 Margaret Murphy	4		
51 Mary Grealish Pat	5	Lisheenavalla	
52 Bridget Morris	7	Carnmore	
53 Mary Kenny Michael	12	Carnmore	
54 Bridget Lally	5	Carnmore	18-6-85
55 Catherine Mullin	12	Lisheenavalla	22-6-85
56 Kate Joyce	13	Cregmore	"
57 Kate Kelly Peter	9	Castlelambert	"
58 Mary Kelly Peter	11	Castlelambert	"
59 Mary Egan	11	Cashla	"
60 Bridget Ward	8	Carnmore	"
61 Winnie Fox	6	Carnmore	"
62 Marie Murphy	6	Ballymurphy	10-7-86
63 Lissie Larner	4	Carnmore	10-7-86
64 Bridget Killalay	7	Caherlay	24-6-85
65 Lissie Murphy	14	Ballymurphy	30-6-85
66 Nora Hynes Ml	5	Carnmore	"
67 Margaret Grealish Pat	7	Lisheenavalla	2-7-85
68 Margaret Mullin	16	Cashla	6-7-85
69 Nora Fahy	8	Carnmore	"
70 Ellen Grealish Peter	4	Carnmore	"
71 Mary Mullin	12	Cashla	8-7-85
72 Anne Ruane	8	Castlelambert	9-7-85
73 Margaret Grealish John	6	Carnmore	15-7-85
74 Mary Killalay	10	Caherlea	20-7-85
75 Margaret Kelly	6	Caherlea	"
76 Julia Mullin	11	Cashla	22-7-85
77 Anne Grealish Ml	7	Carnmore	27-7-85
78 Nora Conway	6	Lisheenavalla	3-8-85
79 Ellen Egan	7	Cashla	10-8-85
80 Sarah Mullins	5	Cashla	11-8-85
81 Julie Mullin Tom	5	Cashla	"
82 Mary Grealish John	5	Carnmore	17-8-85
83 Mary Hynes	8	Carnmore	14-9-85

School Attendance Rolls

84 Mary Sheridan	12	Lydacan	"
85 Sarah Lally	15	Carnmore	"
86 Mary Grealish Pt.	13	Carnmore	30-9-85
87 Bridget Qualter	12	Lydacan	9-11-85
88 Julia Conway	15	Lisheenavalla	"
89 Sarah Kelly	13	Carnmore	11-1-86
90 Julia Carr	13	Carnmore	"
91 Mary Carr	15	Carnmore	26-1-86
92 Mary Silke	9	Carnmore	23-8-86
93 Kate Silke	4	Carnmore	4-10-86
94 Lissie Morris	4	Carnmore	11-10-86
95 Bridget Costoloe	6	Carnmore	"
96 Rose Holmes	6	Carnmore	25-4-87
97 Cath Harte	5	Cashla	2-5-87
98 Bridget Commins	8	Cregmore	4-5-87
99 Julia Murphy	3	Ballymurphy	9-5-87
100 Kate Carr	6	Carnmore	"
101 Julia Lyke?Lynch ?	6	Caherlay	15-5-87
102 Winnie Hanley	4	Carnmore	"
103 Bridget Driggs	6	Cashla	23-5-87
104 Mary Hanley	5	Carnmore	31-8-87
105 Margt. Grealish Jas	4	Carnmore	7-9-87
106 Ellen Grealish	5	Carnmore	"
107 Mary Feeney	10	Newtown	12-9-87
108 Mary Kelly	9	Newtown	"
109 Annie Holland	4	Lisheenavalla	18-4-88
110 Mary Donohue	5	Carnmore	23-4-88
111 Kate Cooney	5	Carnmore	18-4-88
112 Ellen Silke	3	Carnmore	30-4-88
113 Kate Higgins	12	Cashla	"
114 Sarah Forde	4	Lisheenavalla	14-5-88
115 Annie Morrissey	5	Cashla	28-5-88
116 Mary Morrissey	7	Cashla	"
117 Catherine Briggs	6	Cashla	18-6-88
118 Mary Holmes	4	Carnmore	2-7-88
119 Ellen Collins	5	Lisheenavalla	"
120 Julia Hynes	5	Carnmore	"
121 Margaret Hynes	4	Carnmore	"
122 Bridget Grealish	3	Carnmore	"
123 Mary Holland	14	Lisheenavalla	15-4-89
124 Ellen Holland	4	Lisheenavalla	"
125 Catherine Holland	5	Lisheenavalla	"

School Attendance Rolls

126 Bridget Murphy	3	Ballymurphy	"
127 Honarie Kenny	4	Carnmore	"
128 Margaret Hynes Jn.	7	Carnmore	27-5-89
129 Eleanor Spratt	16	Cashla	25-11-89
130 Ellen Hanley	4	Carnmore	9-6-90
131 Anne Conway	4	Lisheenavalla	17-6-90
132 Anne Morris	4	Carnmore	20-9-90
133 Kate Grealish	4	Carnmore	26-9-90
137 Marcella Blackall	7	Cashla	20-5-89
139 Sabina Commins		Carnmore	21-7-90

Appendix B: Deaths and Marriages

Year	Baptisms	Confirmations	Marriages	Deaths
1950	29	--	4	26
1951	39	87	11	17
1952	23	--	9	13
1953	32	--	5	19
1954	27	86	6	24
1955	25	--	4	18
1956	27	--	5	14
1957	31	64	8	19
1958	31	--	7	18
1959	33	--	7	11
1960	33	63	5	13
1961	25	--	9	15
1962	28	-	9	23
1963	29	74	7	11
1964	30	--	13	13
1965	30	--	9	17
1966	29	74	10	17
1967	25	--	9	15
1968	32	--	10	24
1969	30	64	12	19
1970	27	--	11	12
1971	30	--	12	23
1972	37	67	15	14
1973	42	--	5	14
1974	38	--	2	19
1975	41	74	8	22
1976	37	--	6	13
1977	51	--	16	17
1978	55	27	19	15
1979	52	24	19	13
1980	58	32	11	16

Deaths amd Marriages

1981	57	32	14	17
1982	53	25	8	21
1983	57	36	9	17
1984	46	41	9	7
1985	55	37	7	18
1986	56	42	13	18
1987	51	46	9	17
1988	34	46	10	20
1989	46	44	3	13
1990	41	53	15	21
1991	49	46	11	16
1992	34	55	9	16
1993	53	56	5	18
1994	46	49	5	20
1995	40	67	7	12
1996	41	61	11	13
1997	48	46	10	21
1998	48	65	12	19

Deaths in Claregalway from 1959 to 1970

1910 Celia Murphy, Ballymurphy, Mary Grealish, Carnmore and Pat Mooney, Knockdoe.
1912 - 18 deaths
1913 - 13 deaths
1914 - 12 deaths
1915 - 21 deaths
1916 - 21 deaths
1917 - 22 deaths
1918 - 29 deaths
1919 - 22 deaths
1920 - 21 deaths
1930 - 18 deaths
1940 - 16 deaths

The first marriage recorded was in the year 1849. The couple were Patrick Collins and Sarah Ryder, Gortnagoolini.

The first baptism recorded was in the year 1849. Jane Ann Colohan, daughter of Patrick Colohan and Mary Hession, was baptised on 11 November 1849.